AF559739

THE KĀŚYAPAPARIVARTA

Edited and Translated

by

BHIKKHU PĀSĀDIKA

ADITYA PRAKASHAN
New Delhi

First published, 2015

ISBN 978-81-7742-150-7

Printed and Published by Aditya Prakashan, 2/18, Ansari Road,
New Delhi - 110 002.
email: contact@adityaprakashan.com
website: www.adityaprakashan.com
Printed at Replika Press Pvt. Ltd.

In
Memory of
Professor Dr Michael Hahn

कल्याणमित्राय

Acknowledgements

I wish to express my gratitude to Prof. Dr Jens-Uwe Hartmann, the Institute of Indology and Tibetology, Munich University, through whose good offices the publication of this work with Aditya Prakashan has been made possible. Special thanks are due to Dr Mitsuyo Demoto-Hahn, Indica et Tibetica Publisher, Marburg University, for having undertaken the arduous job of completing the final formatting of all the texts. Needless to say, all responsibility for editorial and hermeneutic shortcomings or mistakes – luckily some could be avoided thanks to Dr Demoto-Hahn's alertness – that have escaped my notice lies with me.

Bad Arolsen, Germany
June 2015

Bh. Pā.

Contents

Bibliography and Abbreviations v

Introduction to the Edition and English Translation 1

The Devanāgarī Edition of the *Kāśyapaparivarta* 11

English Translation 99

Bibliography and Abbreviations

Anālayo, Bhikkhu 2011. *A Comparative Study of the* Majjhimanikāya, Vols. 1, 2. Taipei: Dharma Drum Publishing Corporporation (Dharma Drum Buddhist College Research Series 3).

Bagchi, Sitansusekhar (ed.) 1970. *Mahāyāna-Sūtrālaṅkāra of Asaṅga.* Darbhanga: The Mithila Institute of Post-Graduate Studies and Research in Sanskrit Learning (Buddhist Sanskrit Texts - No. 13).

Bhattacharya, Vidhushekhara (ed.) 1931a. *The Catuḥśataka of Āryadeva.* Sanskrit and Tibetan Texts with copious extracts from the commentary of Candrakirti. Calcutta: Visvabharati Bookshop.

--------- 1931b. *Mahāyānaviṃśaka of Nāgārjuna.* Reconstructed Sanskrit Text, Tibetan and Chinese Versions with an English Translation. Calcutta: Visvabharati Studies 1.

Conze, Edward 1954. "Contemplation of Thought" (English translation of *Kāśyapaparivarta*, section 97) in: Conze, E. (ed.), in collaboration with Horner, I.B., Snellgrove, D., Waley, A., *Buddhist Texts through the Ages.* Newly translated from the original Pali, Sanskrit, Chinese, Tibetan, Japanese and Apabhramsa. Oxford: Bruno Cassirer; p. 162.

Edgerton, Franklin 1953. *Buddhist Hybrid Sanskrit Grammar and Dictionary*, Vol. 1: Grammar, Vol. 2: Dictionary. New Haven: Yale University Press.

Harrison, Paul and Watanabe, Shōgo 2006. "Vajracchedikā Prajñāpāramitā" in: Braarvig, Jens (gen. ed.), *Manuscripts in the Schøyen Collection, Buddhist Manuscripts*, Vol. III. Oslo: Hermes Publishing; pp. 89–159.

von Hinüber, Oskar 2009. "Origin and Varieties of Buddhist Sanskrit" in: Falk, Harry and Slaje, Walter (eds.), *Oskar von Hinüber. Kleine Schrif-*

ten, Part 1. Wiesbaden: Harrassowitz Verlag (Veröffentlichungen der Helmuth von Glasenapp-Stiftung, Vol. 47); pp. 554–580.

--------- 2009. "The vocabulary of Buddhist Sanskrit: Problems and perspectives" in: Falk, Slaje (eds.), *Oskar von Hinüber. Kleine Schriften*, Part 2; pp. 589–602.

de Jong, Jan Willem 1977. "Sanskrit Fragments of the Kāśyapaparivarta" in: *Beiträge zur Indienforschung. Ernst Waldschmidt zum 80. Geburtstag gewidmet.* Berlin: Veröffentlichungen des Museums für Indische Kunst Berlin, Vol. 4; pp. 247–255.

Karashima, Seishi 2002. "Some features of the language of the *Kāśyapaparivarta*" in: *Annual Report of the International Research Institute for Advanced Buddhology* (IRIAB) *at Soka University for the Academic Year 2001*. Tokyo; pp. 43–66.

--------- 2004. "Sanskrit Fragments of the *Kāśyapaparivarta* and the *Pañcapāramitānirdeśasūtra* in the Mannerheim Collection" in: *Annual Report of the* IRIAB *at Soka University for the Academic Year 2003*. Tokyo; pp. 105–118 (with facsimiles).

--------- 2009. "Or. 15010/17: H. 143, S.B. 38...", "Or. 15010/38: H. 143, S.B. 68; *Kāśyapaparivarta*" in: Karashima, Seishi and Wille, Klaus (eds.-in-chief), *Buddhist Manuscripts from Central Asia. The British Library Sanskrit Fragments*, Vol. II. 1 (Texts), Vol. II. 2 (Facsimiles). Tokyo: IRIAB at Soka University; pp. 354–356, 391f.; plates 219, 238.

Kashyap, Jagadish Bhikkhu (gen. ed.) 1956. *The Mahāvagga*. Nālandā: Pāli Publication Board (Bihar Government), Nālandā-Devanāgarī-Pāli-Series.

--------- 1958a. *The Dīghanikāya*, Vols. 1–3. Nālandā: Nālandā-Devanāgarī-Pāli-Series.

--------- 1958b. *The Majjhimanikāya*, Vols. 1–3. Nālandā: Nālandā-Devanāgarī-Pāli-Series.

--------- 1959a. *The Saṃyuttanikāya*, Vol. 2. Nālandā: Nālandā-Devanāgarī-Pāli-Series.

--------- 1959b. *The Khuddakanikāya*, Vols. 1–3. Nālandā: Nālandā-Devanāgarī-Pāli-Series.

--------- 1960a. *The Aṅguttaranikāya*, Vols. 1–4. Nālandā: Nālandā-Devanāgarī-Pāli-Series.

--------- 1960b. *The Khuddakanikāya*, Vol. IV, Part 1. Nālandā: Nālandā-Devanāgarī-Pāli-Series.

Kawamura, Leslie 2000. "The Middle Path According to the *Kāśyapaparivarta-sūtra*" in: Silk, Jonathan A. (ed.), *Wisdom, Compassion, and the Search for Understanding*. The Buddhist Studies Legacy of Gadjin M. Nagao. Honolulu: University of Hawai'i Press (Studies in the Buddhist Traditions, a publication of the Institute for the Study of Buddhist Traditions. The University of Michigan, Ann Arbor, Michigan); pp. 221–232.

Klaus, Konrad 2007. "Zu der formelhaften Einleitung der buddhistischen Sūtras" in: Klaus, Konrad and Hartmann, Jens-Uwe (eds.), *Indica et Tibetica. Festschrift für Michael Hahn*. Vienna: Arbeitskreis für tibetische und buddhistische Studien Universität Wien (Wiener Studien zur Tibetologie und Buddhismuskunde Heft 66); pp. 309–322.

Lamotte, Étienne 1962. *L'Enseignement de Vimalakīrti* (Vimalakīrtinirdeśa), traduit et annoté. Louvain: Université de Louvain, Institut Orientaliste (Bibliothèque du Muséon, Volume 51).

Martini, Giuliana 2008. "Tracing the Sources of the *Book of Zambasta*: the Case of the *Yakṣa* Painter Simile and the *Kāśyapaparivarta*" in: *Journal of Inner Asian Art and Archaeology* 3. Brepols (Belgium); pp. 91–97.

--------- 2011. "A Large Question in a Small Place: The Transmission of the *Ratnakūṭa* (*Kāśyapaparivarta*) in Khotan" in: *Annual Report of the* IRIAB *at Soka University for the Academic Year 2010*, Vol. XIV. Tokyo; pp. 135–183.

Mishra, Kameshwar Nath (ed.) 1993. *Aspects of Buddhist Sanskrit.* Proceedings of the International Symposium on the Language of Sanskrit Buddhist Texts, Oct. 1–5, 1991. Sarnath, Varanasi: Central Institute of Higher Tibetan Studies (Samyag-Vāk Series VI).

Negi, J.S., Samdhong Rinpoche, Ngawang Samten (chief eds.) 1993–2005. *Tibetan-Sanskrit Dictionary*, Vols. 1–16. Sarnath, Varanasi: Dictionary Unit, Central Institute of Higher Tibetan Studies.

Ñāṇamoli, Bhikkhu (comp.), Bodhi, Bhikkhu (ed.) 1994. *A Pali-English Glossary of Buddhist Technical Terms.* Kandy: Buddhist Publication Society.

Pandeya, Ramchandra 1971. *Madhyānta-Vibhāga-Śāstra Containing the Kārikās of Maitreya, Bhāṣya of Vasubandhu and Ṭīkā by Sthiramati.* Delhi: Motilal Banarsidass.

Pāsādika, Bhikkhu 1977–79. "The Dharma-Discourse of the Great Collection of Jewels. The *Kāśyapa*-Section - English Translation and Restoration of the Missing Sanskrit Portions" in: *Linh-Sơn - publication d'études bouddhologiques* Nos. 1–9 (pp. 26–41; 31–42; 41–48; 34–42; 28–39; 35–45; 27–37; 31–43; 26–41). Joinville-le-Pont (Paris): publication du Monastère bouddhique Linh-Sơn.

--------- 1980. "The Kāśyapaparivarta ('Od-srung-gi le'u) - Prolegomena" in: *The Tibet Journal,* Vol. 5, No. 4; pp. 48–58.

--------- 1993. "Remarks on Two Kāśyapaparivarta Translations" in: Grünendal, Reinhold, Hartmann, Jens-Uwe and Kieffer-Pülz, Petra (eds.), *Studien zur Indologie und Buddhismuskunde. Festgabe des Seminars für Indologie und Buddhismuskunde für Prof. Dr. Heinz Bechert zum 60. Geburtstag.* Bonn: Indica et Tibetica Verlag; pp. 213–220.

Roth, Gustav 1970. *Bhikṣuṇī-Vinaya,* Including *Bhikṣuṇī-Prakīrṇaka* and a Summary of the *Bhikṣu-Prakīrṇaka* of the Ārya-Mahāsāṃghika-Lokottaravādin. Patna: K.P. Jayaswal Research Institute (Tibetan Sanskrit Works Series Vol. XII).

--------- 1986. "Mangala-Symbols in Buddhist Sanskrit Manuscripts and Inscriptions" in: Bhattacharya, Gouriswar (ed.), *Deya-dharma: Studies in Memory of Dr D.C. Sircar*. Delhi: Sri Satguru Publications (Sri Garib Dass Oriental Series 33); pp. 239–250.

Rhys Davids, T.W., Stede, W. (eds.) 1921–1925. *The Pali Text Society's Pali-English Dictionary*. London: Luzac & Company, Ltd.

Sakaki, R. (ed.) 1926. *Mahāvyutpatti* (2 vols.). Kyoto.

Sander, Lore 1968. *Paläographisches zu den Sanskrithandschriften der Berliner Turfansammlung*. Verzeichnis der orientalischen Handschriften in Deutschland, Supplementband 8. Wiesbaden: Franz Steiner Verlag.

Sander, Lore, Waldschmidt, Ernst 1980. *Sanskrit Handschriften aus den Turfanfunden*, Teil 4. Wiesbaden: Franz Steiner Verlag (Verzeichnis der Orientalischen Handschriften in Deutschland (VOHD), Vol. X, 4); p. 280 (revised transcription of the MS fragments of the *Kāśyapaparivarta* sections 151–153).

Sastri, N. Aiyaswami 1949. "Chang-Chen Lun. Karatalaratna of Bhavaviveka. Translated into Sanskrit" in: Bagchi, P.C. (ed.), *Visva-Bharati Annals* Vol. II. Santiniketan: Visva-Bharati; pp. 1–124.

Silk, Jonathan, A. 2000. "The *Yogācāra Bhikṣu*" in: Silk, J.A. (ed.), *Wisdom, Compassion, and the Search for Understanding*. The Buddhist Studies Legacy of Gadjin M. Nagao. Honolulu: University of Hawai'i Press (Studies in the Buddhist Traditions, a publication of the Institute for the Study of Buddhist Traditions. The University of Michigan, Ann Arbor, Michigan); pp. 265–314.

--------- 2009. "The Nature of the Verses of the *Kāśyapaparivarta*" in: Altman Bromberg, Carol *et al.*, *Bulletin of the Asia Institute*, Evo ṣuyadi – Essays in Honor of Richard Salomon's 65th Birthday. New Series/Vol. 23. Published with the assistance of the Neil Kreitman Foundation (U.K.), pp. 181–190.

--------- 2010. "Test Sailing the Ship of the Teachings: Hesitant Notes on *Kāśyapaparivarta* §§ 153–154" in: Franco, Eli and Zin, Monika (eds.),

From Turfan to Ajanta, Festschrift for Dieter Schlingloff on the Occasion of his Eightieth Birthday, Vol. 2. Lumbini; pp. 897–924.

Skilling, Peter 2009. "Seeing the preacher as the Teacher: A note on *śāstṛ-saṃjñā*" in *Annual Report of the IRIAB at Soka University for the Academic Year 2008*. Tokyo; pp. 73–100.

Stache-Rosen, Valentina (ed.) 1968. *Das Saṅgītisūtra und sein Kommentar Saṅgītiparyāya*. Nach Vorarbeiten von Kusum Mittal bearbeitet. Berlin: Dogmatische Begriffsreihen im älteren Buddhismus, II (Sanskrittexte aus den Turfanfunden), Deutsche Akademie der Wissenschaften zu Berlin, Institut für Orientforschung.

Staël-Holstein, Baron A. von 1926. *The Kāśyapaparivarta - A Mahāyānasūtra of the Ratnakūṭa Class in the Original Sanskrit, in Tibetan and in Chinese*. Shanghai: Commercial Press.

--------- 1933. *A Commentary to the Kāśyapaparivarta Edited in Tibetan and in Chinese*. Peking: Joint Publication of the National Library of Peking and the National Tsinghua University.

Takahashi, Hisao *et al.* 2006. *Vimalakīrtinirdeśa. A Sanskrit Edition Based upon the Manuscript Newly Found at the Potala Palace*. Tokyo: Taisho University Press.

Vaidya, P.L. 1960a. *Madhyamakaśāstra of Nāgārjuna with the Commentary: Prasannapadā by Candrakīrti*. Darbhanga: The Mithila Institute of Post-Graduate Studies and Research in Sanskrit Learning (Buddhist Sanskrit Texts - No. 10).

--------- 1960b. *Bodhicaryāvatāra of Śāntideva with the Commentary Pañjikā of Prajñākaramati*. Darbhanga: The Mithila Institute of Post-Graduate Studies and Research in Sanskrit Learning (Buddhist Sanskrit Texts - No. 12).

--------- 1961. *Śikṣāsamuccaya of Śāntideva*. Darbhanga: The Mithila Institute of Post-Graduate Studies and Research in Sanskrit Learning (Buddhist Sanskrit Texts - No. 11).

Vorobyov-Desyatovsky, V.S. 1957. "Vnov' naidennye listy rukopisei Kāshyapaparivarty" ('The Newly Found Folios of the Kāśyapaparivarta') in: *Rocznik Orientalistyczny* Vol. 21, pp. 491–500.

Vorobyova-Desyatovskaya, M.I., in collaboration with Karashima, Seishi and Kudo, Noriyuki 2002. *The Kāśyapaparivarta. Romanized Text and Facsimiles.* Tokyo: The International Research Institute for Advanced Buddhology Soka University (Bibliotheca Philologica et Philosophica Buddhica V).

Waldschmidt, Ernst, in collaboration with Clawiter, Walter and Holzmann, Lore 1965. *Sanskrit Handschriften aus den Turfanfunden,* Teil 1. Wiesbaden: Franz Steiner Verlag (VOHD, Vol. X, 1); p. 165 (MS fragments of *Kāśyapaparivarta* sections 151–153, plate 36 - facsimile).

Waldschmidt, Ernst 1957. *Das Catuṣpariṣatsūtra* II. Auf Grund von Turfan-Handschriften herausgegeben und bearbeitet. Berlin: Akademie-Verlag (Abhandlungen der Deutschen Akademie der Wissenschaften zu Berlin, Klasse für Sprachen, Literatur und Kunst, Jahrgang 1956, Nr. 1).

Weller, Friedrich 1965. *Zum Kāśyapaparivarta.* Heft 2, Verdeutschung des sanskrit-tibetischen Textes. Berlin: Akademie-Verlag (Abhandlungen der Sächsischen Akademie der Wissenschaften zu Leipzig, Philologisch-historische Klasse, Band 57, Heft 3).

BHS	Buddhist Hybrid Sanskrit
BHSD	Buddhist Hybrid Sanskrit Dictionary by Edgerton
BHSG	Buddhist Hybrid Sanskrit Grammar by Edgerton
c.m.	contra metrum
CŚV	KP quotations in the *Catuḥśatakavṛtti* (Bhattacharya 1931)
em.	emendation
KP	*Kāśyapaparivarta*
m.c.	metri causa

MS	KP manuscript "SI P/2"
MVŚ	KP quotations in the *Madhyānta-Vibhāga-Śāstra* (Pandeya 1971)
om.	omitted, omission
P	KP quotations in the *Prasannapadā* (Vaidya 1960a)
SH	KP von Staël-Holstein ed. (1926)
SI P/85A	reading of KP fragment (Vorobyov-Desyatovsky 1957, de Jong 1977) (in VD)
ŚS	KP quotations in the *Śikṣāsamuccaya* (Vaidya 1961)
s.v.	sub voce (under the word)
T	Turfan MS fragment of KP (Sander, Waldschmidt 1980) (in VD)
Tib.	Tibetan translation of KP
VD	KP Vorobyova-Desyatovskaya ed. (2002)

Introduction to the Devanāgarī Edition and English Translation

The KP is surely one of the earliest Mahāyāna discourses[1] whose edition and transliteration in Roman script are fairly well-known, whilst this seminal text has as yet never been published in Devanāgarī characters. For many years it has been my intention to prepare a Devanāgarī edition of the KP and to revise thoroughly an earlier English translation of mine. In the following some remarks are made about its attempted realization.

Both the KP edition and transliteration in Roman script are based on a unique Sanskrit manuscript kept in the St. Petersburg Branch of the Institute of Oriental Studies, viz. the MS "SI P/2". This manuscript, written in Brāhmī script, was brought to Russia from Eastern Turkestan at the end of the 19th century; a number of lacunae apart, it is nearly complete and may have been written in Khotan sometime in the 7th or 8th century CE. In 1926 von Staël-Holstein published his edition of the KP together with its corresponding Tibetan translation and four Chinese renderings presupposing more or less different versions of the original Sanskrit. Again, in 2002, the Romanized text of the MS "SI P/2" was brought out by Vorobyova-Desyatovskaya in collaboration with Karashima and Kudo. As Vorobyova-Desyatovskaya states, when comparing the MS "SI P/2" with some other fragments of the KP, belonging to the Central Asian MS collections of the UK, Finland and Germany, the conclusion can be safely drawn that "at least two Sanskrit versions of the KP existed in Eastern Turkestan in the first centuries CE: a brief and apparently earlier version, and an extended one which took shape later. The MS 'SI P/2' represents the extended version" of our text.

---

1 An overview of the contents of the KP and a discussion of the importance of the text are given in Weller 1965 (introduction) and in Pāsādika 1980. An outline of its contents following the structure in the Tibetan translation of Sthiramati's KP commentary is presented in Kawamura 2000. Textual and hermeneutical problems are dealt with, first of all, in Weller 1965 and Karashima 2004, also in Pāsādika 1993 and in Silk 2010. As for the transmission of the KP in Khotan, see Martini 2011.

Whereas von Staël-Holstein refers to his Romanized text as 'edition', Vorobyova-Desyatovskaya calls hers a 'transliteration'. When comparing both scholars' dealing with the MS "SI P/2" with the help of the perfectly legible (apart from illegible, omitted, lost, erased or damaged *akṣaras* or parts of *akṣaras*) facsimiles published at the end of Vorobyova-Desyatovskaya's Romanized text, von Staël-Holstein's can in fact be considered an edition even though he does not give footnotes, and Vorobyova-Desyatovskaya's a very careful transliteration with full notes bearing on difficult readings, proposed emendations, parallel readings found in the other KP fragments, as mentioned, and scribal errors. It should be stated here that von Staël-Holstein had, apart from his informative preface with notes, actually planned to publish numerous notes to his edition in a separate volume which, however, never saw the light of day. In his edition he indicates, of course, the punctuation marks occurring in the MS and missing *akṣaras* or parts of *akṣaras*, but he also makes 'improvements' to the Sanskrit text e.g. by inserting *akṣaras* lost because of damage to the Sanskrit text, but without specifying the insertions. Another editorial procedure of von Staël-Holstein is his normalizing a peculiar spelling not infrequently found in the MS, viz. the doubling of the subscribed *-r*, e.g. *krr, grr, prr* etc., a way of writing 'said to have been influenced by the Khotanese'; see Vorobyova-Desyatovskaya (her transliteration, p. 3, n. 1) who, throughout, transliterates the double *-r* spellings. It goes without saying that such spelling would prove rather awkward for converting it into Devanāgarī script.

For the sake of ready comprehensibility in the present Devanāgarī edition of the KP both spelling and punctuation have been standardized to some extent.[2] Where lacunae in the MS occur, reconstructed words or

[2] As regards standardization, admittedly, every so often it has proved difficult to distinguish between scribal errors on the one hand and BHS usage on the other. In a number of footnotes in her KP edition Vorobyova-Desyatovskaya has indicated wrong spelling in the MS and, accordingly, in the present edition the corrected readings have been incorporated. Two examples of standardized spelling may suffice here: a) *bodhisattva/mahāsattva* for *°satva* and b) *śūnyatā* for *śunyatā*. Two more examples may be given to show that frequently peculiar BHS forms are retained (in accordance with BHSG §§ 6.12, 6.17, e.g.) instead of standardization/emendation: In KP sections 50, 51 we have cases of 'masculine modifier with neuter noun' or 'neuter modifier with feminine noun' respectively. The *daṇḍas* have also been standardized, as far as possible, according to context. Occasionally the structures of the KP verses are irregular, i.e.

akṣaras are indicated by italics, and likewise text, lost in the MS, that has been preserved in KP quotations and drawn upon to fill large lacunae. As in von Staël-Holstein's edition, a division of the Devanāgarī text into paragraphs or sections according to its contents seems preferable to Vorobyova-Desyatovskaya's textual arrangement foliowise. Hers is a meticulous presentation of MS data ('handschriftlicher Befund'), while in its arrangement sectionwise the Devanāgarī text should match that of the English translation following it in order to facilitate its study. Since in Vorobyova-Desyatovskaya's presentation of the Romanized KP text all textual and scribal peculiarities, special features of punctuation, numbers occurring in the MS or the position of string holes are already given and since this Romanized text is widely accessible, in the Devanāgarī edition these items are not considered. In view of the special features of the Devanāgarī script it has not proved practicable to indicate most of the MS data as in Vorobyova-Desyatovskaya who has pointed out all missing, superfluous or reconstructed *akṣaras* or parts of *akṣaras* by means of various types of brackets and italics. As for textual passages or even missing folios that have been reconstructed tentatively, i.e. retranslated *ex hypothesi* from the corresponding Tibetan version of the text, all such retranslations are again given in italics.[3] Although tentative reconstructions of missing text in Buddhist Sanskrit discourses or treatises may seem to be superfluous when translating such works, for example, into English, they are certainly justifiable for the purpose of fascilitating envisaged future renderings of texts such as the KP into modern Indian languages. On the whole also the Devanāgarī edition should represent the Buddhist Hybrid Sanskrit[4] text as it has come down to us in the unique MS from Central Asia. To enhance its com-

different metres occur so that quarter-verses of a stanza are not identical in form. Therefore the presentation of the verses in Staël-Holstein is retained.

3 One exception to this procedure is the text's reconstructed title for reasons of typographic style.

4 Here the term BHS is employed non-committally and without value judgement – 'hybrid' in the neutral sense of 'something that is the outcome of mixing two or more different things' – and due to the fact that a great many grammatical forms and words recorded in Edgerton's BHS Grammar and Dictionary are extremely useful for understanding the KP language. For the pros and cons regarding Edgerton's usage of BHS see the contributions by A. Wayman and others in Mishra 1993. As for an estimation of Edgerton's *magnum opus* and evaluation of the considerable progress made after the publication of his work, as well as prospective future tasks, see von Hinüber 2009.

prehensibility, as said, 'standardized' readings are given in the KP text itself. BHS and non-standardized forms are considered in the notes to the KP translation. Although the text's verse parts play an important role, this is not the place to treat the knotty problems attaching to the verses' origins, to their linguistic shape (BHS features vs. scribal idiosyncrasies or blundering) or metric/hypermetric structures. A special discussion of the KP verses would probably require a separate publication.[5] Furthermore, text-critical remarks, emendations or reconstructions by Weller 1965/Pāsādika 1977–79 referred to by Vorobyova-Desyatovsakya in her notes are often tacitly taken into account but not repeated in the present edition. Newly proposed emendations/reconstructions are referred to in the notes to the KP translation; such have become possible thanks to the MS facsimiles provided in Vorobyova-Desyatovskaya 2002 and with the help of the most useful palaeographic charts in Sander 1968.

For the sake of completeness I had planned before to provide, in an appendix at the end of the present edition, further MS fragments of the KP in Devanāgarī script, viz. the MS fragment "SI P/85A" (St. Petersburg), the fragments in the Hoernle and Mannerheim Collections (London, Helsinki), the fragment in the Turfan Collection (Berlin)[6] (see Vorobyova-Desyatovskaya 2002, pp. 58–64) and a new one made accessible in Karashima 2009. Since these fragments are readily available, as listed in the bibliography, it may be more useful to survey in the following re which KP sections, for readings/passages to fill lacunae, which of the above-mentioned fragments and KP quotations in later Mahāyāna texts have been drawn upon in the Devanāgarī edition in order to facilitate the reading of the BHS text.

[5] Re the above-mentioned problems see de Jong 1977 and Silk 2009 in particular.

[6] I am much obliged to Emeritus Prof. Dr Dieter Schlingloff who kindly sent me his review of Waldschmidt *et al.* 1965 (*Zeitschrift der Deutschen Morgenländischen Gesellschaft* 116, pp. 419–425 (Wiesbaden, 1966–1967)) in which he identified the said Turfan fragment as belonging to the KP and improved its reading so that the revised transcription could appear in Sander, Waldschmidt 1980.

KP sections:	readings/passages from:
3	ŚS 33, 14–16
4	ŚS 33, 17–22
5	ŚS 82, 22–25
6	ŚS 34, 28–30
11	ŚS 34, 19–22
14	SI P/85A
15	ŚS 81, 11–12
16	SI P/85A
17	SI P/85A
24	ŚS 34, 4–5; *Mahāyāna-Sūtrālaṃkāra*, Bagchi 1970: 158, 14
52	MVŚ 174, 25–28; 175, 1
57	P 153, 1–3
58	MVŚ 176, 17f.
59	MVŚ 177, 7f.
62	MVŚ 174, 21f.
63	MVŚ 180, 27–29; P 108, 21–24
64	CŚV 150, 3–5; MVŚ 181, 3f., 18f., 27; P 108, 24–30
65	CŚV 272, 16–23; P 108, 30–109, 5
66	MVŚ 182, 9–13
67	MVŚ 183, 1–4
68	MVŚ 184, 1–3
69	MVŚ 184, 15–17
70	MVŚ 185, 4–8
71	MVŚ 185, 21–186, 1; P 64, 2–17
97–99	ŚS 126, 13–22; *Bodhicaryāvatāra-Pañjikā* (Vaidya 1960b), 245, 23–246, 2
100–101	ŚS 126, 23–28
102	P 14, 23–25; ŚS 126, 28–30; Vaidya 1960b: 246, 2–4
128	de Jong 1977 (fragments in the Hoernle & Mannerheim Collections): 250; ŚS 108, 30–109, 2
129–131	de Jong 1977: 250
133–135	de Jong 1977: 250f.
138–140	P 144, 2–13
141–143	P 15, 16–30; 144, 14–27
144–149	P 15, 30–16, 1–24
153	T

Regarding the English translation of the KP, a thorough revision of Pāsādika 1977–79 has been attempted. In the footnotes to the translation, as mentioned, in the main Buddhist Hybrid Sanskrit specifics pertaining to the KP are considered with references especially to Edgerton 1953 and Karashima 2002. A new feature with the revision is that, for hermeneutically difficult passages, Sthiramati's KP commentary (von Staël-Holstein 1933) has been consulted. A difficult passage is found, for example, in KP section 12: *samadharmadeśanā sarvasatveṣu*, which can be rendered: 'the same *dharma*-exposition to all beings' which, however, seems to contradict a statement in section 11 according to which a *bodhisattva* should not reveal "the sublime teachings of the Buddha to beings who have not become 'a [deserving] vessel' for [them]." As the commentator explains, the said passage in section 12 should be understood in the sense that a conscientious *bodhisattva* teaches Hīnayāna and Mahāyāna followers according to their respective requirements. Lastly it should be noted that, at the beginning of folio ***37a*** of the Devanāgarī edition after a lacuna (the missing folio nos. 34–36)[7] and before the beginning of section 70, *ye (')pi śunyaṃ* (of which there is no Tib. equivalent) is left untranslated.

It seems apposite to mention here the *samādāpaka* of the present undertaking, the late Prof. Dr Lal Mani Joshi, by citing from the introductory remarks in Pāsādika 1977–79: "It was the present writer's *kalyāṇamitra,* Prof. Dr Joshi, who requested many times that the missing Sanskrit portions of this important Mahāyāna discourse should be restored with a view to preparing a Devanāgarī edition of the complete Sanskrit version of the text along with a Hindi translation." As for the above bibliography, it cannot be claimed that it is exhaustive. For further references to and bibliographical information about the Chinese KP translations, Japanese research on our text and additional KP quotes and parallels see the forthcoming new Romanized KP edition and English translation by Jonathan A. Silk. I wish to thank Professor Dr Silk, University of Leiden, for his having generously sent me a draft of his edition and translation. For invaluable editorial suggestions many thanks are due to the late Prof. Dr Michael Hahn and for making accessible special computer programs I am grateful to Dr Jayendra Soni and Bidur Bhattarai, M.A., all of them of Philipp's University Marburg.

---

[7] See VD, p. 27: "However, in fact there are only two pages omitted, and the next folio onwards is mistakenly paginated."

I am very much indebted to the Director of the International Research Institute for Advanced Buddhology at Soka University, Tokyo, and notably to Professor Dr Seishi Karashima, for having sent me the Institute's most welcome publications bearing on the KP. Last but not least, I am much obliged to Dr Giuliana Martini (Sāmaṇerī Dhammadinnā), University of Naples, for having apprised me of and provided with publications – including those from her pen – on the KP from Japan and on KP materials in Khotanese.

Bad Arolsen
4th May 2015

Bhikkhu Pāsādika

I. The Devanāgarī Edition of the *Kāśyapaparivarta*

आर्यकाश्यपपरिवर्तो नाम महायानसूत्रम्

नमः सर्वबुद्धबोधिसत्त्वेभ्यः

(1b) सिद्धम्

एवं मया श्रुतमेकस्मिं समये भगवान् राजगृहे विहरति स्म गृद्धकूटे पर्वते महता भिक्षुसंघेन सार्धमष्टाभिर्भिक्षुसहस्रैः षोडशभिश्च बोधिसत्त्वसहस्रैः नानाबुद्धक्षेत्रसंनिपतितैरेकजातिप्रबद्धै-र्यदुतानुत्तरस्यां सम्यक्संबोधौ॥

१

तत्र भगवान् आयुष्मन्तं महाकाश्यपमामंत्रयति स्म। चत्वार इमे काश्यप धर्मा बोधिसत्त्वस्य प्रज्ञापारिहाणाय संवर्तन्ते। कतमे चत्वारः यदुत अगौरवो *भवति* धर्मे च *धर्मभाणके* च। *धर्ममत्सरी* (2a) च भवति। धर्माचार्यमुष्टिञ्च करोति धर्मकामानाञ्च पुद्गलानां धर्मान्तरायं करोति। *विच्छन्दयति* विक्षिपति। न देशयति। प्रतिच्छादयति। आभिमानिकश्च भवत्या-त्मोत्कर्षी परपंसकः *इमे* काश्यप चत्वारो धर्मा बोधिसत्त्वस्य प्रज्ञापारिहाणाय संवर्तन्ते। तत्रेदमुच्यते॥

अगौरवो भवति च धर्मभाणके
धर्मेषु मात्सर्यरतो च भोति।
आचार्यमुष्टिं च करोति धर्मे
धर्मार्थिकाना च करोति *विघ्नम्*।
विच्छंदयन्तो विविधं क्षिपन्तो
धर्मं न देशयति *जिनप्रशस्तान्*।

सो *आत्मज*(2b)त्कर्षणि नित्त्ययुक्तो
परपंसने चाभिरतः कुसीदो।
चतुरो इमे धर्मा जिनेन प्रोक्ता
प्रज्ञाप्रहाणाय जिनोरसानाम्।
एतां हि चत्वारि जहित्व धर्मांश्
चतुरौ परां धर्म जिनोक्त भावयेत्॥

२

चत्वार इमे काश्यप धर्मा बोधिसत्त्वस्य महाप्रज्ञतायै संवर्तंते। कतमे *चत्वारः* यदुत सगौरवो भवति धर्मे च धर्मभाणके च। यथाश्रुतांश्च धर्मान् यथापर्याप्तान् परेभ्यो विस्तरेण संप्रकाशयति। निरामिषेण चित्तेन न प्रतिकांक्षयति (3a)[1]लाभसत्कारश्लोकं बाहुश्रुत्येन च प्रज्ञागमं विदित्वा। *आदीप्तशिरश्चैलोपमः श्रुतं* पर्येषते श्रुताश्च धर्मान् धारयति। प्रतिपत्तिसारश्च भवति न व्याहारपदवाक्यपरमः इमे काश्यप चत्वारो धर्माः बोधिसत्त्वस्य महाप्रज्ञतायै संवर्तंते। इदमुवाच भगवांस्तत्रेदमुच्यते॥

सगौरवो भवति च धर्मभाणके
यथाश्रुतान् धर्म परेषु[2] भाषते।
निरामिषश्चाप्रतिकांक्षमाणो
न लाभसत्कारशिलोक(3b)*चिन्तः*[3]।
श्रुतेन प्रज्ञागम सो विदित्वा
आदीप्तशीर्षः श्रुतमेषते सदा।

---

1 Folio 3a begins with an illegible *akṣara* preceded by a lacuna. At the given place Tib. does not provide a clue to a reconstruction.

2 m.c. for परेषां (VD n. 7).

3 ... ण्तः MS; ... य्.तः VD; Tib.: *mi sems par.*

यथाश्रुतान् धारयती च धर्मान्
धारित्व धर्मा प्रतिपत्तिया स्थितः।
प्रतिपत्तिसारो च स भोति पण्डितो
न *वाक्परो उक्तपरो* च भोति।
चत्वारिमा धर्म भजंत पण्डिताः
प्रज्ञामनाप्नोति[4] जिनप्रशस्ता॥

३

चतुर्भिः काश्यप धर्मैः समन्वागतस्य बोधिसत्त्वस्य बोधिचित्तं मुह्यति। कतमैश्चतुर्भिः यदु-
ताचार्यगुरुदाक्षिणीयविसंवादनतया[5]। परेषामकौकृत्ये कौकृत्योपसंहारणतया महायानसंप्र-
स्थिता (4a) *नां* च सत्त्वानामवर्णायशोऽकीर्तिशब्दश्लोकनिश्चारणतया[6] मायाशाठ्येन च *पर-*
मुपचरति नाध्याशयेन। एभिः काश्यप चतुर्भिः धर्मैः समन्वागतस्य बोधिसत्त्वस्य बोधि-
चित्तं मुह्यति। इदमुवाच भगवान्। तत्रेदमुच्यते॥

गुरुदाक्षिणीये न करोति प्रोक्तुं
परेषु कौकृत्युपसंहरन्ति।
बोधाय संप्रस्थित ये च सत्त्वास्
तेषामवर्णं अयशं भणंति।
मायाय शाठ्येन च कैतवेन
परं च सेवन्ति च नाशयेन।
चतुरो *इमे धर्म निषेव्यमाणा*
मोहेन्ति चित्तं वरबुद्धबोधये।

---

4 m.c. for अन्वाप्नोति (VD n. 8).

5 ŚS 33, 15: °दक्षिणीय°.

6 °यशकीर्ति° MS; Tib.: *brjod pa ma yin pa'i ...*

तस्मादिमान् *धर्म निषे*(4b)वमाणो
वराग्रबोधीय सुदूरि[7] *वर्तते*।
तद्विपरीतस्तु निषेवमाणो
वराग्रबोधिं स्पृशति प्रशास्ताम्॥

४

चतुर्भिः काश्यप धर्मैः समन्वागतस्य बोधिसत्त्वस्य सर्वासु जातिषु जातमात्रस्य *बोधिचित्तमामुखीभवति*[8] न चान्तरा मुह्यति यावद्बोधिमण्डनिषदनात्। कतमैश्चतुर्भिः यदुत जीवितहेतोरपि संप्रजानमृषावादं न भाषते अन्तमश हास्यप्रेक्ष्यमपि। अध्याशयेन च सर्वसत्त्वानामंतिके तिष्ठत्यपगतमायाशाठ्यतया। सर्वबोधिसत्त्वेषु च शास्तृसंज्ञामुत्पादयति। चतुर्दिशं च तेषां *वर्णं निः*(5a)चारयति[9]। यांश्च सत्त्वान् परिपाचयति तान् सर्वाननुत्तरायां सम्यक्संबोधौ समादापयति *प्रादेशिकयानास्पृहणतया*[10]। एभिः काश्यप चतुर्भिः धर्मैः समन्वागतस्य बोधिसत्त्वस्य *सर्वासु* जातिषु जातमात्रस्य बोधिचित्तमामुखीभवति न चान्तरा मुह्यति यावद्बोधिमण्डनिषदनात्। *तत्रेदम्* उच्यते॥

न जीवितार्थे अनृतं वदन्ति
भाषंति वाचं सद् अर्थयुक्तां।
मायाय शाठ्येन च नित्य वर्जिता
अध्याशयेन सद् सत्त्व पश्यति।
बोधाय ये प्रस्थित शुद्धसत्त्वा
शास्तेति तान्मन्यति बोधिसत्त्वान्।

---

7 m.c. for सुदूरे (VD n. 19).
8 See ŚS 33, 18.
9 See ŚS 33, 21.
10 See ŚS 33, 22; °यानस्पृहणतया MS.

(5b) वर्णं च तेषां भणते चतुर्दिशं
शास्तार संज्ञां सदुपस्थपित्वा।
यांश्चापि सत्त्वान् परिपाचयति
अनुत्तरे *ज्ञानि*[11] समादपेति।
एतेषु धर्मेषु प्रतिष्ठितानां
चित्तं न बोधाय कदाचि मुह्यति॥

५

चतुर्भिः काश्यप *धर्मैः* समन्वागतस्य बोधिसत्त्वस्योत्पन्नोत्पन्ना कुशला धर्माः पर्यादीयंते[12] यैर्न विवर्धति *कुशलैर्* धर्मैः। कतमैश्चतुर्भिः। यदुत अभिमानिकस्य लोकायतमन्त्रपर्येष्ट्या[13]। *लाभसत्काराध्यवसितस्य* कुलप्रत्यवलोकनेन। बोधिसत्त्वविद्वेषाभ्याख्यानेन। अश्रुतानामनुद्दिष्टानां च *सूत्रान्तानां प्रतिक्षेपे*(6a)*ण*। एभिः काश्यप चतुर्भिर्धर्मैः समन्वागतस्य बोधिसत्त्वस्योत्पन्नोत्पन्ना कुशला *धर्माः पर्यादीयन्ते यैर्न* विवर्धते कुशलैर्धर्मैः तत्रेदमुच्यते॥

लोकायिकं एषति आभिमानिको
कुलानि *चा योजयते लभार्थो*[14]।
बुद्धौरसा द्विषते च बोधिसत्त्वान्
तेषामवर्णं भणते समंतात्।
नोद्दिष्ट नो चापि श्रुतान् *स सूत्रान्*
प्रतिक्षिपीत[15] इमि जिनेन प्रोक्तान्।
तमेहि धर्मेहि समन्वितस्य

---

11 m. c. for ज्ञाने (VD n. 28).
12 ŚS 82, 23: परिहीयन्ते.
13 See ŚS 82, 24; लोकायतन° MS.
14 m.c. for च योजयति लाभार्थो.
15 [pRVt] क्षिपीत (?), Tib. *spoṅ bar byed.*

कुशलेषु धर्मेषु न वृद्धिरस्ति।
तस्माद् *हि यः पण्डित* बोधिसत्त्वो
दूरान् विजह्याच्चतुरो ऽपि धर्मान्।
इमा निषेवन्त सुदूरि बोधये
नभं व भूमीय सुदूरदूरे॥

६

च(6b)तुर्भिः काश्यप धर्मैः समन्वागतो बोधिसत्त्वः अपरिहाणधर्मो भवति विशेषगामितायै। कतमैश्चतुर्भिः *सुश्रुतं* पर्येषते न दुश्रुतं। यदुत षट्पारमिताबोधिसत्त्वपिटकपर्येष्टि। श्वसदृशश्च भवति *निर्मानतया* सर्वसत्त्वेषु। धर्मलाभसंतुष्टश्च भवति। सर्वमिथ्याजीवपरिवर्जितः आर्यवंशसंतुष्टः नापत्त्या चापत्त्या[16] न परांश्चोदयति। न च दोषान्तरस्खलितगवेषी भवति। येषु *चास्य गम्भीरेषु बुद्धिर्नावगाहते*[17] तत्र तथागतमेव साक्षीति कृत्वा न प्रतिक्षिपति। तथागत एव जानाति नाहं *जाने*। *अनन्ता बुद्धबो*(7a)धिर्नानाधिमुक्तिकानां सत्त्वानां यथाधिमुक्तिकतया धर्मदेशना प्रवर्तते। एभिः *काश्यप चतुर्भिः धर्मैः समन्वागतो* बोधिसत्त्वः अपरिहाणधर्मो भवति विशेषगामितायै। तत्रेदमुच्यते॥

नित्यं च सो *पारमितासु* युक्तो
उपायकौशल्यथ बोधिपीटके।
निर्मानतायाश्च श्वचित्तसादृशो
सर्वे च सत्त्वेषु *निहातमानो*[18]।
तुष्टश्च लाभेन स धार्मिकेन
आजीवशुद्धो स्थित आर्यवंशे।

---

16 नापताया चापत्या MS.
17 See ŚS 34, 28: for °नावहगाहते read °नावगाहते.
18 m.c. for निहत°.

परं च नापत्तिषु चोदयंतो
स्खलितं *परेषां* न गवेषमाणो।
न गाहते यत्र च बुद्धिरस्य
तथागतं साक्षिकरोति तत्र।
नाहं प्रजानामि जिनो *प्रजानते*
(7b) अनन्त बोधी[19] सुगतेन भाषिता।
इमा तु धर्माश्चतुरो विदित्वा
न हापये जातु विशेषमुत्तमम्।
इमेषु धर्मेषु प्रतिष्ठितस्य
न दुर्लभा बोधि जिनप्रशस्ता॥

७

चत्वार इमे काश्यप कुटिलाश्चित्तोत्पादास्तेन बोधिसत्त्वेन परिवर्जितव्याः कतमे चत्वार। यदुत कांक्षा विमतिर्विचिकित्सा सर्वबुद्धधर्मेषु। मानमदम्रक्षक्रोधव्यापादाः सर्वसत्त्वेषु। ईर्ष्यामात्सर्यं परलाभेषु। अवर्णायशोऽकीर्तिशब्दश्लोकनिश्चारणतया *बोधिसत्त्वेषु*। इमे काश्यप चत्वारः कुटिलाश्चित्तोत्पादास्तेन बोधिसत्त्वेन परिवर्जितव्याः तत्रेदमुच्यते॥

धर्मेषु कांक्षां वि(8a)मतिं च कुर्वति
सत्त्वेषु मानं मदक्रोध सेवति।
मात्सर्यमिर्ष्या परलाभ कुर्वते
जिने प्रसादं च न *कुर्वते क्वचित्*।
अकीर्त्यवर्णं अयशं च चारयी
सो बोधिसत्त्वेषु सदा अविद्वान्।

---

19 बोधि MS.

चत्वारि चित्ता कुटिला विवर्जयेत्
स्यात् सत्त्वपक्षं सद बोधिसत्त्वः ॥

८

चत्वार इमे काश्यप ऋजुकस्य बोधिसत्त्वस्य ऋजुकलक्षणानि भवन्ति। कतमानि चत्वारि। यदुत आपत्त्यापन्नो न प्रच्छादयत्याचष्टे विवृणोति निष्पर्युत्थानो भवति। येन सत्यवचनेन राज्यपारिहाणिर्वा धनपारिहाणिर्वा कायजीवितान्तरायो भवेत्तत् सत्यवचनं न *विगूहति*[20] (8b)नान्येनान्यं प्रतिनिसृत्य वाचा भाषते। सर्वपरोपक्रमेषु चाक्रोशपरिभाषणकुंसनपंसनताडनतर्जनवधबन्धनापराधेष्वात्मापराधी भवति कर्मविपाकप्रतिसरणो न परेषां कुप्यति नानुशयं वहति। स श्रद्धाप्रतिष्ठितश्च भवति। सर्वाश्रद्धेयानपि बुद्धधर्मान् श्रद्दधाति आशयशुद्धतामुपादाय। इमे काश्यप चत्वारो ऋजुकस्य बोधिसत्त्वस्य ऋजुकलक्षणानि भवंति। तत्रेदमुच्यते॥

आपत्तिमापन्न न च्छादयंति
कथेन्ति विवरंति च एति दोषात्[21]।
धनराज्यहेतो न च जीवितार्थं
मृषा (9a) वदंते विदधीय संज्ञाम्।
आक्रोशनाकुत्सनपंसनासु
वधेषु बन्धेष्ववरोधनेषु।
आत्मापराधी न परेषु कुप्यते
कर्मस्वको नानुशयं वहंतो।
स श्रद्दधाति सुगतान बोधिं
श्रद्धास्थितो आशयि शुद्धि युक्तो।

---

[20] After SH; Tib. *mi 'khyud cin* – see Negi 1993ff. s.v. *'khyud pa.*

[21] em. एते दोषान् (VD n. 55f.); Tib., however, *ñes pa 'dor.*

ऋजुकलक्षणा ह्येति जिनेन प्रोक्ता
वराग्रसत्त्वेन निषेवितव्याः॥

९

चत्वार इमे काश्यप बोधिसत्त्वखडुंकाः कतमे चत्वारः श्रुतोद्धतधर्मविहारी च भवति न च प्रतिपद्यते धर्मानुधर्मप्रतिपत्तिं। अनुशासनेनोद्धतधर्मविहारी च भवति। न च शुश्रूषत्याचार्योपाध्यायानां। श्रद्धादेयं विनिपातयति *च्युत*(9b)प्रतिज्ञश्च श्रद्धादेयं परिभुंक्ते। दान्ताजानेयप्राप्तांश्च बोधिसत्त्वां दृष्ट्वा अगौरवो भवति मानग्राही। इमे काश्यप चत्वारो बोधिसत्त्वखडुंकाः तत्रेदमुच्यते॥

श्रुतेन औद्धत्यविहारि भोति
न चोद्धतो गच्छति आनुशासनिं।
सो उद्धतो सेवति सर्वधर्मान्
शुश्रूषते न च आर्यां कथंचित्।
च्युतप्रतिज्ञो परिभुंजते सदा
श्रद्धाय दिन्नानि सुभोजनानि।
आजन्यप्राप्तानपि बोधिसत्त्वान्
पश्यित्व नो गौरवता करोति।
मानं च सो बृंहयते खडुंको
निर्मान[22] नो[23] सेवति बोधिसत्त्वान्।
एते खडुंका सुगतेन प्रोक्ता
जिनात्मजैस्ते परि(10a)वर्जनीयाः[24]॥

---

22 m.c. for निर्मानान्; निर्माण MS.

23 em. after VD n. 64; तो MS.

24 em. after Tib.; °आत्मजास्ते ... °वर्जनीयात् MS.

१०

चत्वार इमे काश्यप आजानेया बोधिसत्त्वाः कतमे चत्वारः सुश्रुतं श्रुणोति तत्र च प्रतिपद्यते। अर्थप्रतिसरणश्च भवति न व्यंजनप्रतिसरणः प्रदक्षिणग्राही भवत्यववादानुशासने। सुवचाः सुकृतकर्मकारी च भवति। गुरुशुश्रूषनिर्यातः आजानेय भोजनानि च परिभुंक्ते। अच्युतशीलसमाधिर्दान्ताजानेयप्राप्तांश्च[25] बोधिसत्त्वां दृष्ट्वा सगौरवो भवति सप्रतीशः तन्निम्नः तत्प्रवणः तत्प्राग्भारः तद्गुणप्रतिकांक्षी। इमे काश्यप चत्वारो आजानेया बोधिसत्त्वाः तत्रेदमुच्यते॥

श्रुणोति यं सुश्रुत (10b) तं करोति
धर्मार्थसारो प्रतिपत्तिसुस्थितः।
प्रदक्षिणं गृह्णति आनुशासनीं
सुवचो गुरु सेवति धर्मकाम।
शीले समाधौ च सदा प्रतिष्ठितो
स भोजनं[26] भुंजति शीलसंवृतः।
सगौरवो भवति च सप्रतीशो[27]
तन्निम्न तत्प्रोणु गुणाभिकांक्षि।
आजन्यप्राप्ताश्च जिनोरसा ये
प्रेमेण तां पश्यति नित्यकालम्।
चत्वार एते सुगतोपदिष्टा
आजन्यप्राप्ता सुगतस्य पुत्राः॥

---

[25] em. after SH and VD n. 65; °जानेयाप्राप्तश्च MS.
[26] सुभोजनं MS; Tib.: *de ni bza' ba za* (VD n. 66: reference to Weller 1965).
[27] em. after VD n. 67 (Tib.: *rje sar bcas pa*); सप्रदेशो MS.

११

चत्वार इमे काश्यप बोधिसत्त्वस्खलितानि। कतमानि चत्वारि। अपरिपाचितेषु सत्त्वेषु विश्वासो बोधिसत्त्वस्य स्खलितं। अभाजनीभूतेषु सत्त्वेषूदारबुद्धधर्मसंप्रकाश(11a)नता बोधिसत्त्वस्य स्खलितं। उदाराधिमुक्तिकेषु सत्त्वेषु हीनयानसंप्रकाशना बोधिसत्त्वस्य स्खलितं। सम्यक्प्रत्युपस्थितेषु सत्त्वेषु शीलवत्सु कल्याणधर्मेषु[28] प्रतिविमानना दुःशीलपापधर्मसंग्रहो बोधिसत्त्वस्य स्खलितं। इमानि काश्यप चत्वारो बोधिसत्त्वस्खलितानि। तत्रेदमुच्यते॥

न विश्वसेयापरिपाचितेषु
अभाजने धर्म उदार नो भणे।
उदारधर्मेषु न हीनयाने
प्रकाशये जातु स बोधिसत्त्वो।
सम्यक्स्थितां शीलगुणोपपेतान्
कल्याणधर्मा न विमानयेत।
दुःशीलसत्त्वा न परिग्रहेया
पापं च धर्मन् परिवर्जयेत।
स्ख(11b)लितानि चत्वारि इमानि ज्ञात्वा
विवर्जयेद्दूरत बोधिसत्त्वः।
इमा निषेवंतु न बोधि बुध्यते
तस्माद्विवर्जेदिमि धर्म पण्डितः॥

[28] See ŚS 34, 22; कल्याणधर्म MS.

१२

चत्वार इमे काश्यप बोधिसत्त्वमार्गाः कतमे चत्वारः समचित्तता सर्वसत्त्वेषु। बुद्धज्ञानसमादापनता सर्वसत्त्वेषु। समधर्मदेशना सर्वसत्त्वेषु। सम्यक्प्रयोगता सर्वसत्त्वेषु। इमे काश्यप चत्वारो बोधिसत्त्वमार्गाः तत्रेदमुच्यते॥

समचित्त सत्त्वेषु भवेत नित्यं
समादपेयादिह बुद्धयाने।
धर्मं च देशेत जिनप्रशस्तं
सर्वेषु सत्त्वेषु प्रसन्नचित्तो।
सम्य(12a)क्प्रयुक्ता प्रतिपत्तिसुस्थितो
सर्वेषु सत्त्वेषु समं चरेत।
मार्गानिमांश्चतुर जिनप्रशस्तां
जिनोरसा सद तं भावयन्ति॥

१३

चत्वार इमे काश्यप बोधिसत्त्वस्य कुमित्राणि कुसहायास्ते बोधिसत्त्वेन परिवर्जयितव्या। कतमानि चत्वारि। श्रावकयानीयो भिक्षु आत्महिताय प्रतिपन्नः प्रत्येकबुद्धयानीयो ऽल्पार्थो ऽल्पकृत्यः लोकायतिको विचित्रमन्त्रप्रतिभाणः यं च पुद्गलं सेवमान ततो लोकामिषसंग्रहो भवति न धर्मसंग्रहः इमे काश्यप चत्वारो बोधिसत्त्वस्य कुमित्राणि कुसहायास्ते बोधिसत्त्वेन परिव(12b)र्जयितव्याः तत्रेदमुच्यते॥

ये श्रावका आत्महिताय युक्ता
योगं च ये प्रव्रजिताश्चरंति।
प्रत्येकबुद्धापि च ये ऽल्पकृत्या

अल्पार्थ संसर्ग विवर्जयंति।
लोकायतं ये च पठंति बाला
विग्राहिका यत्र कथोपदिष्टा।
यं सेवमानामिषसंग्रहो भवेद्
भवेन्न धर्मस्य च संग्रहो यहिम्।
तान्बोधिसत्वाश्चतुरो प्रहाय
कल्याणमित्राश्चतुरो भजंति।
एते कुमित्रा कुसहाय उक्ता[29]
जिनेन दूरात्परिवर्जनीया॥

१४

चत्वार इमे काश्यप बोधिसत्त्वस्य भूतकल्याणमित्राणि। कतमानि चत्वारि। याचनको बोधि(**13a**)सत्त्वस्य भूतकल्याणमित्रं बोधिमार्गोपस्तंभाय संवर्तते। धर्मभाणको बोधिसत्त्वस्य भूतकल्याणमित्रं श्रुतप्रज्ञोपस्तंभाय संवर्तते। प्रव्रज्यासमादपको बोधिसत्त्वस्य भूतकल्याणमित्रं सर्वकुशलमूलोपस्तंभाय संवर्तते। बुद्धो भगवां[30] बोधिसत्त्वस्य भूतकल्याणमित्रं सर्वबुद्धधर्मोपस्तंभाय संवर्तते। इमे काश्यप बोधिसत्त्वस्य भूतकल्याणमित्राणि। तत्रेदमुच्यते॥

कल्याणमित्रं स च दायकानां
प्रतिग्राहको बोधिपरिग्रहाय।
धर्मार्थवादी श्रुतप्रज्ञकारी
कल्याणमित्रं सुगतेन (**13b**)प्रोक्तं।
प्रव्रज्य ये चापि समादपेन्ति

[29] युक्ता MS; Tib.: *gsuṅs te.*
[30] em. after SI P/85A 5r.3 (VD n. 76); बुद्धा भगवन्तो MS.

ते मित्र मूलं सुकृतस्य[31] वुक्ताः।
बुद्धाश्च मित्रं सुगतात्मजानां
संबुद्धमार्गस्युपस्तंभनाय।
एते हि चत्वारि जिनप्रशस्ता
कल्याणमित्रा सुगतात्मजानां।
एतान्[32] निषेवन्त सदाप्रमत्ता
प्राप्नोति बोधी सुगतोपदिष्टा॥

१५

चत्वार इमे काश्यप बोधिसत्त्वप्रतिरूपकाः कतमे चत्वारः लाभसत्कारार्थिको भवति न धर्मार्थिकः कीर्तिशब्दश्लोकार्थिको भवति न गुणार्थिकः आत्मसुखार्थिको भवति न सत्त्वदुःखापनयनार्थिकः[33] पर्षद्गणार्थिको[34] भवति *न* (14a) विवेकार्थिकः इमे काश्यप चत्वारो बोधिसत्त्वप्रतिरूपकाः तत्रेदमुच्यते॥

लाभार्थिको भवति *न* धर्मकामो
कीर्त्यर्थिको न्नेव गुणैभिरर्थिकः।
न सत्त्वदुःखापनयेन चार्थिको
यो चात्मनो नित्य सुखेन चार्थिकः।
पर्षद्गणार्थी न विवेककामो
सुखे प्रसक्तो न गुणेषु सक्तो।

31 सुगतस्य MS; Tib.: *dge rtsa yin pas.*
32 em. after VD n. 79; एता MS.
33 ŚS 81, 12: सर्वसत्त्वदुःखा°.
34 em. after VD n. 83; °गुणा° MS.

चत्वार एते प्रतिरूपकोक्ताः
ते बोधिसत्त्वात्परिवर्जनीया[35]॥

१६

चत्वार इमे काश्यप बोधिसत्त्वस्य भूतगुणाः[36] कतमे चत्वार। शून्यतां चाधिमुच्यते कर्मविपाकं चाभिश्रद्दधाति। नैरात्म्यं चास्य क्षमते सर्वसत्त्वेषु महाकरुणा। (14b)निर्वाणगतश्चास्याशयः संसारगतश्च प्रयोगः सत्त्वपरिपाकाय च दानं विपाकाप्रतिकांक्षणता च। इमे काश्यप चत्वारो धर्मा बोधिसत्त्वस्य भूतगुणाः तत्रेदमुच्यते॥

शून्याश्च धर्मानधिमुच्यते सदा
विपाक पत्तीयति कर्मणं च।
नैरात्म्यक्षान्त्या समताप्रतिष्ठितो
करुणां च सत्त्वेषु जनेति नित्यं।
निर्वाणि भावो सद[37] तस्य भोति
प्रयोग संसारगतश्च तस्य।
परिपाचनार्थं च ददाति दानं
विपाक नाकांक्षति कर्मणां च॥

१७

चत्वार इमे काश्यप बोधिसत्त्वस्य महानिधानप्रतिलंभाः[38] कतमे *चत्वारः* (15a)बुद्धोत्पादारागणता। षट्पारमिताश्रवणः अप्रतिहतचित्तस्य धर्मभाणकदर्शनं। अप्रमत्तस्यारण्यवा-

[35] m.c. for बोधिसत्त्वेन परि°; Tib. *byaṅ chub sems dpas.*
[36] em. after SI P/85A 5r.6 (VD n. 86); भूता बोधिसत्वगुणा MS.
[37] m. c. for सदा (VD n. 88); सत MS.
[38] °निदान° MS.

साभिरतिः[39] इमे काश्यप चत्वारो बोधिसत्त्वस्य महानिधानप्रतिलंभाः तत्रेदमुच्यते॥

बुद्धानमारागण सर्वजातिषु
श्रवश्च षण्णामपि पारमीणां।
प्रसन्नचित्तो ऽपि च धर्मभाणकं
संपश्यते गौरव जातु नित्यम्।
सदाप्रमत्तस्य चारण्यवासो
तत्रैव सो भोति रतिः सदास्य।
चत्वार धर्मा सुगतेन प्रोक्ता
महानिधानानि जिनात्मजानाम्॥

१८

चत्वार इमे काश्यप बोधिसत्त्वमारपथसमतिक्रमा[40] धर्माः (15b)कतमे चत्वारः बोधिचित्त-स्यानुत्सर्गः सर्वसत्त्वेष्वप्रतिहतचित्तता। सर्वदृष्टीकृतानामवबोधः[41] अनतिमन्यना सर्वसत्त्वे-षु। इमे काश्यप चत्वारो बोधिसत्त्वस्य मारपथसमतिक्रमा धर्माः तत्रेदमुच्यते॥

बोधाय चित्तं न परित्यजंति
सत्त्वेषु च प्रतिघ जहंति नित्यम्।
सर्वांश्च दृष्टीगतन्[42] उत्सृजंति
न चाधिमन्यन्ति ह सत्त्वकायम्।
चत्वार एते सुगतेन प्रोक्ता
धर्मा हि मारस्य अतिक्रमाय।

---

39 em. after SI P/85A 5v.3; °आभिरतः MS.
40 °समतिक्क्रमणा MS.
41 em. after SI P/85A 5v.5 (VD n. 94); अवबोधना MS.
42 em. after VD n. 96; दृष्टिगतन् MS.

एतान् निषेविब जिना भवंति
अंगीरसा अप्रतिमा विनायका॥

१९

चब्रार इमे काश्यप धर्मा बोधिसत्त्वस्य सर्वकुश(16a)लधर्मसंग्रहाय संवर्तन्ते। कतमे चब्रा-र। निष्कुहकस्यारण्यवासाभिरतिः प्रतिकाराप्रतिकांक्षिणश्चब्रारि संग्रहवस्तूनि। सर्वसत्त्वेषु कायजीवितोत्सर्गः सद्धर्मपर्यैष्टिमारभ्यातृप्तिता सर्वकुशलमूलसमुदाननाय। इमे काश्यप चब्रारो धर्मा बोधिसत्त्वस्य सर्वकुशलधर्मसंग्रहाय संवर्तन्ते। तत्रेदमुच्यते॥

अरण्यवासे कुहनाविवर्जितो
सत्त्वेषु चा संग्रहयो जिनोक्ता।
उत्सर्ग कायस्य च जीवितस्य
सद्धर्मपर्यैष्टि समारभिब्रा।
समुदाननायाश्च सदा अतृप्तो
कुशलान मूलान अन(16b)ल्पकानां।
कुशलान धर्माण च संग्रहार्थे
चब्रार धर्मा सुगतेन प्रोक्ता॥

२०

चब्रार इमे काश्यप बोधिसत्त्वस्याप्रमेया पुण्यसंभाराः कतमे चब्रारः निरामिषचित्तस्य धर्मदानं। दुःशीलेषु च सत्त्वेषु महाकरुणा। सर्वसत्त्वेषु बोधिचित्तारोचनता। दुर्बलेषु सत्त्वेषु क्षान्त्या सेवनता। इमे काश्यप चब्रारो बोधिसत्त्वस्याप्रमेया पुण्यसंभाराः तत्रेदमुच्यते॥

दानं च धर्मस्य जिनप्रशस्तं
चित्तेन शुद्धेन निरामिषेण।

अपेतशीले करुणा च तीव्रा
परेषु बोधाय जनेति चित्तम्।
क्षान्त्याधिसेवेति च दुर्बलेषु
धर्मेष्व् *अमी* (17a) संग्रहताय[43] चोक्ता।
एता निषेवित्व जिना भवंति
ते बोधिसत्त्वे सद सेवितव्याः॥

चतुष्कका अष्ट जहित्व पापका
बोधाय ये आवरणं करोन्ति।
तथापरा द्वादश सेव्य पण्डिता
प्राप्नोति बोधिं अमृतं स्पृशित्वा।
ये चाग्रसत्त्वा इम धर्मनेत्री
धारेन्ति वाचेन्ति प्रकाशयन्ति।
तेषा जिनो पुण्यमनन्तु भाषते
येषामप्रमाणं जिन वर्णयंति।
ये क्षेत्रकोट्यो यथ गंगवालिका
रत्नान पूरित्वन तेषु[44] दद्यात्।
यो वा इतो गाथ चतुष्पदी पठेद्
इमस्य पुण्यस्य न एति संख्या॥

[43] m.c. for संग्रहाय; संग्रहता- *य* MS.
[44] m.c. for तेषां (VD n. 110).

२१

चत्वार इमे काश्यप धर्मा बोधिसत्त्वस्य अविद्या(17b)भागीयक्लेशसमतिक्रमाय संवर्तते। कतमे चत्वारः शीलसंवरः सद्धर्मपरिग्रहः प्रदीपदानमन्तमशः संस्तुतेभ्यः इमे काश्यप चत्वारो धर्मा बोधिसत्त्वस्य अविद्याभागीयक्लेशसमतिक्रमाय संवर्तते॥

२२

चत्वार इमे काश्यप धर्मा बोधिसत्त्वस्य अनावरणज्ञानताये संवर्तते। कतमे चत्वारः यदुत इन्द्रियसंवरः गंभीरार्थविवरणता स्वलाभेनानवमन्यना। परलाभेश्वनध्यवसानता। इमे काश्यप चत्वारो धर्मा बोधिसत्त्वस्यानावरणज्ञानताये संवर्तन्ते॥

२३

न खलु *पुनः* (18a)काश्यप नाममात्रेण बोधिसत्त्वो महासत्त्व इत्युच्यते। धर्मचर्यया समचर्यया कुशलचर्यया धर्माश्रिताभिः काश्यप समन्वागतो बोधिसत्त्वो महासत्त्व इत्युच्यते। द्वात्रिंशद्भि काश्यप धर्मैः समन्वागतो बोधिसत्त्वो इत्युच्यते। कतमे द्वात्रिंशद्भिः यदुत हितसुखाध्याशयतया सर्वसत्त्वेषु। सर्वज्ञज्ञानावतारणतया। किमहमर्घामीति[45] परेषां ज्ञानाकुत्सनतया निरधिमानतया। दृढाध्याशयतया। अकृत्रिमप्रेमतया। अत्यंतमित्रता[46]। मित्रामित्रेषु समचित्ततया। यावन्नि(18b)र्वाणपर्यंतताये।

---

[45] em. after Weller 1965: 82, n. 4; अर्गामीति MS.

[46] em. °तया; the qualities enumerated in the following mostly appear in the nom. in lieu of the instr.

२४

सूनृतवाक्यता[47] स्मितमुखपूर्वाभिभाषणता। उपादत्तेषु[48] भारेष्व् *अविषादनतया*। सर्वसत्त्वेष्वपरिच्छिन्नमहाकरुणता अपरिखिन्नमानसतया। सद्धर्मपर्येष्टिमारभ्यातृप्तता श्रुतार्थतया। आत्मस्खलितेषु दोषदर्शनतया परस्खलितेष्वरुष्टापत्तिचोदनतया। सर्वेर्यापथेषु बोधिचित्तपरिकर्मणतया[49]। विपाकाप्रतिकांक्षिण त्यागः[50] सर्वभवगत्युपपत्त्यनिःश्रितं शीलम्। सर्वसत्त्वेष्वप्रतिहता क्षांतिः

२५

सर्वकुशलमूलसमुदाननाय वीर्यं। आरूप्यधातु(19a)परिकर्षितं ध्यानं। उपायसंगृहीता प्रज्ञा चतुःसंग्रहवस्तुसंप्रयुक्ता उपाय। शीलवद्दुःशीलाद्वयतया मैत्रता। सत्कृत्य धर्मश्रवणं सत्कृत्यारण्यवासः सर्वलोकविचित्रिकेष्वनभिरतिः *कु*-[51]दृष्टिविगतं। हीनयानास्पृहणता[52] महायाने चानुशंससंदर्शितया। पापमित्रविवर्जनता कल्याणमित्रसेवनता। चतुब्रह्मविहारनिष्पादनता। पंचाभिज्ञविक्क्रीडनता। ज्ञानप्रतिसरणता। प्रतिपत्तिविप्रतिपत्तिस्थिताना सत्त्वनामनुत्सर्गः एकांशवचनता। सत्यगुरुकता। *सर्व*(19b)कुशलमूलसमुदानतया अतृप्तता। बोधिचित्तपूर्वंगमता।

---

47 em. after Weller 1965: 82, n. 11; अनृत° MS.
48 I.e. उपात्तेषु ; नुपादत्तेषु MS.
49 em. after ŚS 34, 4–5; सर्वैर्यापथेषु बोधिचित्तपरिकर्मतया MS.
50 Cf. the KP quotation/quasi-quotation in the *Mahāyāna-Sūtrālaṃkāra* (Bagchi 1970: 158, 14): विपाको (*sic*) ऽप्रतिकाङ्क्षिणो दानेनेति.
51 After VD n. 127.
52 °यानस्पृहणता MS.

२६

एभिः काश्यप द्वात्रिंशद्भिर्धर्मैः समन्वागतो बोधिसत्त्वो महासत्त्व इत्युच्यते। तत्रेदमुच्यते॥

सर्वेषु सत्त्वेषु हितं सुखं च
अध्याशयेनाप्यधिमुच्यमानाः।
सर्वज्ञज्ञानोतरणाय किं नु
अर्घामि नार्घाम्यहं ज्ञानमाना।
अकुत्सनतयानधिमानताया
दृढाशयाकृत्रिमप्रेमताया।
सत्त्वेषु चात्यन्तसुमित्रताया[53]
यावन्न निर्वाणपरायणत्वं।
मित्रे अमित्रे समचित्तताया
स्मितोमुखत्वं सूनृता च वाणी।
उपात्तभारे ... (20a)दार्यणत्वं
करुणापरिच्छिन्न तथेव सत्त्वे॥

२७

सद्धर्मपर्येष्टिय नास्ति खेदः
श्रुतेष्वतृप्ते स्खलिते *त्मदोषदृक्*[54]।
परश्च रुष्टेन न चोदनीयः
ईर्यापथे चित्तसुकर्मताया।
त्यागो विपाकाप्रतिकांक्षणं च

---

53 em. after Weller 1965: 85, n. 5; °अमित्रताया MS.
54 I.e. स्खलित *आत्म*°; after Tib. *lta* (Negi 1993ff. s.v.).

अनिश्रितं शील भवंगतीषु।
सत्त्वेषु क्षांति प्रतिघातवर्जिता
समुदाननाया कुशलस्य वीर्यम्।
आरूप्यधात्ववकृष्टं च ध्यानं
उपायतो संगृहीता च प्रज्ञा।
चतुःसंग्रहेः संग्रहीतोपायो
दुःशीलशीले (ऽ)द्वयता च मैत्र्या।
सत्कृत्य धर्मश्रवणं च कालं
सत्कृत्य वासो च अरण्यशान्ते।
लोकेषु चित्रेषु रतिर्न कार्यं
हीनेषु (20b) यानेषु रतिर्न कार्यम्।
उदारयानेषु स्पृहा जनेया
पापाणि मित्राणि विवर्जयेया।
कल्याणमित्राणि सदा च सेवे
चत्वार ब्रह्माश्च विहार भावयेत्॥

२८

क्रीडेतभिज्ञेहि च पंचभिः सदा
ज्ञानानुसारी च भवेत *नित्यं*।
न उत्सृजेया प्रतिपत्तियुक्ता
न च द्वितीयापि कदाचिदन्या।
एकांतवादी च भवेत नित्यं
सत्ये च से गौरव नित्य भोति।
भावेति धर्मांश्च जिनप्रशस्ता

पूर्वंगमं बोधयि चित्त कृत्वा।
द्वात्रिंशदेते सुगतेन प्रोक्ता
धर्मा निषेव्या सुगतोरसेभि[55]।
इमेहि धर्मेहि समन्विता ये
ते बोधिसत्त्वा सुगतेन प्रोक्ता॥

२९

उपमो(21a)पन्यासनिर्देशांस्ते[56] काश्यप निर्देक्ष्यामि यैरुपमोपन्यासनिर्देशेभिः बोधिसत्त्व-महासत्त्वगुणान्[57] *विज्ञापयेत्*। तद्यथा काश्यप इयं महापृथिवी सर्वसत्त्वोपजीव्या निर्विकारा निष्प्रतिकारा। एवमेव काश्यप प्रथमचित्तोत्पादिको बोधिसत्त्वो यावद्बोधिमण्डनिषदना ताव-त्सर्वसत्त्वोपजीव्यो निर्विकारो निष्प्रतिकारो भवति। तत्रेदमुच्यते॥

पृथिवी यथा सर्वजनोपजीव्या
प्रतिकार नाकांक्षति निर्विकारा।
चित्ते तथाद्ये स्थित बोधिसत्त्वो
यावन्न बुद्धो भविता जिनोत्तम।
अनुत्तरा सर्वजनोपजीव्यो
प्रतिका(21b)र नाकांक्षति निर्विकारो।
पुत्रे च शत्रुंहि च तुल्यमान सो[58]
पर्येषते नित्य वराग्रबोधिम्॥

---

55 em. after VD n. 145; °रसेति MS.

56 °शास्ते MS.

57 em. after Weller 1965: 86, n. 19; बोधिसत्वो महासत्वगुणान् MS.

58 After SH, Weller 1965: 87, n. 1; तुल्यमानसो (VD n. 147).

३०

तद्यथा काश्यप अब्धातु सर्वतृणगुल्मोषधिवनस्पतयो रोहापयति। एवमेव काश्यप आशयशुद्धो बोधिसत्त्वः सर्वसत्त्वानि मैत्रतया स्फरित्वा विहरन् सर्वसत्त्वानां सर्वशुक्लधर्मान् विरोहयति। तत्रेदमुच्यते॥

यथापि आब्धातु तृणगुल्ममौषधी
वनस्पतीनौषधिधान्यजातान्[59]।
एमेव शुद्धाशयबोधिसत्त्वो
मैत्र्याय सत्त्वान् स्फरते अनंतान्।
स्फरित्व धर्मान् विविधा क्रमेण
शुक्लेहि धर्मेहि विवर्धमानः।
अनुपू(22a)र्व प्राप्नोति जिनान बोधिं
निहत्य मारं सबलं ससैन्यम्॥

३१

तद्यथा काश्यप तेजोधातुः सर्वसस्यानि परिपाचयति। एवमेव काश्यप बोधिसत्त्वस्य प्रज्ञा सर्वसत्त्वानां सर्वशुक्लधर्मान् परिपाचयति। तत्रेदमुच्यते॥

यथापि तेजो परिपाचयंति
सस्यानि सर्वाणि तृणौषधींश्च।
एमेव प्रज्ञा सुगतात्मजानान्
धर्मान् शुभा वर्धयते जनस्य॥

---

[59] em. after VD n. 147; °जाताम् MS.

३२

तद्यथा काश्यप वायुधातुः सर्वबुद्धक्षेत्राणि विठपयति। एवमेव काश्यप बोधिसत्त्वस्योपाय-कौशल्यं सर्वबुद्धधर्मान् विठपयति। तत्रेदमुच्यते॥

वायु(22b)र्यथेव विठपेति क्षेत्रान्
बुद्धान नानाविध आशयातो।
उपाय एवं हि जिनोरसानाम्
विठपंति धर्मान् सुगतोक्तमग्रान्॥

३३

तद्यथापि नाम काश्यप मारस्य पापीमतश्चतुरंगं बलसैन्य सर्वदेवैर्न शक्यमभिभवितुं पर्यादतुं वा। एवमेव काश्यप शुद्धाशयो बोधिसत्त्व सर्वमारैर्न शक्यमभिभवितुं पर्यादत्तुं वा॥

३४

तद्यथापि नाम काश्यप शुक्लपक्षे चन्द्रमण्डलं परिपूर्यते वर्धते च। एवमेव काश्यप आशय-शुद्धो बोधिसत्त्वः सर्वशुक्लधर्मैर्वर्धते। तत्रेदमुच्यते॥

शुक्लपक्षे यथा चन्द्रमण्डलं *परि-*[60]
(23a)पूर्यते वर्धति नो च हीयते।
एमेव शुद्धाशय बोधिसत्त्वो
शुद्धेहि धर्मेहि सदा विवर्धते॥

---

[60] After Tib. *yoṅs su gaṅ 'gyur.*

३५

तद्यथापि *नाम* काश्यप सूर्यमण्डलमेकप्रमुक्ताभि सूर्यरश्मिभिः सत्त्वानामवभासं करोति। एवमेव काश्यप बोधिसत्त्वमेकप्रमुक्ताभिः प्रज्ञारश्मिभिः सत्त्वानां ज्ञानावभासं करोति। तत्रेदमुच्यते॥

एकप्रमुक्ताभि यथेव सूर्यो
रश्मीभि सत्त्वान करोति भासम्।
एवं जिनानां सुत ज्ञानरश्मिभि
प्रज्ञाय सत्त्वान (ऽ)वभास कुर्वति॥

३६

तद्यथापि नाम काश्यप सिंहो मृगराजा यतो यत एव प्रक्रमते सर्वत्रा(23b)भीतो ऽनुत्त्रस्त एव प्रक्रमति। एवमेव काश्यप शीलश्रुतगुणधर्मप्रतिष्ठितो बोधिसत्त्वो यतो यत एव प्रक्रमते सर्वत्राभीतो ऽनुत्त्रस्त एव प्रक्रमते। तत्रेदमुच्यते॥

यथा हि सिंहो मृगराज केसरी
येनेच्छकं याति असंत्रसंतो।
एमेव शीलश्रुतज्ञानसुस्थितो
येनेच्छकं गच्छति बोधिसत्त्वो॥

३७

तद्यथापि नाम काश्यप सुदान्तः कुंजरो नागस्सर्वभारवहनतया न परिखिद्यते। एवमेव काश्यप सुदान्तचित्तो बोधिसत्त्व सर्वसत्त्वानां सर्वभारवहनता न परिखिद्यते। तत्रेदमुच्यते॥

(24a)यथापि नागो बलवान् सुदान्तो
भारं वहंतो नदुपेति खेदं।
सुदान्तचित्तो तथ बोधिसत्त्वो
सत्त्वान भारेण न खेदमैति॥

३८

तद्यथापि नाम काश्यप पद्ममुदके जातमुदकेन न लिप्यते। एवमेव काश्यप बोधिसत्त्वो लोके जातो लोकधर्मैहि न लिप्यते। तत्रेदमुच्यते॥

पद्मं यथा कोकनदं जलेरुहं
जलेन नो लिप्यति कर्दमेन वा।
लोकेस्मि जातो तथ बोधिसत्त्वो
न लोकधर्मैहि कदाचि लिप्यते॥

३९

तद्यथापि नाम काश्यप विटपच्छिन्नो वृक्षो मूले ऽनुपहते पुनरेव विरोहति। एवमेव काश्यप उपायकौशल्यक्लेशच्छिन्नो बोधि(24b)सत्त्वः सर्वकुशलमूलसंयोजने ऽनुपहते पुनरेव त्रैधातुके विरोहति। तत्रेदमुच्यते॥

यथापि वृक्षो विटपस्मि छिन्नो
विरोहते मूल दृढे ऽनुपद्रुते।
एवं उपायो ऽपहतो विरोहते
मूलस्मि संयोजन अप्रहीणे[61]॥

---

[61] em. after VD n. 161; सुप्रहीणे MS.

४०

तद्यथापि नाम काश्यप नानादिग्विदिक्षु महानदीष्वाप्स्कन्धो महासमुद्रे प्रविष्टः सर्वमेकरसो भवति यदुत लवणरसः एवमेव काश्यप नानामुखोपचितं कुशलमूलं बोधिसत्त्वस्य बोधाय परिणामितं सर्वमेकरसं भवति यदिदं विमुक्तिरस। तत्रेदमुच्यते॥

नानानदीनामुदकं प्रविष्टं
महासमु(25a)द्रेकरसं यथा स्यात्।
कुशलानि नानामुखसंचितानि
परिणामितान्येकरसानि बोधये॥

४१

तद्यथापि नाम काश्यप सुमेरुप्रतिष्ठिता चतुर्महाराजकायिकास्त्रयस्त्रिंशाश्च देवाः एवमेव काश्यप बोधिचित्तकुशलमूलप्रतिष्ठिता बोधिसत्त्वस्य सर्वज्ञता। तत्रेदमुच्यते॥

चतुर्महाराजिकस्त्रायस्त्रिंशा
यथा सुमेरुस्थित देवसंघा।
तथ बोधिसत्त्वा कुशले प्रतिष्ठाः
सर्वज्ञता प्राप्य वदंति धर्मान्॥

४२

तद्यथापि नाम काश्यप आमात्यसंगृहीता राजानः सर्वराजकार्याणि कुर्वन्ति। एवमेव काश्यप उपायसंगृही(25b)ता बोधिसत्वस्य प्रज्ञा सर्वबुद्धकार्याणि करोति। तत्रेदमुच्यते॥

यथा हि राजान अमात्यसंग्रहा
सर्वाणि कार्याणि करोंति नित्यं।

तथ बोधिसत्त्वस्य उपायसंग्रहो[62]
बुद्धार्थ प्रज्ञाय[63] करोन्ति नित्य॥

४३

तद्यथापि नाम काश्यप व्यभ्रे देवे विगतवलाहके नास्ति वर्षस्यायद्वारं। एवमेव काश्यप अल्पश्रुतस्य बोधिसत्वस्यान्तिका नास्ति सद्धर्मवृष्टेरायद्वारं। तत्रेदमुच्यते॥

व्यभ्रे यथा विगतवलाहके नभे
वर्षस्य *आयो* न कदाचि विद्यते।
अल्पश्रुतस्यान्तिक धर्मदेशना
न बोधिसत्त्वस्य कदाचि लभ्यते॥

४४

तद्यथापि नाम काश्यप*अ*(26a)भ्रघनमेघसमुत्थिता वर्षधारा सस्यान्यभिवर्षति। एवमेव काश्यप महाकरुणाधर्ममेघसमुत्थिता बोधिसत्त्वस्य सद्धर्मवृष्टिस्सत्त्वानामभिवर्षति। तत्रेद-मुच्यते॥

यथापि मेघो विपुलो सविद्युतो
सस्यानु[64] वर्षेण करोति तृप्तिम्।
सद्धर्ममेघोत्थितवर्षधारा
तर्पेति सत्त्वास्तथ बोधिसत्त्वः॥

---

62 em. °संग्रहा? (VD).
63 VD n. 165: 'Nom. pl. fem.?'
64 m.c. for सस्यानां (VD n. 166).

४५

तद्यथापि नाम काश्यप यत्र राजा चक्रवर्ति उत्पद्यते तत्र सप्त रत्नान्युत्पद्यंते। एवमेव काश्यप *यत्र* बोधिसत्त्व उत्पद्यते तत्र सप्तात्रिंशद्बोधिपक्ष्या धर्मा उत्पद्यंते। तत्रेदमुच्यते॥

उत्पद्यते यत्र हि *चक्रव*(26b)र्ति
तत्रास्य रत्नानि भवंति सप्त।
उत्पद्यते यत्र च बोधिसत्त्वस्
तत्रास्य बोध्यंग भवंति सप्त॥

४६

तद्यथापि नाम *काश्यप* यत्र मणिरत्नायद्वारं भवति बहूनां तत्र कर्षापणशतसहस्राणामायद्वारं भवति। एवमेव काश्यप यत्र बोधिसत्त्वस्यायद्वारं भवति बहूनां तत्र श्रावकप्रत्येकबुद्धशतसहस्राणामायद्वारं भवति। तत्रेदमुच्यते॥

यथापि यस्मिं मणिरत्न भोति
कर्षापणायो बहु तत्र भोति।
संबोधिचित्तस्य च यत्र आयो
आयो बहू तत्र च श्रावकानाम्॥

४७

तद्यथापि नाम काश्यप मिश्रकावनप्रति(27a)ष्ठिताना त्रायस्त्रिंशानां देवानामुपभोगपरिभोगाः समाः संतिष्ठंते। एवमेव काश्यप आशयशुद्धस्य बोधिसत्त्वस्य सर्वसत्त्वानामन्तिके सम्यक्प्रयोगो भवति। तत्रेदमुच्यते॥

यथापि देवान समा प्रयोगा
मिश्रावने संस्थिहते स्थिताना।
एमेव शुद्धाशय बोधिसत्त्वो
सत्त्वेषु सम्यक्कुरुते प्रयोगम्॥

४८

तद्यथापि नाम काश्यप मंत्रौषधपरिगृहीतं विषं न विनिपातयति। एवमेव काश्यप ज्ञानोपायकौशल्यपरिगृहीतो बोधिसत्त्वस्य क्लेशविषं न शक्नोति विनिपातयितुं। तत्रेदमुच्यते॥

यथा विषं मं(27b)त्रपरिग्रहेण
जनस्य दोषं क्रिययासमर्थं।
एवं हि ज्ञानी इह बोधिसत्त्वो
क्लेशैर्न शक्यं विनिपातनाय॥

४९

तद्यथापि नाम काश्यप यो महानगरेषु संकारकूटो[65] भवति स इक्षुक्षेत्रेषु शालिक्षेत्रेषु मृद्वीकाक्षेत्रेषु चोपकारीभूतो भवति। एवमेव काश्यप यो बोधिसत्त्वस्य क्लेशः स सर्वज्ञतायामुपकारीभूतो भवति। तत्रेदमुच्यते॥

नगरेषु संकारु यथा अचोक्षो[66]
सो इक्षुक्षेत्रेषुपकार कुर्वति।
एमेव क्लेशो उपकार कुर्वति
यो बोधिसत्त्वस्य जिनान धर्मे॥

---

65 em. यं … संकरकूटं MS.
66 After Tib. *mi gtsaṅ*; सुचोक्षो MS.

५०

तद्यथापि नाम काश्यप इष्वस्त्रे अशिक्षितस्य शस्त्रग्रह(28a)णं। एवमेव काश्यप अल्पश्रुतस्य बोधिसत्त्वस्य धर्मप्रविचयकौशल्यमीमांसार्थग्रहणज्ञानं[67] द्रष्टव्यः॥

५१

तद्यथापि नाम काश्यप कुंभकारस्य बालभाजनेषूदाराग्निदानं। एवमेव काश्यप बालप्रज्ञेषु बोधिसत्त्वस्योदारधर्मदेशना वेदितव्यः॥

५२

तस्मिन्तर्हि काश्यप इह महारत्नकूटे धर्मपर्याये शिक्षितुकामेन बोधिसत्त्वेन योनिशोधर्मप्रयुक्तेन भवितव्यं। तत्र काश्यप कतमश्च योनिशोधर्मप्रयोगः[68] यदुत सर्वधर्माणां भूतप्रत्यवेक्षा। कतमा च काश्यप सर्वधर्माणां भूतप्रत्यवेक्षा। या[69] काश्यप नात्मप्रत्यवे(28b)क्षा नसत्त्वनजीवनपोषनपुद्गलनमनुजनमानवप्रत्यवेक्षा। इयमुच्यते काश्यप मध्यमा प्रतिपद्धर्माणां भूतप्रत्यवेक्षा।

५३

पुनरपरं काश्यप मद्यमा प्रतिपद्धर्माणां भूतप्रत्यवेक्षा या रूपस्य न नित्यमिति प्रत्यवेक्षा नानित्यमिति[70] प्रत्यवेक्षा। या वेदनायाः संज्ञायाः संस्काराणां विज्ञानस्य न नित्यमिति प्रत्यवेक्षा नानित्यमिति प्रत्यवेक्षा। इयमुच्यते काश्यप मध्यमा प्रतिपद्धर्माणां भूतप्रत्यवेक्षा।

---

67 em. after VD n. 173; °मीमास-द्-अर्थ° MS.
68 See MVŚ 174, 26f.; कतमो योनिश° MS.
69 See *ibid.*; यत्र MS.
70 नानित्यानीति MS.

५४

या पृथिवीधातोर्न नित्यमिति प्रत्यवेक्षा नानित्यमिति प्रत्यवेक्षा। याब्धातोस्तेजोधातोर्वायुधातो न नित्यमित्ति प्रत्य(29a)वेक्षा नानित्यमिति प्रत्यवेक्षा। या आकाशधातोर्विज्ञानधातो न नित्यमिति प्रत्यवेक्षा नानित्यमिति प्रत्यवेक्षा। इयमुच्यते काश्यप मध्यमा प्रतिपद्धर्माणां भूतप्रत्यवेक्षा।

५५

पुनरपरं काश्यप मध्यमा प्रतिपद्धर्माणां भूतप्रत्यवेक्षा या चक्षुरायतनस्य न नित्यमिति प्रत्यवेक्षा नानित्यमिति प्रत्यवेक्षा। इयमुच्यते काश्यप मध्यमा प्रतिपद्धर्माणां भूतप्रत्यवेक्षा। एवं यावच्छ्रोत्रघ्राणजिह्वाकायमनायतनस्य न नित्यम् *इति प्रत्यवेक्षा* नानित्यमिति प्रत्यवेक्षा। इयमुच्यते काश्यप मध्यमा प्रतिपद्धर्माणां भूतप्रत्यवेक्षा।

५६

नित्यमिति काश्यप अयमेको ऽन्तः अनि(29b)त्यमिति काश्यप अयं द्वितीयो ऽन्तः यदेतयोर्द्वयो नित्यानित्ययोर्मध्यं तदरूप्यमनिदर्शनमनाभासमविज्ञप्तिकमप्रतिष्ठमनिकेतमियमुच्यते काश्यप मध्यमा प्रतिपद्धर्माणां भूतप्रत्यवेक्षा।

५७

आत्मेति काश्यप अयमेको ऽन्तः नैरात्म्यमित्ययं द्वितीयो ऽन्तः यदात्मनैरात्म्ययोर्मध्यं[71] तदरूप्यमनिदर्शनमनाभासमविज्ञप्तिकमप्रतिष्ठमनिकेतमियमुच्यते काश्यप मध्यमा प्रतिपद्धर्माणां भूतप्रत्यवेक्षा।

---

71 P 153, 1: यदेतदनयोरन्तयोर्मध्यं.

५८

भूतचित्तमिति काश्यप अयमेको ऽन्तः अभूतचित्तमिति काश्यप अयं द्वितीयो ऽन्तः यत्र काश्यप न चेतना[72] न मनो न विज्ञानमियमुच्यते का(30a)श्यप मध्यमा प्रतिपद्धर्माणां भूतप्रत्यवेक्षा।

५९

एवं सर्वधर्माणां कुशलाकुशलानां लौकिकलोकोत्तराणां सावद्यानवद्यानां सास्रवानास्रवानां संस्कृतासंस्कृतानां संक्लेश इति काश्यप अयमेको ऽन्तः व्यवदानमित्ययं काश्यप द्वितीयो ऽन्तः यो ऽस्यान्तद्वयस्यानुपगमो[73] ऽनुदाहारो ऽप्रव्याहार[74]। इयमुच्यते काश्यप मध्यमा प्रतिपद्धर्माणां भूतप्रत्यवेक्षा।

६०

अस्तीति काश्यप अयमेको ऽन्तः नास्तीत्ययं द्वितीयो ऽन्तः यदेतयोर्द्वयोरन्तयोर्मध्यमियमुच्यते काश्यप मध्यमा प्रतिपद्धर्माणां भूतप्रत्यवेक्षा।

६१

यदपि काश्यप युष्माकं मयाख्यात। यदु(30b)त अविद्याप्रत्यया संस्काराः संस्कारप्रत्ययं विज्ञानं विज्ञानप्रत्ययन्नामरूपन्नामरूपप्रत्ययं षडायतनं षडायतनप्रत्यय स्पर्शः स्पर्शप्रत्यया वेदना वेदनाप्रत्यया तृष्णा तृष्णाप्रत्ययमुपादानमुपादानप्रत्ययो भवः भवप्रत्यया जातिः जातिप्रत्यया जरामरणशोकपरिदेवदुःखदौर्मनस्योपायासाः संभवंत्येवमस्य केवलस्य महतो दुःखस्कन्धस्य समुदयो भवति।

---

72 Tib., MVŚ 176, 17: न चित्तं न चेतना...
73 em. after MVŚ 177, 7–8 (and Tib.); °अनुगमो MS.
74 em. after *ibid.* (and Tib.); प्रव्याहार SH, VD.

६२

अविद्यानिरोधा संस्कारनिरोधः संस्कारनिरोधाद्विज्ञाननिरोधः विज्ञाननिरोधान्नामरूपनिरोधः नामरूपनिरोधात् षडायतननि[31a,b]*रोधः षडायतननिरोधात् स्पर्शनिरोधः स्पर्शनिरोधाद्वेदनानिरोधः वेदनानिरोधात्तृष्णानिरोधः तृष्णानिरोधादुपादाननिरोधः उपादाननिरोधाद्भवनिरोधः भवनिरोधाज्जातिनिरोधः जातिनिरोधाज्जरामरणशोकपरिदेवदुःखदौर्मनस्योपायासा निरुध्यन्ते । एवमस्य केवलस्य महतो दुःखस्कन्धस्य निरोधो भवतीति । अत्र काश्यप विद्या चाविद्या चाद्वयमेतद्*[75] *असम्भिन्नं द्विधा*[76]। *यदत्र ज्ञानमियमुच्यते काश्यप मध्यमा प्रतिपद्धर्माणां भूतप्रत्यवेक्षा । एवमेव संस्काराश्चासंस्कृतं च विज्ञानं च विज्ञाननिरोधश्च नामरूपं च नामरूपनिरोधश्च षडायतनं च षडायतननिरोधश्च स्पर्शश्च स्पर्शनिरोधश्च वेदना च वेदनानिरोधश्च तृष्णा च तृष्णानिरोधश्चोपादानं चोपादाननिरोधश्च भवश्च भवनिरोधश्च जातिश्च जातिनिरोधश्च जरामरणं च जरामरणनिरोधश्चाद्वयमेतदसम्भिन्नं द्विधा। यदत्र ज्ञानमियमु*(32a)च्यते काश्यप मध्यमा प्रतिपद्धर्माणां भूतप्रत्यवेक्षा॥

६३

पुनरपरं काश्यप धर्माणां भूतप्रत्यवेक्षा यन्न शून्यताया धर्मा शून्या[77] करोति धर्मा एव शून्या[78]। यन्नानिमित्तेन धर्माननिमित्तान् करोति धर्मा चैवानिमित्ताः यन्नाप्रणिहितेन धर्मानप्रणिहितान्[79] करोति धर्मा एवाप्रणिहिताः यन्नानभिसंस्कारेण धर्माननभिसंस्कृतान्[80] करोति धर्मा चैवानभिसंस्कृताः[81] एवं नानुत्पादेन धर्माननुत्पन्नान्[82] करोति धर्मा चैवानुत्पन्नाः

---

[75] As for विद्या चाविद्या चाद्वयमेतद् , see MVŚ 174, 21f.

[76] See Negi 1993ff. s.v. *dbyer med pa*; cf. the gloss at MVŚ 178, 19, 21: अद्वैधीकारम् (*gñis su byar med pa*).

[77] P 108, 21: शून्यतया धर्मान् शून्यान्.

[78] *Ibid.*: अपि तु दर्मा एव शून्याः.

[79] After *ibid.*, 108, 22; MS धर्मा। प्रणिहितान्.

[80] धर्मानभिसंस्करोति MS.

[81] Cf. Weller 1965: 100, n. 10; चवानभिसंस्कृताः MS.

एवं नाजाता[83] धर्मानजातीकरोति धर्मा चैवाजाताः एवं यन्न अग्राह्या धर्मान्नग्राह्या करोति धर्मा चैवाग्राह्या। (32b) एवं नानास्रवा[84] धर्माननास्रवा करोति धर्मा चैवानास्रवा। एवं यन्नास्वभावेन धर्मानस्वभावीकरोति धर्मा चैवास्वभावा[85]। एवं यन्नास्वभावेन धर्मास्वभावता। धर्माणां यत्स्वभावं नोपलभते। या एवं प्रत्यवेक्षा इयमुच्यते काश्यप मध्यमा प्रतिपद्धर्माणां भूतप्रत्यवेक्षा॥

६४

न खलु पुनः काश्यप पुद्गलभावविनाशाय शून्यता। पुद्गलश्चैव शून्यता शून्यता चैव शून्यता। अत्यन्तशून्यता। पूर्वान्तशून्यता। अपरान्तशून्यता प्रत्युत्पन्नशून्यता। शून्यता काश्यप प्रतिसरथ[86] मा पुद्गलम्। ये खलु पुन काश्यप शून्यतोप(33a)लंभेन शून्यता[87] प्रतिसरंति तानहं काश्यप नष्टप्रनष्टानिति वदामि। इतो[88] प्रवचनात् वरं खलु पुन काश्यप सुमेरुमात्रा पुद्गलदृष्टिराश्रिता न त्वेवाधिमानिकस्य[89] शून्यतादृष्टिमालीना[90]। तत्कस्माद्धेतो। पुद्गलदृष्टिगतानां काश्यप शून्यता निःसरणं। शून्यतादृष्टि पुन काश्यप केन निःसरिष्यति[91]॥

---

82 धर्मान्नानुत्पादा MS.

83 न जाता MS.

84 After Weller 1965: 100, n. 20; एवमनास्रवा MS.

85 MVŚ 180, 28: यन्नास्वभावतया धर्मानस्वभावान् करोति धर्मा एवास्वभावा इति.

86 MVŚ 181, 27: शून्यतां काश्यप प्रतिसरतेति.

87 P 108, 24: शून्यतां.

88 *Ibid.*, 108, 26: इति.

89 *Ibid.*, 108, 28: त्वेव अभावाभिनिवेशिकस्य; see also CŚV 150, 3: त्वेवाभिमानिकस्य.

90 I.e. °दृष्टिरामलीना – cf. Weller 1965: 101, n.15; cf. CŚV 150, 4: शून्यतादृष्टिः। तत्कस्माद्धेतोः.

91 P 108, 29f. (Tib. accordingly): सर्वदृष्टिकृतानां हि काश्यप शून्यता निःसरणम्। यस्य खलु पुनः शून्यतैव दृष्टिः, तमहमचिकित्स्यमिति वदामि। CŚV 150, 4f.: सर्वदृष्टिगतानां ... शून्यतादृष्टिस्तमहमचिकित्स्यम् ...

६५

तद्यथापि नाम काश्यप कश्चिदेव पुरुषो ग्लानो भवेत्तस्मै वैद्यो भैषज्यं दद्यात्तस्य तद्भैषज्यं सर्वदोषानुचाल्य कोष्ठगत न निर्गच्छेत्[92]। तत्किं मन्यसे काश्यप। अपि नु स ग्लान-पुरुषस्तस्माद् ग्लान्या परिमुक्तो[93] भवेत् यस्य तद्भैषज्यं (33b)सर्वकोष्ठगता दोषानुच्चाल्य कोष्ठगतो न निःसरेत्। आह नो भगवान्। गाढतरश्च तस्य पुरुषस्य तद्ग्लेलान्यं[94] भवेत् यस्य तद्भैषज्यं सर्वदोषानुचाल्य कोष्ठगतं न निःसरेत्। भगवानाह। एवमेव काश्यप सर्वदृष्टि-गतानां शून्यता निःसरणं। यस्य खलु पुनः काश्यप शून्यतादृष्टिस्तमहमचिकित्स्यमिति वदामि। तत्रेदमुच्यते॥

यथा हि वैद्यो पुरुषस्य दद्याद्
विरेचनं रोगविनिग्रहाय।
उच्चाल्य दोषाश्च न निःसरेत
ततो निदानं च न चोपशान्ति।
एमेव दृष्टीगहनाश्रितेषु
या शून्यता निःसरणं परं हि।
सा शू*न्यता दृष्टिगतैव यस्य*
जिनेन उक्तः अचिकित्स्य सो हि ॥

६६

[95]*तद्यथा काश्यप कश्चिदेव पुरुष आकाशजो*[96] *भीतः सोरस्ताडं क्रन्देदेवञ्च वदेदपनयै-तदाकाशमिति। तत्किं मन्यसे काश्यप शक्यमाकाशमपनेतुम्। आह। नोहीदं भगवन्।*

---

92 P 109, 1 (cf. also CŚV 272, 17): उच्चार्य स्वयं कोष्ठगतं न निःसरेत्.
93 P 109, 2 (CŚV 272, 18): तु स पुरुषस्ततो ग्लान्यान्मुक्तो.
94 P 109, 2f. (CŚV 272, 20): नो हीदं भगवन्। गाढतरं … ग्लान्यं.
95 Quoted at MVŚ 182, 9–13.

भगवानाह। एवमेव काश्यप एते श्रमणब्राह्मणाः शून्यतायामुत्त्रसन्ति तानहं महाविक्षेपप्राप्तानिति वदामि। तत्कस्माद्धेतोः शून्यतायामेव हि ते काश्यप विचरन्ति तस्या एव बिभ्यन्तीति[97] *। तत्रेदमुच्यते*[98] *॥...*

६७

[99] *तद्यथा काश्यप चित्रकरः स्वयमेव भीषणं यक्षरूपं कृत्वा तस्मादेव भीतस्त्रस्तो*[100] *ऽधोमुखो निपत्य सम्मोहं निगच्छेत्। एवमेव काश्यप सर्वबालपृथग्जनाः स्वयमेव रूपशब्दगन्धरसस्पर्शान् कृत्वा तेभ्यः संसारे भ्राम्यन्ति न च तान् धर्मान् यथाभूतं प्रजानन्तीति। तत्रेदमुच्यते*[101] *॥ ...*

६८

तद्यथा काश्यप मायाकारः पुरुषो मायाकृतं निर्मिमीते। अथ स मायानिर्मितस्तमेव मायाकारं खादेत। एवमेव काश्यप योगाचारो भिक्षुर्यद्यदेवारम्बणं मनस्करोति तत्सर्वमस्य रिक्तकमेव ख्याति[102] *। तुच्छकं शून्यमसारं चैव ख्याति। तत्रेदमुच्यते॥*[103] *...*

---

96 Tib. आकाशाद्.

97 MVŚ 182, n. 11: em. बिभ्यति.

98 Folio nos. 34–36 (sections 66–69) are lost; only the prose parts of the lost sections are quoted in MVŚ. The missing verses, retranslated in prose from Tib., are given in the notes. – *यथा ह्याकाशभीतिपीडितः पुरुषः। मूढो ऽपनयैतदाकाशमिति वदति। आकाशमपनेतुन्न शक्यमपि। मोहपृथग्जना एवं भाषन्ते। एवमेव ये श्रमणब्राह्मणाः। शून्यतायास्त्रसन्ति विक्षिप्तचित्ताः। शून्यतायां हि ते पृथग्जना विचरन्ति। क्वचिदपि शून्यता न शक्या व्युदसितुम्॥*

99 Quoted at MVŚ 183, 1–4.

100 MVŚ 183, 2: भीतस्त्रस्तो.

101 After Tib.: *यथा हि चित्रकरः। भीषणं यक्षरूपं कृत्वा। तस्माद्भीतो ऽधोमुखः। निपत्य सम्मोहं निगच्छति। एवमेव सर्वबालपृथग्जनाः। स्वयमेव रूपशब्दादीन् कृत्वा। तेभ्यः प्रमुह्य षड्गतिकेषु भ्राम्यन्ति॥*

102 Quoted at MVŚ 184, 1–3.

103 After Tib.: *यथा हि मायाकारो ऽभिनिर्मितं[कृत्वा]। तेन मायाकृतेन खाद्यते। एवमेव योगाचारो यन्मनस्करोति। तत्तस्य रिक्तकमेव तुच्छकं ख्याति॥*

६९

[104]*तद्यथा काश्यप काष्ठद्वयं प्रतीत्याग्निर्जायत इति जातश्च समानस्तदेव काष्ठद्वयं दहति। एवमेव काश्यप भूतप्रत्यवेक्षां प्रतीत्यार्यं प्रज्ञेन्द्रियं जायते जातं च तामेव भूतप्रत्यवेक्षां दहति। तत्रेदमुच्यते*[105]॥... (37a)ये (ऽ)पि शून्यं।

७०

तद्यथापि नाम काश्यप तैलप्रदीपस्य नैवं[106] भवत्यहमन्धकारं विधमामीति। अथ च पुनस्तैलप्रद्योते कृते आलोकं प्रतीत्य तमोऽन्धकारं विगच्छति। यश्च काश्यप तैलप्रद्योतो यच्च तमो(ऽ)न्धकारमुभयमेतच्छून्यता अग्राह्या शून्या निश्चेष्टा। एवमेव काश्यप *ज्ञान उत्पन्ने ऽज्ञानं विगच्छति। न खलु पुनः काश्यप ज्ञानस्यैवं भवत्यहमज्ञानं विधमामीति। अपि तु खलु ज्ञानं प्रतीत्याज्ञानं विगच्छति*[107]। यं च ज्ञानं चाज्ञानं च उभयमेतच्छून्यता अग्राह्या शून्या निश्चेष्टा[108]। *तत्रेदमुच्यते*[109]॥

७१

तद्यथापि नाम काश्यप गृहे वा लयने वा अववरके[110] वा वर्षसहस्रस्यात्ययेन न केन[111]-चित्तैलप्रद्योतः कृतो भवेत्। अथ च तत्र कश्चिदेव पुरुषः तैलप्रदीपं कुर्यात्। तत्किं मन्यसे

---

104 Quoted at MVŚ 184, 15–17.

105 Retransl. in prose from Tib.: *यथा हि काष्ठद्वयवायुसंघर्षात्। जातो ऽग्निस्तदेव [काष्ठद्वयं] दहति। एवमेव प्रज्ञेन्द्रिये जाते ऽपि। तामेव भूतप्रत्यवेक्षां दहति॥*

106 °प्रदीपस्यैवं MS; MVŚ 185, 4–5: न ... °प्रद्योतस्यैवं.

107 Italicized passage, missing in MS, after Tib. and MVŚ 185, 6–8.

108 दग्राह्या ... निश्चेष्ट्या MS.

109 Tib. has verses retransl. in prose: *यथा हि प्रदीपेन तमो ऽन्धकारं सर्वम्। विगच्छति किं तु न (तस्य्) आगमनगमने। एवमेव ज्ञान उत्पन्ने ऽज्ञानं विगच्छति। तस्यापि कुतश्चिदागमनं वा गमनं वा न स्तः। न प्रदीपस्य्(आहम्) अन्धकारं विधमामीति। किं त्वालोक उत्पन्ने ऽन्धकारं विगच्छति। [प्रदीपान्धकारे] शून्ये ऽग्राह्ये खपुष्पोपमे। एवमेव ज्ञानाज्ञाने शून्यतोभे॥*

110 MVŚ 185, 21: वा ऽवचरके.

111 After MVŚ, *ibid.*; तत्कदा° MS.

(37b) काश्यपापितु[112] तस्य तमोऽन्धकारस्यैवं भवेद्[113] वर्षसहस्रं संचितो ऽहं नाहमितो विगमिष्यामीति । आह नो हीदं भगवं । न हि तस्य तमोऽन्धकारस्य शक्तिरस्ति तैलप्रद्योते[114] कृते न विगंतुमवश्यं तेन विगन्तव्यम्[115]। भगवानाह । एवमेव काश्यप कल्पकोटीनयुतशतसहस्रसंचितो ऽपि कर्मक्लेश एकेन योनिशोमनसिकारप्रज्ञाप्रत्यवेक्षणेन विगच्छति । तैलप्रद्योत इति काश्यप आर्यस्यैतत् प्रज्ञेन्द्रियस्याधिवचनं । तमोऽन्धकार इति काश्यप[116] कर्मक्लेशस्याधिवचनम् । तत्रेदमुच्यते॥

यथापि दीपो लयने चिरस्य
कृतो भवेत[117] पुरुषेण केनचित् ।
[118] *तत्रान्धकारस्य न भोति एवं*
चिरस्थितो नाहमितो गमिष्ये ॥
तमो(ऽ)न्धकारस्य न शक्तिरस्ति
कृते प्रदीपे न विगच्छनाय ।
प्रतीत्य दीपं च विनश्यते तम
उभयं पि शून्यं न च कीं च मन्यति ॥
ज्ञानं तथा आर्य प्रतीत्य नास्रवं
अज्ञान क्लेशोपचितं विगच्छति ।
संपर्क तेषां न कदाचि विद्यते
ज्ञानस्य क्लेशस्य च नित्यकालम् ॥

---

112 After MVŚ 185, 23; काश्यप मैवां MS.
113 After MVŚ, *ibid.*; तमोन्धकारस्य भूद्ग MS.
114 यस्तैलप्रद्योत MS (VD n. 195).
115 After MVŚ 185, 25; विगतव्यं MS.
116 MVŚ 186, 1: इति शबलस्यैतत्.
117 Read with P 64, 3: कृतो हि गेहे.
118 Quoted at P 64, 4–17.

ज्ञानं न कल्पेति अज्ञानु नो भवेत्
ज्ञानं प्रतीत्यैव विनश्यते तमो।
भयं पि अग्राह्य खपुष्पसंनिभ
ज्ञानं तथाज्ञानु भयं पि शून्यम् ॥

७२

[119]*तद्यथापि नाम काश्यप आकाशे बीजानि नोत्पद्यन्ते। एवमेव काश्यप यो ऽसंस्कृताद्बोधिसत्त्वस्य बुद्धधर्मोत्पादः [सो] ऽभावो ऽसंभवः तत्रेदमुच्यते*[120]... ॥

७३

तद्यथापि नाम काश्यप संकारसम्पूर्णायां भूम्यां सर्वबीजान्युत्पद्यन्ते। एवमेव काश्यप क्लेशसंकारसम्पूर्णे लोकसंनिवेशे बोधिसत्त्वस्य बुद्धधर्मा उत्पद्यन्ते। तत्रेदमुच्यते[121] ॥...

७४

तद्यथापि नाम काश्यप कान्तारजंगलेषु पद्मं नोत्पद्यते। एवमेव काश्यप यो ऽसंस्कृताद्बोधिसत्त्वस्य बुद्धधर्मोत्पादः [सो] ऽभावो ऽसंभवः तत्रेदमुच्यते[122] ॥ ...

---

[119] Folio nos. 38–39 (sections 71 (verses), 72–77 (including beginning of verse part)) are lost. Retranslated text after Tib.; the verse parts, also retransl. in prose, are given in the notes.

[120] After Tib.: *यथाप्याकाशाद्बीजोत्पादः। अतीतानागतप्रत्युत्पन्ने नास्ति। एवमसंस्कृतात्कचित्। बुद्धधर्मोत्पादो ऽभावो न संभवति॥*

[121] After Tib.: *ससंकारायां सार्द्रायां च [भूम्याम्]। बीजोत्पादो यथा न तु जंगलेषु। एवमेव क्लेशमिथ्याबोपेते जगति। जिनपुत्राणां जिनधर्मा उत्पद्यन्ते॥*

[122] After Tib.: *पुष्करतडागेषु यथा पद्मोत्पादः। न कदाचिज्जङ्गलेषु। एवमसंस्कृतात्कचित्। बुद्धधर्मोत्पादो ऽभावो न संभवति॥*

७५

तद्यथापि नाम काश्यप संकारभूतपंकात्पद्ममुत्पद्यते। एवमेव काश्यप क्लेशसंकारभूतपंके मिथ्यात्वनियतसत्त्वेषु बोधिसत्त्वस्य बुद्धधर्मा उत्पद्यन्ते। तत्रेदमुच्यते[123] *॥ ...*

७६

तद्यथापि नाम काश्यप चतुर्महासमुद्राः सर्पिःपरिपूर्णाः। एवमेव बोधिसत्त्वस्य कुशलमूलाभिसंस्कारो द्रष्टव्यः। तत्रेदमुच्यते[124] *॥ ...*

७७

तद्यथापि नाम काश्यप कश्चिदेव पुरुषः शतशकलस्फुट-[125] *वालस्य [एकशकलस्य-] आग्रेण चतुर्महासमुद्रेभ्य एकजलबिन्दुमुद्धरेत्। एवमेव काश्यप श्रावकस्य कुशलमूलाभिसंस्कारो द्रष्टव्यः तत्रेदमुच्यते॥*

यथा हि बिन्दुं जलराशितो [नरः]
शतभागाग्रेण **(40a)** वालमुद्धरेत्।
कुशलान्वितं श्रावकमेव पश्यथ
कुशलेन युक्तं अभिसंस्कृतेन॥

---

[123] After Tib.: *ससंकाराद्यथा पंकजलात्। पद्मोत्पादो न जातु स्थलात्। एवं क्लेशमिथ्यात्वोपेते जगति। जिनपुत्राणां जिनधर्मा उत्पद्यन्ते॥*

[124] After Tib.: *यथापि चतुःसमुद्रास्सर्पिषा। परिपूर्णाः शुद्धसमन्तेष्टाश्च। एवमेव बोधिसत्त्वः सुगतात्मजः। सदा कुशलनदीपूर्णो द्रष्टव्यः॥*

[125] Cf. Negi 1993ff. s.v. *gśog pa* – स्फुटन.

७८

तद्यथापि नाम काश्यप घुणखादितस्य सर्षपाभ्यन्तरे आकाशधातु। एवमेव काश्यप श्रावकस्याभिसंस्कृतं ज्ञानं द्रष्टव्य। तत्रेदमुच्यते॥

घुणखादितस्यैव हि सर्षपस्य
आकाशमभ्यंतरितो परित्तं।
अभिसंस्कृतं ज्ञान तथा विजानथ
यं श्रावकस्य लघुकं परित्तकं॥

७९

तद्यथापि नाम काश्यप दशसु दिक्ष्वाकाशधातुरेवं बोधिसत्त्वस्याभिसंस्कृतं ज्ञानं द्रष्टव्यं। तत्रेदमुच्यते॥

यथापि आकाश दशद्दिशासु[126]
अनावृतं तिष्ठति स(40b)र्वलोके।
अभिसंस्कृतं पश्यथ बोधिसत्त्वे
ज्ञानं तथा सर्वजगत्प्रधान॥

८०

तद्यथापि नाम काश्यप राज्ञः क्षत्रियस्य मूर्ध्नाभिषिक्तस्याग्रमहिषी दरिद्रपुरुषेण सार्धं विप्रतिपद्येत। तस्य ततः पुत्रो जायेत। तत् किं मन्यसे काश्यप। अपि नु स राजपुत्र इति वक्तव्यः आह नो हीदं भगवन्। भगवानाह। एवमेव काश्यप किं चापि मम श्रावकार्धर्मधातुनिर्जाता न च पुनस्ते तथागतस्याभिषेक्यपुत्रा इति वक्तव्याः तत्रेदमुच्यते॥

---

126 em. after VD n. 200; दशदिशासु MS.

यथापि राज्ञो महिषी मनापी
दरिद्रसत्त्वेन सहा वसेत।
तस्या सुतस्तेन च जायते यो
(41a)स राजपुत्रो न तु राज भेष्यती।
एमेव ये श्रावक वीतरागा
न ते ऽभिषेक्या मम जातु पुत्राः।
तथा हि ते आत्महिताय युक्ता
स्वपरोभयार्थैकर बुद्धपुत्राः॥

८१

तद्यथापि नाम काश्यप राजा क्षत्रियो मूर्धाभिषिक्तः प्रत्यवरया चेटिकया सह प्रतिपद्येत। तस्य तत पुत्र उत्पद्येत। किं चापि काश्यप स प्रत्यवरया चेटिकया संतिकादुत्पन्नो ऽथ च पुन स राजपुत्र इति वक्तव्यः एवमेव काश्यप किं चापि प्रथमचित्तोत्पादिको बोधिसत्त्वः अप्रतिबलः संसारे संसरन् सत्त्वान् विनयितुं काममथ च पुन स तथाग(41b)तपुत्रो इति वक्तव्यः तत्रेदमुच्यते॥

चेटीय सार्धं यथ चक्रवर्त्ती
संवासं गत्वा जनयेत पुत्रं।
किं चापि चेटीय सकाश जातो
तं राजपुत्रेति वदेति लोके।
चित्ते तथा प्रथमे बोधिसत्त्वो
बलेन हीनो त्रिभवे भ्रमंतो।

दानेन सत्त्वा विनयंनुपायैर्[127]
जिनात्मजो वुच्चति शुद्धसत्त्वो॥

८२

तद्यथापि नाम काश्यप राज्ञश्चक्रवर्तिनः पुत्रसहस्रं भवेत्। न चात्र कश्चि चक्रवर्तिलक्षणसमन्वागतो भवेत् न तत्र राज्ञश्चक्रवर्तिनः पुत्रसंज्ञोत्पद्येत[128]। एवमेव काश्यप किं चापि तथागतो कोटीशतसहस्रपरिवारः श्रावकैर्[129] न चात्र कश्चि(**42a**)द्बोधिसत्त्वो भवति न तत्र तथागतस्य पुत्रसंज्ञोत्पद्यते। तत्रेदमुच्यते॥

यथा सहस्रं नृपते सुतानां
न चेक पुत्रो ऽपि सलक्षणः स्यात्।
न तत्र संज्ञा नृवरस्य तेषु
वोढू यतस्ते न धुरं समर्थाः।
तथा हि बुद्धो बहुकोटिनिर्वृतः[130]
स्यात्तेषु कश्चिन्न च बोधिसत्त्वः।
न पुत्रसंज्ञा सुगतस्य तेषु
न बोधिसत्त्वो ऽस्ति यतो ऽत्र कश्चित्॥

८३

तद्यथापि नाम काश्यप राज्ञश्चक्रवर्तिनो अग्रमहिष्या कुक्षे सप्तरात्रोपपन्नः कुमारश्चक्रवर्तिलक्षणसमन्वागतः तस्य कुक्षिगतस्यापरिपक्केन्द्रियस्य कललमहाभूतगतस्य बलवन्ततरा

[127] After VD; सत्त्वाविन° SH.
[128] em. after Tib. (Weller 1965: 109, n. 8); पुत्रसंज्ज्ञ मन्येत MS.
[129] em. after VD n. 206; श्रावकेर् MS.
[130] m.c. for निवृतः (cf. Weller 1965: 109, n. 12).

तत्र देवता स्पृह(42b)मुत्पादयंति। न त्वेव तेषु बलजवनवेगस्थामप्राप्तेषु कुमारेषु। तत् कस्माद्धेतो। स हि चक्रवर्तिवंशस्यानुपच्छेदाय स्थास्यति। एवमेव काश्यप प्रथमचित्तोत्पादिको बोधिसत्त्वः अपरिपक्वेन्द्रिय कललमहाभूतगत एव समानो। अथ[131] च पुनर्बलवंततरा तत्र पूर्वबुद्धदर्शना[132] देवा स्पृहामुत्पादयंति। न त्वेवाष्टविमोक्षध्यायीष्वर्हत्सु। तत् कस्माद्धेतोः स हि बुद्धवंशस्यानुपच्छेदाय स्थास्यति। तत्रेदमुच्यते॥

यथाग्रदेवीय तु चक्रवर्तिनो
कुक्षिस्थितो लक्षणपुण्यसत्त्वो।
बलवंतरं देवा स्पृहा करोन्ति
न स्थामप्राप्तान कुमारकानां।
ए(43a)काग्रचित्ते स्थितबोधिसत्त्वे
संसारसंस्थे घटमान बोधये।
जनेन्ति तस्य स्पृह देवनागा
न श्रावकेषु त्रिविमोक्षध्यायिषु॥

८४

तद्यथापि नाम काश्यप करविङ्कपोतक आण्डकोशप्रक्षिप्तः अनिर्भिन्ने नयने सर्वपक्षिगणमभिभवति यदुत गंभीरमधुरनिर्घोषरुतरवितेन। एवमेव काश्यप प्रथमचित्तोत्पादिको बोधिसत्त्वो अविद्याण्डकोशप्रक्षिप्त कर्मक्लेशतमस्तिमिरपटलपर्यवनद्धः नयनो ऽपि सर्वश्रावकप्रत्येकबुद्धानभिभवति। यदुत कुशलमूलपरिणामनाप्रयोगनिर्हाररुतरवितेन॥ [133]तद्यथापि नाम काश्यप रा(43b)ज्ञश्चक्रवर्तिन अग्रमहिष्याः तत्क्षणजातं कुमारं सर्वश्रेष्ठिनैगमजा-

[131] समानोदथ MS.
[132] em. after Tib. (VD n. 208); पूर्वदर्शनो MS.
[133] Re the foll., cf. the prose part of section 86 below.

नपदाः कोट्टराजानश्च नमस्यंत्येवमेव काश्यप प्रथमचित्तोत्पादिको बोधिसत्त्वः सदेवको लोको नमस्करोन्ति॥

८५

तद्यथापि नाम काश्यप एकं वैडूर्यं मणिरत्नं सुमेरुमात्रं राशि काचमणिकानभिभवति। एवमेव काश्यप प्रथमचित्तोत्पादिको बोधिसत्त्वः सर्वश्रावकप्रत्येकबुद्धानभिभवति। तत्रेद-मुच्यते॥

यथापि वैडूर्यमणि प्रभास्वरः
काचामणीनभिभवते प्रभूतान्।
एमेव चित्ते प्रथमे बोधिसत्त्वो
अभीभवति पृथक्च्छ्रावकान् गणान्॥

८६

(44a)तद्यथापि नाम काश्यप राज्ञो ऽग्रमहिष्याः तत्क्षणजातं कुमार सर्वश्रेष्ठिनैगमजान-पदाः कोट्टराजानश्च नमस्यन्ति। एवमेव काश्यप प्रथमचित्तोत्पादिको बोधिसत्त्वः सदेवको लोको नमस्यन्ति। तत्रेदमुच्यते॥

यथापि रज्ञो पृथिवीश्वरस्य
पुत्रो भवेल्लक्षणचित्रिताङ्गं।
दृष्ट्वेव तं जातमात्रं कुमारं
सकोट्टराजा प्रणमंति पौराः।
उत्पन्नमात्रे तथ बोधिसत्त्वे
सल्लक्षणं तं जिनराजपुत्रं।

लोकस्सदेवो (ऽ)पि नमस्करोन्ति
प्रसन्नचित्तं बहुमानपूर्वम्॥

८७

तद्यथापि नाम काश्यप यानि हिमवति पर्वतराजे[134] भैषज्यानि विरोहंति सर्वान्य(44b)म-मान्यपरिग्रहान्यविकल्पानि। यत्र च पुनर्व्याध्या व्युपनाम्यंते तं व्याधिं प्रशमयंति। एवमेव काश्यप प्रथमचित्तोत्पादिको बोधिसत्त्वो य ज्ञानभैषज्यं समुदानयति तत्सर्वं निर्विकल्प समुदानयति। समचित्तता सर्वसत्त्वेषु चिकित्सा प्रयोजयति[135]। तत्रेदमुच्यते॥

हिमवंत ये पर्वतराज भेषजा
रोहंति ते निर्मम निर्विकल्पा।
यत्रोपनाम्यंति च तं शमेन्ति
व्याधिं जरा चापनयन्ति केचित्।
जिनात्मजा पी समुदानयंति
यं ज्ञानभेषज्य विकल्प मुक्ता।
हितार्थ सर्वं समुदानयंति
समचित्त सत्त्वेषु चिकित्स कुर्वन्॥

८८

तद्यथापि (45a)नाम काश्यप नवचन्द्रो नमस्क्रियते सो[136] चेव पूर्णचन्द्रो न तथा नमस्कृ-यते। एवमेव काश्यप ये मम श्रद्दधंति तैर्बलवंततरं बोधिसत्त्वो नमस्कर्तव्य न तथागतः तत्कस्य हेतो। बोधिसत्त्वनिर्जाता हि तथागताः तत्रेदमुच्यते॥

---

134 हिमवन्त्रः पर्वतराजा MS.
135 प्रयति MS.
136 em. after VD n. 220; °कृयते सा MS.

चन्द्रं नवं सर्व नमस्करोन्ति
तमेव पूर्णं न नमस्करोन्ति।
एमेव यः श्रद्दधते जिनात्मजो
स बोधिसत्त्वं नमतां[137] जिना न तु॥

८९

तद्यथापि नाम काश्यप मात्रिका सर्वशास्त्रग्रहणज्ञाने पूर्वंगमा। एवमेव काश्यप प्रथम-चित्तोत्पादिको बोधिसत्त्वः सर्वबुद्धविकुर्विताधिष्ठाने (ऽ)नुत्तरे पूर्वंगमः॥

९०

तद्यथापि (45b)नाम काश्यप न जातु केनचिच्चन्द्रमण्डलमुत्सृज्य तारकरूपं नमस्कृत पूर्वं। एवमेव काश्यप न जातु पण्डितो मम शिक्षाप्रतिपन्न बोधिसत्त्वं रिञ्चित्वा श्रावकं नमस्करोति। तत्रेदमुच्यते॥

न केनचिच्चन्द्र विवर्जयित्वा
नमस्कृता तारगणा कदाचित्।
न जातु शिक्षाप्रतिपन्न एवं
ममात्मजं त्यज्य नमेत श्रावकम्॥

९१

तद्यथापि नाम काश्यप सदेवको लोको काचमणिकस्य परिकर्म कुर्यात्। न जातु स काचमणिको वैडूर्यमणिरत्नो भविष्यति। एवमेव काश्यप सर्वशीलशिक्षाधुतगुणसमाधिसमन्वा-

137 em. after VD n. 223: ‘imper. 3rd sg. medium?’; नमता MS.

गतो (ऽ)पि श्रावको न जातु स (46a)बोधिमण्डे निषद्यानुत्तरा सम्यक्संबोधिमभिसंभोत्स्यते। तत्रेदमुच्यते॥

यथापि लोको परिकर्म कुर्यात्
सदेवकः काचमणिस्य शुद्धये।
न काच वैडूर्य कदाचि भेष्यते
अन्यादृशी तस्य सदेव जातिः।
एवं हि शीलाश्रुतध्यानयुक्तो
यः श्रावकः सर्वगुणान्वितो ऽपि।
न बोधिमण्डस्थित मार जित्वा
बोधिं स्पृशित्वा सुगतो भविष्यति॥

९२

तद्यथापि नाम काश्यप वैडूर्यस्य महामणिरत्नस्य परिकर्म क्रियमाणे[138] बहूनां तत्र कर्षापणशतसहस्राणामायद्वारं भवति। एवमेव काश्यप यत्र बोधिसत्त्वस्य परिकर्म क्रियमाणे (46b) बहूनां तत्र श्रावकप्रत्येकबुद्धशतसहस्राणामायद्वारं भवति। तत्रेममुच्यते॥

वैडूर्यरत्ने परिकर्म नीयते
कर्षापणानां च बहायु भोति।
बुद्धोरसानां परिकर्मनं तथा
आयो बहू श्रावकनां तथेव[139]॥

[138] em. after VD n. 229.; °माणैर् MS.
[139] em. after Karashima 2002: 55, n. 75; बहूनां श्रावकानां MS.

९३

अथ खलु भगवान् पुनरेवायुष्मंतं महाकाश्यपमामंत्रयति स्म। यस्मिं काश्यप देशे उष्ट्रधूमक कृष्णशिर उत्तानशायी भवति स देश सोपद्रवः सोपक्लेश सोपायासो भवति। सचेत् पुन काश्यप यस्मिं देशे बोधिसत्त्वो भवति। स देश निरुपद्रव निरुपक्लेश निरुपायासो भवति। तस्मात्तर्हि (47a)काश्यप सत्त्वार्थोद्युक्तेन बोधिसत्त्वेन भवितव्यं। तेन सर्वकुशलमूलानि सर्वसत्त्वानामुत्स्त्रष्टव्यं। सर्वं च कुशलमूल सम्यक्समुदानयितव्यं। यच्च ज्ञानभेषज्यं पर्येषते तेन चतुर्दिशं गत्वा सर्वसत्त्वानां भूतचिकित्सा कर्तव्या। भूतचिकित्साया च सत्त्वा चिकित्सितव्याः।

९४

तत्र काश्यप कतमा भूतचिकित्सा। यदुत रागस्य अशुभा चिकित्सा। द्वेषस्य मैत्री चिकित्सा। मोहस्य प्रतीत्यसमुत्पादप्रत्यवेक्षणा चिकित्सा। सर्वदृष्टीगतानां शून्यता चिकित्सा। सर्वकल्पविकल्पपरिकल्पारंभणवितर्कमनसिकाराणां आनिमित्त चिकित्सा। (47b)सर्वकामधातुरूपधात्वारूप्यधातुप्रहाणाय अप्रणिहित चिकित्सा। सर्वविपर्यासाना चत्वारो ऽविपर्यास चिकित्सा। अनित्ये नित्यसंज्ञायाः अनित्याः सर्वसंस्कारा इति चिकित्सा। दुःखे सुखसंज्ञाया दुःखा सर्वसंस्कारा इति चिकित्सा। अनात्मीये आत्मीयसंज्ञाया अनात्मान सर्वधर्मा इति चिकित्सा। अशुभे शुभसंज्ञायाः शांतं निर्वाणमिति चिकित्सा।

९५

चत्वारि स्मृत्युपस्थानानि कायवेदनाचित्तधर्मसंनिश्रितानां चिकित्सा। काये कायानुपश्यी विहरति न च काये कायानुपश्यनायामात्म्यदृष्ट्यां पतति। वेदनायां वेदनानुप(48a)श्यी[140]

[140] Karashima 2009: 391: °नुदर्शी.

विहरति न च वेदनानुपश्यनाया[141] आत्मदृष्टीगते पतति। चित्ते चित्तानुपश्यी विहरति न च चित्तानुपश्यनायां जीवदृष्टीये पतति। धर्मे धर्मानुपश्यी विहरति न च धर्मानुपश्यनायां पुद्गलदृष्टीये पतति। चत्वारि सम्यक्प्रहाणानि सर्वाकुशलधर्मप्रहाणाय चिकित्सा। सर्वकुशलधर्मपारिपूर्यै संवर्तते। चत्वारोदृद्धिपादाः[142] कायचित्तपिण्डग्राहोत्सर्गाय संवर्तन्ते चिकित्सा। पंचेन्द्रियाणि पंच बलानि अश्राद्धकौसिद्यमुषितस्मृतिचित्तविक्षेपासम्प्रजन्यतादुष्प्रज्ञतानां चिकित्सा। सप्त बोध्यंगानि धर्मसमू(48b)हाज्ञानस्य[143] चिकित्सा। आर्याष्टांगो मार्ग दौष्प्रज्ञसर्वपरप्रवादिनां कुमार्गप्रतिपन्नानां चिकित्सा। इयमुच्यते काश्यप भूतचिकित्सा। तत्र काश्यप बोधिसत्त्वेन योगः करणीयः।

९६

यावंत काश्यप जंबुद्वीपे वैद्या वा वैद्यांतेवासिनो वा सर्वेषां तेषां जीवको वैद्यराजा अग्रोमाख्यायते। यावंतः काश्यप त्रिसाहस्रमहासाहस्रायां लोकधातौ सत्त्वाः ते सर्वे जीवकवैद्यराजसदृशा भवेयुः ते सर्वे परिपृच्छेरन् दृष्टिकौकृत्यप्रतिष्ठितस्य प्रपतितस्य किं भैषज्यमिति। ते न समर्था न च शक्नोति तमर्थ आख्यातुं वा निर्देष्टुं वा (49a)विज्ञातुं[144] वा। तत्र काश्यप बोधिसत्त्वेनैवमुपपरीक्षितव्य। न मया लोकिकभैषज्यसंतुष्टिर्वेदितव्या। लोकोत्तर मया ज्ञानभैषज्यं पर्येष्टितव्यं सर्वकुशलमूलं च सम्यक्समुदानयितव्यमित्येवं चोपपरीक्षितव्यः यच्च ज्ञानभैषज्यं समुदानयित्वा तेन चतुर्दिशं गत्वा सर्वसत्त्वानां भूतचिकित्सा कर्तव्याः भूतचिकित्सया च सत्त्वानि चिकित्सितव्याः।

---

141 *Ibid.*: °नुदर्शनेन.
142 *Ibid.*: 392: चत्वार ऋद्धि°.
143 *Ibid.*: 392: °समोहज्ञानस्य.
144 em. after Tib.; ज्ञानविज्ञाता MS.

९७

तत्र कतरं लोकोत्तरं ज्ञानभैषज्यं। यदिदं हेतुप्रत्ययज्ञानः नैरात्म्ये निःसत्त्वनिर्जीवनिष्पोषनिष्पुद्गलेषु धर्मेष्वधिमुक्तिज्ञानं। शून्यतानुपलंभेषु धर्मेष्वनुत्रासः चित्त(49b)परिगवेषतायै वीर्यं। [145]स एवं चित्तं परिगवेषते। कतरं चित्तं रज्यति वा दुष्यति वा मुह्यति वा। अतीतं[146] वा अनागतं वा प्रत्युत्पन्नं वा। यदि तावदतीतं चित्तं तत् क्षीणं। यदनागतं चित्तं तदसंप्राप्तः[147] अथ प्रत्युत्पन्नस्य चित्तस्य स्थितिर्नास्ति।

९८

चित्तं हि काश्यप नाध्यात्मं न बहिर्धा नोभयमन्तरेणोपलभ्यते। चित्तं हि काश्यप अरूप्यनिदर्शनमप्रतिघमनाभासमविज्ञप्तिकमप्रतिष्ठितमनिकेतम्। चित्तं हि काश्यप सर्वबुद्धैर्न दृष्टं न पश्यंति न पश्यिष्यन्ति न द्रक्ष्यन्ति। यत् सर्वबुद्धैर्न (50a) दृष्टं न पश्यंति न द्रक्ष्यंति कीदृशस्तस्य प्रचारो द्रष्टव्यं नान्यत्र वितथविपर्यासपतिताया संतत्या[148] धर्माः प्रवर्तंते। चित्तं हि काश्यप मायासदृशमभूतं विकल्प्य विविधोपपत्तिं[149] परिगृह्णाति। चित्तं हि काश्यप वायुसदृशं दूरंगममग्राह्यमप्रचारम्। चित्तं हि काश्यप नदीस्रोतसदृशमनवस्थितमुत्पन्नं भग्नविलीन[150]। चित्तं हि काश्यप प्रदीपार्चिःसदृशं हेतुप्रत्ययतया प्रवर्तते ज्वलति च।

---

145 The foll. quoted at ŚS 126, 13–30, and in Vaidya 1960(b): 245, 23–246, 4.
146 ŚS 126, 14: किमतीतम्.
147 ŚS 126, 15: °प्राप्तम्.
148 ŚS 126, 18: द्रष्टव्यः – अन्यत्र वितथपतितया संज्ञया.
149 ŚS 126, 19: °सदृशमभूतपरिकल्पनया विविधामुपपत्तिं.
150 ŚS 126, 20: °स्रोतःसदृशमनवस्थितमुत्पन्नभग्नविलीनम्.

९९

चित्तं हि काश्यप विद्युसदृश क्षणभंगाव्यवस्थितं[151]। चित्तं हि काश्यप आकाशसदृशमागंतुकेरुपक्लेशो सं(50b)क्लिश्यते[152]। चित्तं हि काश्यप वानरसदृश विषयाभिलाषि विचित्रकर्मसंस्थानतया। चित्तं हि काश्यप चित्रकरसदृश विचित्रकर्माभिसंस्करणतया। चित्तं हि काश्यप अनवस्थितं नानाक्लेशप्रवर्तनतया। चित्तं हि काश्यप एकचरमद्वितीयचित्ताभिसन्धानतया। चित्तं हि काश्यप राजसदृशं सर्वधर्माधिपतेया। चित्तं हि काश्यप अमित्रसदृशं[153] सर्वदुःखसंजननतया।

१००

चित्तं हि काश्यप पांस्वागारसदृशमनित्ये नित्यसंज्ञया। चित्तं हि काश्यप नीलमक्षिकासदृशमशुचो शुचिसंज्ञाया[154]। चित्तं हि का(52a)[155]श्यप मत्स्यबडीशसदृश दुःखे सुखसंज्ञाया[156]। चित्तं हि काश्यप स्वप्नसदृशमनात्मीये आत्मीयसंज्ञाया। चित्तं हि काश्यप प्रत्यर्थिकसदृशं विविधकारणाकरणतया। चित्तं हि काश्यप ओजाहारयक्षसदृश सदावतारगवेषणतया[157]। चित्तं हि काश्यप अरिसदृशं सदाच्छिद्रारामगवेषणतया।

१०१

चित्तं हि काश्यप सदा उन्नतावनतमनुनयप्रतिघोपहतम्। चित्तं हि काश्यप चोरसदृशं सर्वकुशलमूलमुषणतया। चित्तं हि काश्यप रूपारामं पतंगनेत्रसदृशम्। चित्तं हि काश्यप

---

151 ŚS 126, 21: विद्युत्सदृशं क्षणभङ्गानवस्थितम्.
152 ŚS 126, 22: °आगन्तुकैः क्लेशैरुपक्लिश्यते.
153 *Ibid.*: पापमित्रसदृशं.
154 ŚS 126, 23: °अशुचौ °संज्ञया.
155 MS erroneously '52a'ff. for '51a'ff. (VD n. 242).
156 ŚS *ibid.*: °बडिशसदृशं ... °संज्ञया.
157 ŚS 126, 24f.: ओजोहार° °सदृशं सदा विवरगवेषणतया.

शब्दारामं संग्रामभे(52b)रीसदृसम्। चित्तं हि काश्यप सदा गन्धारामं वराह इव मीड-कुणपे[158]। चित्तं हि काश्यप रसारामं रसभोज्यचेटीसदृशं[159]। चित्तं हि काश्यप स्पर्शारामं मक्षिकेव तैलपात्रे।

१०२

चित्तं हि काश्यप परिगवेष्यमाणं[160] न लभ्यते। यन्न लभ्यते तन्नोपलभ्यते। *यन्नोपलभ्य-ते*[161] तन्नातीतं नानागतं न प्रत्युत्पन्नं। यन्नातीतं नानागतं न प्रत्युत्पन्नं तत् त्र्यध्व-समतिक्रान्तम्। यत् त्र्यध्वसमतिक्रान्तं तन्नैवास्ति न नास्ति। यन्नैवास्ति न नास्ति तदजातम्। यदजातं तस्य नास्ति स्वभावः यस्य नास्ति स्वभावः तस्य नास्त्युत्पाद। यस्य ना(53a)स्त्युत्पादः तस्य नास्ति निरोधः यस्य नास्ति निरोधः तस्य नास्ति विगमः अविगमस्तस्य न गतिर्नागतिर्न च्युतिर्नोपपत्तिः यत्र न गतिर्नागतिर्न च्युतिर्नोपपत्तिः तत्र न केचित् संस्काराः यत्र न केचित् संस्काराः तदसंस्कृतम्। तदार्याणां गोत्र।

१०३

यदार्याणां गोत्र। तत्र न शिक्षा न निश्रयो नानिश्रयः यत्र न शिक्षा न निश्रयो नानिश्रयः तत्र न शिक्षाव्यतिक्रमः यत्र न शिक्षाव्यतिक्रमः तत्र न संवरो नासंवरः यत्र न संवरो नासंवर तत्र न चारो नाचारः न प्रचारः यत्र न चारो नाचारः न प्रचारः तत्र न चित्तं न चेतसिका धर्माः (53b) यत्र न चित्तं न चेतसिका धर्माः तत्र न मनो न विज्ञानः यत्र न मनो न विज्ञान तत्र न कर्मो न विपाकः यत्र न कर्मो न विपाकः तत्र न सुखं न दुःखं। यत्र न सुखं न दुःखं तदार्याणां गोत्रं। यदार्याणां गोत्रं तत्र न कर्मो न कर्माभिसंस्कारो नापि तत्र गोत्रे कायेन कर्म

---

158 ŚS 126, 27: इवाशुचिमध्ये.

159 *Ibid.*: रसावशेषभोक्तृचेटीसदृशम्.

160 em. after ŚS 126, 28, Vaidya 1960b: 246, 2 and P 14, 23: परिगवेषमानं MS.

161 After ŚS and P; omitted in MS.

क्रियते न वाचा न मनसा। नापि तत्र गोत्रे हीनोत्कृष्टमध्यमव्यवस्थानं। समं तद्गोत्रमाकाशसमतया। निर्विशेषं तद्गोत्रं सर्वधर्मैकरसतया।

१०४

विविक्तं तद्गोत्रं कायचित्तविवेकतया। अनुलोमं तद्गोत्रं निर्वाणस्य। विमलं तद्गोत्रं सर्वक्लेशमलविगतम्। अममं (54a) तद्गोत्रमहंकारममकारविगतं। अविषमं तद्गोत्रं भूताभूतसमतया निर्यातम्। सत्यं तद्गोत्रं परमार्थसत्यया। अक्षयं तद्गोत्र अत्यंततानुत्पन्नं। नित्यं तद्गोत्रं सदाधर्मतथतय। सुखं तद्गोत्रं निर्वाणपरमतया। शुभं तद्गोत्रं सर्वाकारमलविगतं। अनात्मा तद्गोत्रमात्मनः परिगवेष्यमाणानुपलंभात्। विशुद्धं तद्गोत्रमत्यंतविशुद्धतया॥

१०५

अध्यात्मं काश्यप परिमर्गथ मा बहिर्विधावध्वं। तत्कस्माद्धेतोः भविष्यन्ति काश्यप अनागते ऽध्वनि भिक्षवः श्वलेष्ठ्वनुजवनसदृशाः कथं च काश्यप भिक्षवः श्वलेष्ठ्वनुज(54b)वनसदृशा भवति। तद्यथापि नाम काश्यप श्वानो लेष्टुना त्रासितः तमेव लेष्टुमनुधावति। न तमनुधावति येन स लेष्टुः क्षिप्तो भवति। एवमेव काश्यप संत्येके श्रमणब्राह्मणा ये रूपशब्दगन्धरसस्पर्शैर्भयभीता अरण्यायतनेषु विहरंति। तेषा तत्रेकाकिनामद्वितीयानां कायप्रविविक्तविहारिणां रजनीयास्तज्ज्ञक्रिया रूपशब्दगन्धरसस्पर्शा अवभासमागच्छंति। ते तत्रावेक्षकाः सुखल्लिकानुयोगमनुयुक्ता विहरंति।

१०६

ते न जानन्ति न बुद्ध्यंति किं रूपशब्दगन्धरस(55a)स्पर्शानां निःसरणमिति। ते अजानंताः अबुद्ध्यंताः तेषां रूपशब्दगन्धरसस्पर्शानामास्वादं चादीनवं च निःसरणं च अवतीर्णा ग्रामनगरनिगमराष्ट्रराजधानीषु पुनरेव रूपशब्दगन्धरसस्पर्शैर्हन्यंते। सचेदरण्यगता कालं

कुर्वंति। तेषां लोकिकसंवरस्थिताना स्वर्गलोक उपपत्तिर्भवति। ते तत्रापि दिव्यैः पंचभिः कामगुणैर्हन्यंते। ते ततश्च्युता अपरिमुक्ता समानश्चतुर्भिरपायैर्निरयतिर्यग्योनियमलोकासुरैः एवं हि काश्यप भिक्षवः श्वलेष्ट्वनुजवनसदृशा भवं(55b)ति।

१०७

कथं च काश्यप भिक्षुर्न श्वलेष्ट्वनुजवनसदृशो भवति। यः काश्यप भिक्षु आक्रुष्टो न प्रत्याक्रोशति ताडितो न प्रतिताडयति पंसितो न प्रतिपंसयति। भण्डितो न प्रतिभण्डयति। रोषितो न प्रतिरोषयति। आध्यात्मं चित्तनिध्यप्तिं प्रत्यवेक्षते। को वाक्रुष्टो वा ताडितो वा पंसितो वा भण्डितो वा रोषितो वा। एवं हि काश्यप भिक्षुर्न श्वलेष्ट्वनुजवनसदृशो भवति। तत्रेदमुच्यते॥

श्वानो यथा लेष्टुन त्रास्यमानो
अनुधावते लेष्टु न येन क्षिप्तं।
एमेविहेके श्रमणा द्विजा वा
रूपादिभीता वनवासमाश्रिता।
(56a) तेषां च तस्मिन् वसतामरण्ये
रूपादयो दर्शनमेत इष्टा।
उपेक्षकाध्यात्मगते ऽनभिज्ञा
आदीनवान् *निःसरणं*[162] किमेषा।
अजानमाना पुन ग्राममाश्रिता
पुने पि रूपेहि विहन्यमाना।
च्युताश्च देवै मनुजैश्च केचित्
तत्रापि दिव्यानुपभुज्य भोगा।

---

[162] em. after VD n. 254; *निः* सरणे MS.

अपायभूमिः प्रपतंति केचित्
च्युता च्युता दुःखमुपैति मूढाः।
एवं हि ते दुःखशतानुबद्धा
श्वलेष्टतुल्या सुगतेन देशिता।
आक्रुष्ट नाक्रोशति ताडितस्तथा
न पंसितः पंसयते च केचित्।
न भण्डितो भण्डयते तथान्या[163]
न रोषितो रोषयते च सूरतः।
आध्यात्मचित्तं प्रति(**56b**)पक्षतश्च
गवेषते शान्ततवि[164] स्मृतीमान्।
एवंविधः शीलव्रतोपपन्नो
न श्वानतुल्य कथितो जिनेन॥

१०८

तद्यथापि नाम काश्यप कुशलो अश्वदमकसूतो। यत्र यत्र पृथिवीप्रदेशे अश्व स्खलति उत्कुंभति वा खडुंकक्रिया वा करोति तत्र तत्र चैव पृथिवीप्रदेशे निगृह्णाति। स तथा तथा निगृह्णाति यन्न पुनरपि प्रकुप्यते। एवमेव काश्यप योगाचारो भिक्षुर्यत्र यत्रैवं चित्तस्य विकारं पश्यति तत्र तत्रैवास्य निग्रहाय प्रतिपद्यते। स तथा तथा चित्तं निगृह्णाति यथा न पुन प्रकुप्यते। तत्रेदमुच्यते॥

यथाश्वसूत कुशलो भवेत
स्खलितं च अश्वं स(57a)*मभिग्रहेति*।

---

163 After VD; तथान्यान् (!) अरोषितो SH.
164 °तवि? Tib.: *yid źi* (शान्तमानस – Negi 1993ff. s.v.).

योगी तथा चित्त*वि*कार दृष्ट्वा
तथा निगृह्णाति यथा न कुप्यते॥

१०९

तद्यथापि नाम काश्यप गलग्रह सर्वेन्द्रियाणां ग्रहो भवति जीवितेन्द्रियस्योपरोधे वर्तते। एवमेव काश्यप सर्वदृष्टिगतानामात्मग्राहो धर्मजीवितेन्द्रियस्योपरोधेन वर्तते। तत्रेदमुच्यते॥

गलग्रहो वे यथ जीवितेन्द्रिया
निगृह्णते नास्य सुखं ददाति।
दृष्टीकृतानामपि आत्मदृष्टि
विनाशयेत इम धर्मजीवितं॥

११०

तद्यथापि नाम काश्यप पुरुषो यतो यतः बद्धो भवति ततस्तत एव मोचयितव्यो भवति। एवमेव काश्यप यतो यत एव चित्तं सज्यति तत*स्त*(57b)त एव मोचयितव्यं भवति। तत्रेदमुच्यते॥

यथापि बद्धः पुरुषः समंतात्
समंततो मोचयितव्य भोति।
एवं यहिं सज्यति मूढचित्तं
ततस्ततो योगिन मोचनीयम्॥

११११

द्वाविमौ काश्यप प्रव्रजितस्याकाशपलिगोधौ। कतमौ द्वौ। लोकायतमंत्रपर्यैष्टिश्च[165] उत्सद-पात्रचीवरधारणता च। इमौ द्वौ। तत्रेदमुच्यते॥

लोकायतस्याभ्यसनाभियोगो
ततोत्सदं चीवरपात्रधारणं।
आकाशबोधे इमि द्वे प्रतिष्ठिते[166]
तौ बोधिसत्त्वेन विवर्जनीयो॥

११२

द्वाविमौ काश्यप प्रव्रजितस्य गाढबन्धनो। कतमौ द्वौ। यदुतात्मदृष्टिकृतब(58a)न्धनं च लाभसत्कारश्लोकबन्धनं चेतीमे काश्यप द्वौ प्रव्रजितस्य गाढबन्धनं। तत्रेदमुच्यते॥

द्वे बन्धने प्रव्रजितस्य गाढे
दृष्टीकृतं बन्धनमुक्तमार्यैः।
सत्कारलाभोयशबन्धनं च
ते सर्वदा प्रव्रजितेन त्याज्ये॥

११३

द्वाविमो काश्यप प्रव्रजितस्यांतरायकरो धर्मौ। कतमो द्वौ। गृहपतिपक्षसेवना च आर्यपक्ष-विद्वेषणता चेतीमे काश्यप द्वौ प्रव्रजितस्यांतरायकरौ धर्मौ। तत्रेदमुच्यते॥

---

165 Cf. above KP section 5; °पर्यैष्टिता च MS.
166 (ऽ)प्रति° VD.

गृहस्थपक्षस्य च सेवना या
आचार्यपक्षस्य च या विगर्हणा।
द्वावंतरायो परिपन्थभूतो
तौ बोधि(58b)सत्त्वेन विवर्जनीयो॥

११४

द्वाविमौ काश्यप प्रव्रजितस्य मलो कतमौ द्वौ। यदुत क्लेशाधिवासनता च मित्रकुलभेक्षा-ककुलाध्यवसानताग्रहणं चेतीमे काश्यप द्वौ प्रव्रजितस्य मलो। तत्रेदमुच्यते॥

क्लेशांश्च यो प्रव्रजितो ऽधिवासयेत्
मित्रं स भेक्षाककुलं च सेवते।
एतौ जिनेन्द्रेण हि देशितो मलो
तौ बोधिसत्त्वेन विवर्जनीयो॥

११५

द्वाविमो काश्यप प्रव्रजितस्याशनिप्रपातौ। कतमौ द्वौ। सद्धर्मप्रतिक्षेपश्च च्युतशीलस्य च श्रद्धादेयपरिभोगं चेतीमे काश्यप द्वौ प्रव्रजितस्य अशनीप्रपातो धर्मो। तत्रेदमुच्यते॥

सद्धर्मस्य (59a) प्रतिक्षेप।
च्युतशीलस्य भोजनं।
अशनिप्रपातो द्वावेतौ।
वर्जनीयो नृपात्मजैः[167]॥

---

[167] em. after Tib. (Weller 1965: 129, n. 12); कृपात्मकैः MS.

११६

द्वाविमौ काश्यप प्रव्रजितस्य व्रणौ । कतमौ द्वौ । परदौषप्रत्यवेक्षणता च स्वदौषप्रतिच्छादनता चेतीमे काश्यप द्वौ प्रव्रजितस्य व्रणौ तत्रेदमुच्यते॥

वृणुते च स्वका दोषा।
परदोषाश्च वीक्षते।
विषाग्नितुल्यो द्वावेतौ।
व्रणौ त्याज्यौ परीक्षकैः॥

११७

द्वाविमौ काश्यप प्रव्रजितस्य परिदाघो। कतमो द्वौ। यदुत सकषायचित्तस्य[168] च काषायधारणं शीलवंतानां गुणवंतानां चान्तिकादुपस्थानपरिचर्यास्वीकरणं चेतीमे काश्यप द्वौ प्रव्रजितस्य परिदाघो। तत्रेदमु(59b)च्यते॥

सकषायचित्तस्य काषायधारणं
शीलान्वितानां च सकाश सेवना।
परिचर्युपस्थानभिवादनं च
धर्माविमौ द्वौ परिवर्जनीया॥

११८

द्वाविमौ काश्यप प्रव्रजितस्य दीर्घग्लान्यौ। कतमौ द्वौ। यदुत अभिमानिकस्य च चित्तनिध्यप्तिर्महायानसंप्रस्थितानां च सत्त्वाना विच्छन्दना। इमे काश्यप द्वौ प्रव्रजितस्य दीर्घग्लान्यो। तत्रेदमुच्यते॥

---

168 em. after VD n. 272; सकाषायस्य MS.

निध्यप्ति चित्तस्यभिमानिकानां
विच्छन्दना यापि च बुद्धयानं।
इमे हि द्वे प्रव्रजितस्य ग्लान्ये
उक्ते जिनेनाप्रतिपुद्गलेन॥

११९

द्वाविमो काश्यप प्रव्रजितस्य अचिकित्सो ग्लान्यौ। कतमौ द्वौ। य(60a)दुताभीक्ष्णापत्त्यापद्यनता। अव्युत्थानता चेतीमे काश्यप द्वौ प्रव्रजितस्य अचिकित्सो ग्लान्यो॥

१२०

द्वाविमौ काश्यप प्रव्रजितस्य शल्यो कतमौ द्वौ। यदुत शिक्षापदसमतिक्रमं च अनादत्तसारस्य च कालक्रिया। इमे काश्यप द्वौ प्रव्रजितस्य शल्यो। *तत्रेदमुच्यते*[169]॥

१२१

श्रमण श्रमण इति काश्यप उच्यते। कियन्नु तावत्काश्यप श्रमणः श्रमण इत्युच्यते। चत्वार इमे काश्यप श्रमणाः कतमे चत्वारः यदुत वर्णरूपलिङ्गसंस्थानश्रमण। आचारगुप्तिकुहकश्रमणः कीर्तिशब्दश्लोकश्रमणः भूतप्रतिपत्तिश्रमणः इमे काश्यप (60b) चत्वारः श्रमणाः॥

१२२

तत्र काश्यप कतमो वर्णरूपलिङ्गसंस्थानश्रमणः इह काश्यप इहेकत्य श्रमण वर्णरूपलिङ्गसंस्थानसमन्वागतो भवति। संघाटीपरिवेष्टितो मुण्डशिरः सुपात्रपाणिः[170] स च भव-

---

[169] After Tib.: *शिक्षापदसमतिक्रमो भवति। अनादत्तसारस्य च कालक्रिया। इमे द्वे प्रव्रजितस्य शल्ये इति शास्ता देवमनुष्याणां सर्वज्ञो ऽवदत्॥*

[170] Cf. Tib. *lag na lhuṅ bzed thogs*; सुपात्रपाणैः परिगृहीतः MS.

त्यपरिशुद्धकायकर्मसमुदाचार अपरिशुद्धवाक्कर्मसमुदाचारः अपरिशुद्धमनस्कर्मसमुदाचारो भवति। अयुक्त अमुक्तः अदान्तः अशान्तः अगुप्तः अविनीतः लुब्धः अलसो दुःशीलः पापधर्मसमाचारः अयमुच्यते काश्यप वर्णरूपलिङ्गसंस्थानश्रमणः॥

१२३

तत्र काश्यप कतमः आचारगुप्तिकु(61a)हकः श्रमणः इह काश्यप इहैकत्य श्रमणः आचारचारित्रसंपन्नो भवति संप्रजानचारी चतुर्भि ईर्यापथैर्लूहान्नपानभोजी संतुष्टः चतुर्भिरार्यवंशेरसंसृष्टो गृहस्थप्रव्रजितैरल्पभाष्यो ऽल्पमंत्रः ते चास्येर्यापथाः कुहनलपनतया कल्पिता भवंति। नचित्तपरिशुद्धये। न शमाय नोपशमाय। न दमाय। उपलंभदृष्टिकश्च भवति। शून्यतानुपलंभाश्च धर्मेषु श्रुत्वा प्रपातसंज्ञी भवति। शून्यतावादिनां च भिक्षुणामंतिके अप्रसादसंज्ञामुत्पादयति। इयमुच्यते काश्यप आचारगुप्तिकुहक(61b)श्रमणः॥

१२४

तत्र काश्यप कतमः कीर्तिशब्दश्लोकश्रमणः इह काश्यप इहैकत्य श्रमणः प्रतिसंख्याय शीलं रक्षति। कथं मां परे जानीयुः शीलवानिति। प्रतिसंख्याय श्रुतमुद्गृह्णीते कथं मां परे जानीयुर्बहुश्रुत इति। प्रतिसंख्यायारण्ये प्रतिवसति। कथं मां परे जानीयुरारण्यक इति। प्रतिसंख्याय अल्पेच्छः संतुष्टः प्रविविक्तो विहरति यावदेव परोपदर्शनाय न निर्वेदाय न विरागाय न निरोधाय नोपशमाय न संबोधये न श्रामण्याय न ब्राह्मण्याय न निर्वाणाय। अयमुच्य(62a)ते काश्यप कीर्तिशब्दश्लोकश्रमणः॥

१२५

तत्र काश्यप कतमो भूतप्रतिपत्तिः श्रमणः यः काश्यप भिक्षुरनर्थिको भवति कायेन च जीवितेनापि कः पुनर्वादो लाभसत्कारश्लोके। शून्यता आनिमित्ता अप्रणिहिताश्च धर्मा श्रुत्वा

आप्तमनो भवति। तथत्वतायां प्रतिपन्नो निर्वाणे चाप्यनर्थिको ब्रह्मचर्यं चरति कः पुनर्वादस्त्रैधातुकाभिनन्दनतया। शून्यतादृष्ट्याप्यनर्थिको भवति कः पुनर्वाद आत्मसत्त्वजीवपोषपुद्गलदृष्ट्या। धर्मप्रतिसरणश्च भवति। क्लेशानां च अध्यात्मविमोक्ष मर्गति न बहिर्धा धावति। अत्यंतपरिशुद्धश्च (62b)प्रकृत्या सर्वधर्मा असंक्लिष्टान् पश्यति आत्मद्वीपश्च भवत्यनन्यद्वीपः धर्मतो ऽपि तथागतं न समनुपश्यति कः पुनर्वाद रुपकायेन। विरागतो ऽपि धर्मं नाभिनिविशते कः पुनर्वाद रुतवाक्पथोदाहरणेन। असंस्कृतमति चार्यसंघं न विकल्पयति कः पुनर्वादो गणसंनिपाततः नापि कस्यचिद्धर्मस्य प्रहाणायाभियुक्तो भवति न भावनायै न साक्षीक्रियाय। न संसारे विरोहति न निर्वाणमभिनन्दति। न मोक्षं पर्येषते न बन्धं। प्रकृतिपरिनिर्वृता च सर्वधर्मान् विदित्वा न संसरति न परिनिर्वाय(63a)ति। अयमुच्यते काश्यप भूतप्रतिपत्तिः श्रमणः। भूतप्रतिपत्त्या श्रामण्या योगः करणीयो न नामहेतुन भवितव्यो। इमे काश्यप चत्वारः श्रमणाः तत्रेदमुच्यते॥

१२६

यो कायवाक्चित्तमनेरशुद्धो
अदान्तगुप्तो अविनीत लुब्धो।
मुण्डःशिरश्चीवरपात्रपाणी
संस्थानलिङ्गा श्रमणेषु वुक्तो।
आचारचर्यापि समन्वितो ऽपि
रूक्षान्नभोजी कुहनादिसेवी।
चतुरार्यवंशेहि समन्वितो ऽपि
संसर्ग दूरात् परिवर्जयंतो।
ते चास्य सर्वे न दमाय भोन्ति
न शान्तये नापि च निर्विदाय।
शून्यानिमित्तेषु प्रपातसंज्ञी

आ(63b)चारगुप्तिः कुहको द्वितीयो।
धुतागुणा शील श्रुतं समाधिः
परस्य विस्मापनहेतु कुर्वति।
न शान्तये नापि च निर्विदाय
कीर्तीयश्लोकश्रमणो तृतीय।
कायेन यो ऽनर्थिक जीवितेन वा
यो लाभसत्कारपराङ्मुखश्च।
विमोक्ष उत्पादमुखं च श्रुत्वा
अनर्थिका सर्वभवद्गतीषु।
अत्यंतशून्याश्च परीक्ष्य धर्मान्
न निर्वृतिं पश्यति नाप्यनिर्वृतिं।
विरागतो धर्ममवेक्षते सदा
असंस्कृतं धर्ममवेक्ष्य[171] निर्वृतः॥

१२७

तद्यथापि नाम काश्यप दरिद्रपुरुषस्य समृद्धकोश इति नामधेयं भवेत्। तत्किं मन्यसे काश्यप। अनुरूपं (64a)तस्य दरिद्रपुरुषस्य तन्नामधेयं भवेत्। आह नो हीदं भदंत भगवन्। भगवानाह। एवमेव काश्यप ये ते श्रमणब्राह्मणा इत्युच्यंते न च श्रमणब्राह्मण-गुणसमन्वागता[172] भवंति। तानहं दरिद्रपुरुषानिति वदामि। तत्रेदमुच्यते॥

यथा दरिद्रस्य भवेत नामं
समृद्धकोशं ति न तच्च शोभते।

171 em. after Tib. (Weller 1965: 136, n. 2); अनित्य MS.
172 em. after Tib. (Weller 1965: 136, n. 5); °ब्राह्मणसमन्वागता MS.

श्रामण्यहीन श्रमणो न शोभते
दरिद्र आढ्येति व उच्यमानः॥

१२८

तद्यथापि नाम काश्यप कश्चिदेव पुरुषो महता उदकार्णवेनोह्यमानः उदकतृष्णया[173] कालं कुर्यात् । एवमेव काश्यप इहेकत्ये श्रमणब्राह्मणो[174] बहून्धर्मान् पर्याप्नुवंति[175] न रा-(64b)गतृष्णान्[176] विनोदयंति । न द्वेषतृष्णा न मोहतृष्णा[177] शक्नुवंति विनोदयितुं । ते महता धर्मार्णवेनोह्यमाना क्लेशतृष्णया कालगता दुर्गतिगामिनो भवंति। तत्रेदमुच्यते॥

यथा मनुष्यो उदकार्णवेन
उह्याति तृष्णाय करेय कालम्।
तथा पठंता बहुधर्मतृष्णया
धर्मार्णवस्था पि व्रजंत्यपायं॥

१२९

तद्यथापि नाम काश्यप वैद्यो औषधभस्त्रां[178] गृहीत्वा अनुविचरेत् । तस्य कश्चिदेव व्याधि उत्पद्येत न च तं व्याधि शक्नुयाच्चिकित्सितुं। एवमेव काश्यप बहुश्रुतस्य क्लेशव्याधि द्रष्टव्यो यस्तेन श्रुतेन न शक्नोति आत्मनः क्लेशव्याधि चिकित्सितुं। निरार्थकं तस्य तच्छ्रु(65a)तं भविष्यति। तत्रेदमुच्यते॥

---

173 em. after ŚS 108, 31; तृषया MS.
174 de Jong 1977: 250: काश्यपैकत्याः …°ब्राह्मणा; ŚS 108, 32: इहैके …°ब्राह्मणा.
175 de Jong, *ibid.*: पर्याप्य; ŚS 108, 32–109, 1: उद्गृह्य पर्यवाप्य.
176 de Jong, *ibid.*, ŚS 109, 1: °तृष्णां.
177 *Ibid.*: °तृष्णां.
178 em. after de Jong 1977: 250; ओषधभारं MS.

यथेव वैद्यौषधभस्त्रसंस्थे
परिभ्रमेत निखिलंहि लोके।
उत्पन्नव्याधिन्न निवर्तये च
निरर्थकं तस्य भवेत तं हि।
भिक्षुस्तथा शीलगुणैरुपेतः
श्रुतेन युक्तो ऽपि न चा चिकित्सेत्।
अयोनिश क्लेशसमुत्थिता रुजा
वृथा श्रमस्तस्य श्रुताभियोगः॥

१३०

तद्यथापि नाम काश्यप ग्लानः पुरुषो राजार्हं भैषज्यमुपयुज्यासंवरेण कालं कुर्यात्। एवमेव काश्यप बहुश्रुतस्य क्लेशव्याधिर्द्रष्टव्यः यस्तेनासंवरेण कालं करोति। यो राजार्हं भैषज्यं पर्यापुनित्वा असंवरेण अपायगामी भवति। तत्रेदमुच्यते॥

यथापि राजार्हं पीत्व भै(65b)षजं
व्रजेन्नरो ऽसंवरतो निपातं।
बहुश्रुतस्येष तु क्लेशव्याधिर्
यो ऽसंवरेणेह करोति कालम्॥

१३१

तद्यथापि नाम काश्यप अनर्घं वैडूर्यमहामणिरत्नमुच्चारे पतितमकार्योपकं भवति। एवमेव काश्यप बहुश्रुतस्य लाभसत्कारोच्चारपतनं द्रष्टव्यं निष्किंचनं देवमनुष्येषु। तत्रेदमुच्यते॥

रत्नं यथोच्चारगतं जुगुप्सितं
यथा स्यान्न तथा यथा पुर।

बहुश्रुतस्यापि वदामि भिक्षोः
सत्कारमीढे पतनं तथैव॥

तद्यथापि नाम काश्यप तदेव वैडूर्यं महामणिरत्नममेध्यावस्करादुद्धृतं भवेत् सुधौतं सुप्रक्षालितं सुपरिमार्जितं। तं मणिरत्न(66a)स्वभावमेव न विजहात्येवमेव काश्यप बहुश्रुतो ऽल्पप्रयत्नेन सर्वक्लेशान् विशोधयति महाप्रज्ञारत्नस्वभावमेव न विजहाति॥

१३२

तद्यथापि नाम काश्यप मृतकस्य शिरसि सुवर्णमाला। एवमेव काश्यप दुःशीलस्य काषायधारणं द्रष्टव्यं। तत्रेदमुच्यते॥

सुवर्णमालेव मृतस्य शीर्षे
न्यस्ता यथा स्यादथ पुष्पमाला।
काषायवस्त्राणि तथा विशीले
दृष्ट्वा न कुर्यान्मनसः प्रदोषं॥

१३३

तद्यथापि नाम काश्यप अवदातवस्त्रप्रावृतस्य[179] प्रवरचन्दनानुलिप्तस्य श्रेष्ठिपुत्रस्य वा राजपुत्रस्य वा शिरसि चम्पकमाला[180] बद्धा भवेत्। एवमेव *काश्यप* (66b)*शीलवतो*[181] बहुश्रुतस्य काषायधारणं द्रष्टव्य। तत्रेदमुच्यते॥

सुस्नातस्यानुलिप्तस्य।
श्रेष्ठिपुत्रस्य शोभनं।

[179] de Jong 1977: 250: सुस्नातस्य सुविलिप्तस्य सुछिन्नकेशनखस्यावदात°.
[180] em. after *ibid.*; चणपकमालाबद्धं MS.
[181] *Ibid.* and VD: दुःशील°.

शीर्षे चम्पकमालेव।
शुभगन्धा मनोरमा॥
यथा तथैव काषायं।
संवरस्थे बहुश्रुते।
द्रष्टव्यं शीलसंपन्न।
जिनपुत्रे गुणान्विते॥

१३४

चत्वार इमे काश्यप दुःशीला शीलवंतप्रतिरूपकाः[182] कतमे चत्वारः इह काश्यप एकत्यो भिक्षुः प्रातिमोक्षसंवरसंवृतो विहरति । आचारगोचरसंपन्न अणुमात्रेष्ववद्येषु[183] भयदर्शी समादाय शिक्षते शिक्षापदेषु। परिशुद्धकायकर्मवङ्मनस्कर्मणा समन्वागतो विहरति। परिशुद्धाजीवः स च भव(67a)त्यात्मवादी। अयं काश्यप प्रथमो दुःशीलः शीलवंतप्रतिरूपको द्रष्टव्यः। पुनरपरं काश्यप इहेकत्यो[184] भिक्षुर्विनयधरो भवति । प्रवर्तविनयो[185] विनयगुप्तिप्रतिष्ठितः सत्कायदृष्टिरस्यानुचलिता भवति । अयं काश्यप द्वितीयो दुःशीलः शीलवंतप्रतिरूपकः। पुनरपरं काश्यप इहेकत्यो भिक्षुः मैत्राविहारि सत्त्वारंबणया[186] समन्वागतः स च अजाति सर्वधर्माणां श्रुत्वा उत्त्रसति संत्रसति संत्रासमापद्यते। अयं काश्यप तृतीयो दुःशीलः शीलवन्तप्रतिरूपकः। पुनरपरं काश्यप इहेकत्यो भिक्षुः द्वादश धुतगुण[187]-*समादाय वर्तते*। (67b)उपलंभदृष्टिकश्च भवत्यहंकारस्थितः अयं काश्यप चतुर्थो दुःशीलः शीलवन्तप्रतिरूपको *द्रष्टव्यः इमे काश्यप* चत्वारो दुःशीला शीलवंतप्रतिरूपका द्रष्टव्याः॥

---

182 de Jong 1977: 250: शीलवत्प्रति°.
183 *Ibid.*: °त्रेष्वपि वद्येषु.
184 *Ibid.*: 251: काश्यपेहैकत्यो.
185 *Ibid.*: प्रवृतविनयो; em. प्रवृत्त°/प्रवर्तित° (VD n. 310).
186 de Jong 1977: 251: °रंबणया करुणया; Tib. *byams pa daṅ ldan pa* – मैत्रतया (cf. Negi 1993ff. s.v.).
187 de Jong *ibid.*: द्वादश धुतगुणान्.

१३५

शीलं शीलमिति काश्यप उच्यते। यत्र नात्मा[188] नात्मीयं। न क्रिया नाक्रिया। न करणं नाकरणं। न चारो नाचारः न प्रचारो नाप्रचारः न नामं न रूप। न निमित्तं नानिमित्तं। न शमो न प्रशमः न ग्राहो नोत्सर्गः न ग्राह्यं नाग्राह्य। न सत्त्वो न सत्त्वप्रज्ञप्तिः न वाङ्ग वाक्प्रज्ञप्तिः न चित्तं न चित्तप्रज्ञप्तिः न लोको नालोकः न निश्रयो नानि(68a)श्रयः नात्मशीलोत्कर्षणा। न परशीलपंसना[189]। न शीलमन्यना। न शीलकल्पना। न विकल्पना। न संकल्पना। न परिकल्पना। इदमुच्यते काश्यप आर्याणां शील। अनास्रवमपर्यापंनं त्रैधातुकापगतं सर्वनिश्रयविगतम्[190]।

१३६

अथ भगवांस्तस्यां वेलायामिमां गाथामभाषतः॥

न शीलवन्तस्य मलं न किंचन
न शीलवन्तस्य मदो न निश्रयः।
न शीलवन्तस्य तमो न बन्धनम्
न शीलवन्तस्य रजो न *दोषः*।
शान्तप्रशान्तोपशान्तमानसो
कल्पःविकल्पापगतो निरंगणः।
सर्वेञ्जनामन्यनविप्रमुक्तः
स शीलवा(68b)न् काश्यप बुद्धशासने।
न कायसापेक्षि[191] न जीवितार्थिको

---

188 The foll. lacuna in MS; according to Tib. and de Jong, *ibid.*, no lacuna.
189 em. after de Jong, *ibid.* (tallying with Tib.); परदुःशील° MS.
190 em. after *ibid.*; °आनुगतं सर्वनिश्रयापगतमं MS.
191 em. afterVD n. 316; °सावेक्षि MS.

ह्यनर्थिकः सर्वभवोपपत्तिभिः।
सम्यग्गतः *सैव विधि* प्रतिष्ठितः
स शीलवान् काश्यप बुद्धशासने।
न लोकलिप्तो न च लोकनिश्रितो
आलोकप्राप्तो अममो अकिञ्चनः।
न चात्मसंज्ञी न परेषु संज्ञी
संज्ञापरिज्ञाय विशुद्धशीलः।
यस्या न ऽपारं न च पारमध्यम्
अपारपारे च न जातु सक्तः।
अबद्ध् असक्तो अकुहो अनास्रवः
स शीलवान् काश्यप बुद्धशासने।

१३७

नामे च रूपे च असक्तमानसः
समाहितस्सो हि सुदान्तचित्तः।
यस्येह आत्मा न च आत्मनीया
एतावता शीलस्थि(69a)तो निरुच्यते।
न शिक्षया मन्यति प्रातिमोक्षे
न चापि तेन भवतेह तन्मयो।
अथोत्तरं मर्गति आर्यमार्गे
विशुद्धशीलस्य इमे निमित्ता।
न शीलपरमो न समाधितन्मयो
पर्येषते दुत्तरि प्रज्ञभावना।
अनोपलंभं अरियाण गोत्रं

विशुद्धशीलं सुगतप्रशस्तम्।
सत्कायदृष्टे हि विमुक्तमानसो
अहं ममेतीह न तस्य भोति।
अधिमुच्यते शून्यत बुद्धगोचरम्
इमस्य शीलस्य समो न विद्यते।
शीले प्रतिष्ठाय समाधि शुद्धः
समाधिप्राप्तस्य च प्रज्ञभावना।
प्रज्ञाय ज्ञानं भवते विशुद्धं
विशुद्धज्ञानस्य च शीलसंपदा॥

१३८

अस्मिन् खलु पुनर्गाथाभिनिर्हारे (69b)भाष्यमाणे अष्टानां भिक्षुशतानामनुपादायास्त्रवेभ्यश्चित्तानि विमुक्तानि। द्वात्रिंशतीनां च प्राणसहस्त्राणां विरजो विगतमलं धर्मेषु धर्मचक्षुर्विशुद्धं। पंच भिक्षुशतानि ध्यानलाभीनि[192] उत्थायासनेभ्यः प्रक्रान्तानि इमां गंभीरां धर्मदेशनामनवतरन्ति अनवगाहमानानि अनधिमुच्यमानानि[193]।

१३९

अथायुष्मान् महाकाश्यपो भगवंतमेतदवोचत्। इमानि भगवां पंच भिक्षुशतानि ध्यानलाभीन्युत्थायासनेभ्यः प्रक्रांतानि। इमां गंभीरां धर्मदेशनामनवतरन्ति अनवगाहमानानि अनधिमुच्यमानानि। भगवानाह। तथा ह्येते काश्यप भिक्षवः (70a)आभिमानिकाः[194] ते ऽनधिमुच्यमाना इमं गंभीरं गाथाभिनिर्हारमनास्त्रवं शीलविशुद्धिनिर्देशं श्रुत्वा नावतरंति

---

[192] em. after P 144, 2; °लाभी MS.
[193] em. after P 144, 2f.; अवतरंतो नावगाहमानाः अनधिमुच्यमानाः MS.
[194] em. after P 144, 4; अनधिमानिका MS.

नाधिमुच्यंति नावगाहंति। तत्कस्माद्धेतोः गंभीरो ऽयं काश्यप गाथाभिनिर्हारो गंभीरा बुद्धाना भगवंतानां बोधिः सा न शक्या अनवरोपितकुशलमूलैः सत्त्वैः पापमित्रपरिगृहीतैरनधिमुक्तिबहुलैरधिमोक्तुं[195] वा पर्यापुनितुं वा अवतरितुं वा।

१४०

अपि च काश्यप एतानि पंच भिक्षुशतानि काश्यपस्य तथागतस्यार्हतः सम्यक्संबुद्धस्य प्रवचने अन्यतीर्थिकश्रावका अभूवन्। तैः काश्यपस्य तथाग(70b)तस्यांतिकादुपारंभाभिप्रायैरेका[196] धर्मदेशना श्रुता। श्रुत्वा चेव चित्तप्रसादो लब्ध आश्चार्यं[197] यावन्मधुरप्रियभाणी खल्वयं काश्यपस्तथागतो ऽर्हन् सम्यक्संबुद्ध इति। ते ततश्च्युत समाना एकचित्तप्रसादेन कालगताः त्रायस्त्रिंशेषु देवेषूपपन्नाः तेनैव हेतुना इह मम शासने प्रव्रजिताः तान्येतानि काश्यप पंच भिक्षुशतानि दृष्टिगतप्रस्कन्दितानि[198] इमां गंभीरा धर्मदेशना नावतरंति नावगाहंति नाधिमुच्यंते न श्रद्दधंति। कृतं पुनरेषामनया[199] धर्मदेशनाया परिकर्म। न भूयो विनिपातगामिनो भवि(71a)ष्यंति। एभिरेव स्कन्धैः परिनिर्वास्यंति।

१४१

तत्र भगवानायुष्मंतं सुभूतिमामन्त्रयति स्म। गच्छ त्वं सुभूते एतान् भिक्षु संज्ञपय। सुभूतिराह। भगवत एव तावदेते भिक्षवो भाषितं प्रतिविलोमयंति कः पुनर्वादो मम। अथ खलु भगवांस्तस्यां वेलायां येन मार्गेण ते भिक्षवो गच्छंति स्म। तस्मिन् मार्गे द्वौ भिक्षू निर्मिमीते स्म। अथ तानि पंच भिक्षुशतानि येन मार्गेण तौ द्वौ भिक्षू निर्मितकौ[200] तेनोपसंक्रामन्ति

---

[195] em. after P 144, 6f.; शक्यमनवरोपितकुशलमूले ... सत्त्वैरधिमुच्यितुं MS.

[196] P 144, 8: उपालम्भाभिप्रायैरेषा.

[197] P 144, 9: लब्धः। एवं तैर्वाग् भाषिता – आश्चर्यं.

[198] P 144, 12: दृष्टिप्रस्कन्धानि.

[199] em. after P 144, 13; एषामयं MS.

[200] em. after P 15, 18; 144, 17; भिक्षु निर्मितो MS.

स्म[201]। उपसंक्रम्येवमवोचन् । कुत्र आयुष्मन्तौ गमिष्यथः ताववोचताम्[202]। गमिष्याव आवामरण्यायतनेषु (71b) सुखं फाषं विहरिष्यावः तत्कस्माद्धेतोः यं हि भगवान् धर्मं देशयति तामावां धर्मदेशनां नावतरावो नावगाहावहे नाधिमुच्यावहे । उत्त्रसावः संत्रसावः संत्रासमापद्यावहे तावावामरण्यायतनेषु सुखं विहरिष्यावः।

१४२

तान्यपि पंच भिक्षुशतान्येतदवोचन्। वयमप्यायुष्मंतो भगवतो धर्मदेशनां नावतरामो नावगाहामहे नाधिमुच्यामहे। उत्त्रसामः संत्रसामः संत्रासमापद्यामहे। तेन वयमरण्यायतनेषु ध्यानसुखविहारैर्विहरिष्यामः निर्मितकाववोचताम्। संगायिष्याम वयमायुष्मंतो न विवदिष्यामः अवि(72a)वादपरमो हि श्रमणधर्मः यदिहमायुष्मन्त इत्युच्यते परिनिर्वाणमिति। कतमः स धर्मो यः परिनिर्वास्यति कश्चित्पुनरस्मिं काये आत्मा वा सत्त्वो वा जीवो वा जंतुर्वा पोषो वा पुद्गलो वा मनुजो वा मानवो *वा* कर्ता वा कारको वा वेदको वा जानको वा संजानको वा उत्थापको वा समुत्थापको वा यः परिनिर्वास्यति।

१४३

ते आहुः न क्वचिदस्ति अस्मिं काये आत्मा वा सत्त्वो वा जीवो वा जंतुर्वा पुरुषो वा पुद्गलो वा मनुजो वा मानवो *वा* कर्ता वा कारको वा वेदको वा जानको वा संजानको वा उत्थापको वा यः परिनिर्वास्यति । निर्मितकौ प्राहुः *किं* (72b) पुन साक्षीकृयाया परिनिर्वास्यतीति । ते आहुः रागक्षयाय द्वेषक्षयाय मोहक्षयाय आयुष्मन्त परिनिर्वाणमिति। निर्मितकौ प्राहुः किं पुनरायुष्मतां रागद्वेषमोहाः संविद्यंते यां क्षपयिष्यथ। ते आहुः न ते ऽध्यात्मं[203] न बहिर्धा नोभयमंतरेणोपलभ्यंते। नापि ते अपरिकल्पिता उत्पद्यंते। निर्मितकाववोचताम्। तेन-

201 em. after *ibid.*; तेनोपसंक्कामन्नुप° MS.
202 em. after P 15, 19; 144, 18; गमिष्यथ। … अवोचता MS.
203 em. after P 15, 27; आध्यात्मेन MS.

मायुष्मन्तो मा कल्पयत। मा विकल्पयत[204]। यदायुष्मंतो *न* कल्पयिष्यथ न विकल्पयिष्यथ तदायष्मन्तो न रंक्ष्यथ न विरंक्ष्यथ। यश्चायुष्मंतो न रक्तो न विरक्तः *स* (73a) शान्त इत्युच्यते।

१४४

शीलमायुष्मन्तो न संसरति न परिनिर्वाति। समाधिप्रज्ञाविमुक्तिविमुक्तिज्ञानदर्शनम् *आयुष्मन्तो* न संसरति न परिनिर्वाति। एभिश्चेवायुष्मन्तो धर्मै[205] निर्वाणं सूच्यते। एते च धर्मा शून्या विविक्ता[206] *अग्राह्याः* प्रजहीतैतामायुष्मन्तः संज्ञां यदुत परिनिर्वाणमिति। मा च संज्ञायां संज्ञां कार्ष्ट[207]। मा असंज्ञायां *मा* च संज्ञायां संज्ञां परिज्ञासिष्ट[208]। यः संज्ञायां संज्ञां परिजानाति संज्ञा बन्धनमेवास्य तद्भवति। संज्ञावेदयितनिरोधसमापत्तिमायुष्मन्तः समापद्यध्वं मा च कल्पयथ मा विकल्पयथ। संज्ञावेदयितनिरो(73b)धसमापत्तिसमापन्नस्य भिक्षोर्नास्त्युत्तरे करणीयमिति[209] वदावः।

१४५

अस्मिं खलु पुनर्धर्मपर्याये भाष्यमाणे तेषां पंचानां भिक्षुशतानामनुपादायास्रवेभ्यः चित्तानि विमुक्तानि। तानि विमुक्तचित्तानि येन भगवांस्तेनोपसंक्रान्तानि[210]। उपसंक्रम्य भगवतः पादौ शिरसाभिवन्द्यैकान्ते न्यसीदन्[211]। अथायुष्मान् सुभूतिस्तान् भिक्षूनेतदवोचत्। क्व नु खल्वायुष्मंतो गता कुतो वा आगताः ते ऽवोचन्। न क्वचिद्गमनाय न कुतश्चिदागमनाय

---

204 em. after P 15, 28; मास्मान् … मास्मन् विकल्पयत MS.
205 P 16, 1: एभिश्चायुष्मन्तो धर्मैर्.
206 P 16, 2: प्रकृतिविविक्ताः.
207 em. after *ibid.*; संज्ञाया संज्ञा कार्ष्व MS.
208 em. after P 16, 3; संज्ञया संज्ञा परिज्ञासिष्व MS.
209 P 16, 5: °उत्तरीकरणीयमिति.
210 em. after P 16, 6f.; ते विमुक्तचित्ता … °संक्कमन्न् MS.
211 em. after *ibid.*; शिरोभिर्वन्दित्वा एकांते न्यषीदन् MS.

भदन्त सुभूते भगवता धर्मो देशितः सुभूतिराह। को नामायुष्मतां शास्ता। ते आहुः यो नोत्पन्नो[212] *न प*(74a)रिनिर्वास्यति।

१४६

सुभूतिराह। कस्य युष्मे श्रावका कस्य सकाशाद्युष्मे विनीता। ते आहुर्येन न प्राप्त *नाभिसंबुद्धम्*[213]। सुभूतिराह। कस्य सकाशाद्युष्माकं धर्मं श्रुतं। ते आहुर्यस्य न स्कन्धा न धातवो नायतनानि। सुभूतिराह। कथं पुनर्युष्मे धर्मं श्रुतं। ते आहुर्न बन्धनाय न मोक्षाय। सुभूतिराह। कथं यूयं प्रयुक्ता। ते आहुः न योगाय न प्रयोगाय न प्रहाणाय। सुभूतिराह। केन यूयं विनीताः ते आहुः यस्य न कायपरिनिष्पत्तिर्न चित्तप्रचारं। सुभूतिराह। कथं युष्माभिप्रयुज्यमाना[214] विमुक्ताः *ते* (74b)आहुः नाविद्याप्रहाणाय न विद्योत्पादाय।

१४७

सुभूतिराह। (कस्य यूयं श्रावकाः ते आहुः यस्य न प्राप्तो नाभिसंबुद्धः सुभूतिराह।)[215] केवच्चिरेण यूयं परिनिर्वास्यथ[216]। ते आहुः यावच्चिरेण तथागतनिर्मितकाः परिनिर्वास्यंति तावच्चिरेण वयं परिनिर्वास्यामः सुभूतिराह। कृतं युष्माभि स्वकार्थं। ते आहुः अर्थानुपलब्धत्वात्। सुभूतिराह। कृतं युष्माभिः करणीय। ते आहुः कारकानुपलब्धित्वात्। सुभूतिराह। के युष्माकं सब्रह्मचारिणः ते आहुः ये त्रैधातुके नोपचरंति न प्रचरंति।

---

212 em. after P 16, 10; योत्पन्नो MS.
213 P 16, 13: प्राप्तं नाभिसंबुद्धम्.
214 युष्माभि प्रयुज्यमाना SH, VD.
215 See above beginning of section 146.
216 P 16, 14: कियच्चिरेणायुष्मन्तः परिनिर्वास्यन्ति.

१४८

(75a)सुभूतिराह ।क्षीणा युष्माकं क्लेशाः ते आहुरत्यंतक्षयत्वात्सर्वधर्माणां । सुभूतिराह । धर्षितो युष्माभिर्मारः ते आहुः स्कन्धमारानुपलब्धित्वात् । सुभूतिराह । परिचीर्णो युष्माभिस्तथागतः ते आहुर्न कायेन *न वाचा*[217] न चित्तेन। सुभूतिराह। स्थिता युष्माकं दाक्षिणेयभूमौ[218]। ते आहुः अग्राहतः अप्रतिग्राहतः सुभूतिराह । छिन्ना यूयं संसारं । ते आहुः अनुच्छेदतो ऽशाश्वततः[219] सुभूतिराह । प्रतिपन्ना यूयं श्रमणभूमौ । ते पुनराहुः असंगाविमुक्तौ[220]। सुभूतिर् *आह* । (75b)किंगामिन आयुष्मन्तः ते आहुः यद्गामिनस्तथागतनिर्मिताः[221]॥

१४९

इति ह्यायुष्मतः सुभूतेः परिपृच्छतः तेषां *च* भिक्षूणां विसर्जयन्तानां तस्यां पर्षदि अष्टानां भिक्षुशतानां पंचानां च भिक्षुणीशतानामनुपादायास्रवेभ्यश्चित्तानि विमुक्तानि। द्वात्रिंशतीनां च प्राणिसहस्राणां सदेवमानुषिकायां प्रजायां विरजो *विगतमलं* धर्मेषु धर्मचक्षुर्विशुद्धम्॥

१५०

अथ खलु समन्तालोको नाम बोधिसत्त्वो महासत्त्वो भगवंतमेतदवोचत् । *इह* भगवन् महारत्नकूटे धर्मपर्याये शिक्षितुकामेन बोधिसत्त्वेन कथं स्थातव्यं कथं प्रतिपत्तव्यं कथं शिक्षितव्यम् । *भग*(76a)वानाह । उद्गृह्य कुलपुत्र इह धर्मपर्याये शिक्षा आख्याता प्रतिपत्तिसाराणां सत्पुरुषाणां इयं धर्मपर्यायो बह्वर्थकरो भविष्यति।

---

217 After P 16, 18.
218 P 16, 19: विशोधिता युष्माभिर्दक्षिणीयभूमिः.
219 em. after P 16, 20; अनुच्छेद-अशाश्वतत्वात् MS.
220 P 16, 21: सर्वग्राहविनिर्मुक्तितः.
221 P 16, 22: यंगामिनस्.

१५१

तद्यथापि नाम कुलपुत्र कश्चिदेव पुरुषः मृन्मयीन्नावमभिरुह्य[222] गंगानदीमुत्तर्तुकामो भवेत्। तत् किं मन्यसे कुलपुत्र कीदृशेन वीर्येण तेन पुरुषेण सा नौर्वाहयितव्या भवेत्। आह। बलवता भगवन् वीर्येण। तत्कस्माद्धेतोः मा मे असंप्राप्तपारस्यैवांतरेण नौर्विपद्येत। महौघार्णवप्राप्तो ऽस्मि। मा हैवांतरेणायं नावा विकीर्येत। भगवानाह। एवमेव समन्तालोक अतो बहुतरेण (76b)बलवन्ततरेण वीर्येण बोधिसत्त्वेन बोधिः समुदानयितव्या। महाबलवीर्येण च बुद्धधर्माः समुदानयितव्याः।

१५२

एवंमनसिकारेण अनित्यो बतायं कायः चतुर्महाभूतिकः मातापितृकललसंभूतः अध्रुवो ऽनाश्वासिकः विपरिणामधर्मः उच्छदस्नपनपरिमर्दनभेदनविकिरणविध्वंसनधर्मः ओदनकुल्माषोपचितः अचिरस्थायी अनाहारो न तिष्ठति। जर्जरगृहसदृशो दुर्बलः मा हैव अनादत्तसारस्यान्तरेण कालक्रिया भविष्यति। महोघार्णवप्राप्तो ऽस्मि चतुरुत्तररोगशतप्राप्तानां सत्त्वानामुह्यमानाना(77a)मुत्तारणाया बोधिसत्त्वेन[223] महाधर्मनावं समुदानयिष्यामि यया धर्मनावा सर्वसत्त्वान् संसारार्णवप्राप्तानुह्यमानानुत्तारयिष्यामि।

१५३

तत्र समंतालोक कीदृशी धर्मनौर्बोधिसत्त्वेन समुदानयितव्या। इह समंतालोक बोधिसत्त्वेन धर्मनावा समुदानयितव्या यदुत सर्वसमचित्तसंभाराः भवंति अनन्तपुण्योपचिता शीलफलनिर्जाता दानपरिवारालंकारालंकृता। आशयदृढसारबन्धनसुबद्धा। क्षान्तिसोरत्यस्मृतिशल्यबद्धा। सप्तबोध्यंगसंभारदृढवीर्यकुशलधर्मदारुसमुदानिता[224] *ध्यानचि*(77b)त्तक्रमणीय-

---

222 मृन्मयीनाव° MS.

223 To be inserted preferably at the beginning of this section: एवंमनसीकारेण बोधि°.

224 em. after T; °अकुशलधर्म° MS.

कर्मणीकृता । दान्तशान्ताजानेयकुशलशिल्पसुनिष्ठिता[225]। अत्यंताकोप्यधर्ममहाकरुणा-संगृहीता चतुःसंग्रहवस्तुशूरतुरगवाहिणी प्रत्यर्थिकप्रज्ञाज्ञानसुप्रतिरक्षिता। उपायकौशल्य-सुकृत*विचिता* चतुब्रह्मविहारसुशोधिता।

१५४

चतुस्मृत्युपस्थानसुचिन्तितकायोपनीता । सम्यक्प्रहाणप्रसठा । ऋद्धिपादजवजविता । इ-न्द्रियसुनिरीक्षिता दानवक्रविगता बलवेगसमुद्गता अन्तरेणाशिथिला बोध्यंग*विबोधका*[226] अरिशत्रुमारपथजहनी मार्गक्रमवाहिनी[227]। कुतीर्थ्यतीर्थजहनी । शमथनिध्यप्तिनिर्दिष्टा वि-पश्यनाप्रयो(78a)गा । उभयोरन्तयोरसक्तवाहिनी । हेतुधर्मयुक्ता । विपुलविस्तीर्णाक्षय-प्रहाणाबन्धा । विघुष्टशब्दा दशसु दिक्षु शब्दमादायत्यागच्छतागच्छताभिरुहत महाधर्म-नावं। निर्वाणपुरगामिनी। क्षेममार्गगामिनी। *अपारिम*[228]तीरसत्कायदृष्टिंजहनी। पारिम-तीरगामिनी लघुसर्वदृष्टिगतविगता।

१५५

ईदृशी कुलपुत्र धर्म*नौर्* बोधिसत्त्वेन समुदानयितव्या। अपरिमाणकल्पकोटिनयुतशतसह-स्रापरिखिन्नमानसेन[229] सर्वसत्त्वानामर्थाय अनया सद्धर्मनावा सर्वसत्त्वा तारयितव्या चतुर्भि-रोघैरुह्यमाना। ईदृशी (78b)नावा कुलपुत्र बोधिसत्त्वेन समुदानयितव्या। तत्र समंतालोक कतमा बोधिसत्त्वस्य क्षिप्राभिज्ञता। यदुत अकृत्रिमः प्रयोगः सर्वसत्त्वेषु। तीव्रछन्दिकता आशयशुद्ध्या। उत्तप्तवीर्यता सर्वकुशलमूलसमुदानय*नाय*। कुशलछन्दिकता योनिशोमन-

---

225 em. after T; दान्ताशान्ता° MS.
226 VD n. 373: विबोधना/विबोधनी?
227 em. after Weller 1965: 155, n. 7; मानोक्क्रम° MS.
228 After Tib. *tshu rol gyi 'gram* – म ... [आ] ... MS.
229 Tib.: *yoṅs su mi skyo bar*; °सहस्रपरिखिन्न° MS.

सिकारेण। श्रुतातृप्तता प्रज्ञापारिपूर्यै। निर्मानता प्रज्ञोप*स्तम्भाय*। प्रव्रज्यानिम्नता सर्वगुणपारिपूर्यै। अरण्यवासः कायचित्तविवेकतया।

१५६

असंसर्गो दुर्ज*नान* विवर्जनतया। धर्मार्थिकता परमार्थार्थप्रतिसरणतया। ज्ञानार्थो ऽत्यंताकोपनार्थतया[230]। धर्मार्थो *ज्ञा*(79a)नार्थतया। सत्यार्थो अविसंवादनार्थतया। शून्यतार्थो सम्यक्प्रयोगार्थतया। विवेकार्थो अत्यंतोपशमार्थतायेति। इयमुच्यते समंतालोक बोधिसत्त्वस्य महासत्त्वस्य क्षिप्राभिज्ञता॥

१५७

अथ खल्वायुष्मान् महाकाश्यपो भगवंतमेतदवोचत्। आश्चर्यं भगवन् आश्चर्यं सुगत यावच्चायं महारत्नकूटो सूत्रान्त*राज* उपकारीभूतो महायानसंप्रस्थितानां कुलपुत्राणां च कुलदुहितृणां च। कियद्भगवन् स कुलपुत्रो *वा* कुलदुहिता वा पुण्यं प्रसवति य इतो रत्नकूटात् सूत्रान्तराज्ञ एकगाथामप्युपदिशेत्[231]।

१५८

एवमुक्ते भगवाना(79b)युष्मंतं महाकाश्यपमेतदवोचत्। यो हि काश्यप कुलपुत्रो वा कुलदुहिता वा गंगानदीवालुकासमेषु लोकधातुषु परमाणुरजांसि भिन्देय। भित्वा तात्तका चैव वारा वापेय। तात्तका चैव तां सर्वलोकधातवः सप्तरत्नपरिपूर्णां कृत्वा तथागतेभ्यो ऽर्हद्भ्यः सम्यक्संबुद्धेभ्यो दानं दद्यात्। गंगानदीवालुकासमानां च बुद्धानां भगवन्तानां एकेकस्य च तथागतस्य गंगानदीवालुकासमान् विहारान् कारापयेत्।

---

[230] em. after VD n. 379; त्यंतकोप° MS.

[231] °राज्ञा-द्-एक° MS.

१५९

गंगानदीवालुकासमानां च बुद्धानां भगवतामेकेकं च तथागतस्याप्रमेयश्रावकसंघं गंगानदीवालुकासमान् कल्पां *च सर्व*(80a)सुखोपधानैः परिचरेत्। तेषां च बुद्धानां भगवतां (यावज्जीव मनापेन कायकर्मेण वाक्कर्मेण मनस्कर्मेण उपस्थानपारिचर्याय तात्तका चैव गंगानदीवालुकासमां लोकधातवः परमाणुरजांसि तात्तका भिद्य भित्वा वा तात्तका चैव वारा वापेय। तान् सर्वं लोकधातुः सप्तरत्नपरिपूर्णं कृत्वा दानं दद्याद्बुद्धानां भगवतां)[232] यावज्जीवं च मनापेन कायकर्मणा वाक्कर्मणा मनस्कर्मणा उपस्थानपारिचर्याय तात्तका चैव गंगानदीवालुकासमानपि तात्तका चैव बुद्धानां भगवतां सत्कुर्याद् *गुरुकुर्या*(80b)त् मानयेत् पूजयेत् तेषां च परिनिर्वृतानां सप्तरत्नमया स्तूपा कारापयेत्। यश्च कुलपुत्रो वा कुलदुहिता वा इतो महारत्नकूटात् सूत्रान्तराज्ञः सर्वबुद्धभाषितादेकामपि गाथा उद्गृह्णेय धारयेत्। अस्य पुण्यस्कन्धस्य स पूर्वकपुण्यस्कन्धः शतिमामपि कलां नोपैति। सहस्त्रिमामपि कोटिशतसहस्त्रिमामपि संख्यामपि कलामपि गणनामपि उपमापि उपनिषामपि न क्षमते। यश्च श्रुणेय श्रुत्वा च न परिक्षिपेय। अयं ततो बहुतरः पुण्यस्कन्धः प्रसूतो[233] भवेत्। यश्च मातृग्राम *उ*(81a)*द्दिश्यमाने*[234] श्रृणुयाद्वा लिखापयेद्वा पर्याप्नुयाद्वा तस्य न जातु विनिपातो भविष्यति। स एव तस्य *पश्चिमकः भावो* भविष्यति।

१६०

यत्र च पृथिवीप्रदेशे अयं रत्नकूटो धर्मपर्यायो भाष्यते वा देश्यते वा लिख्यते वा *लिखितो* वा पुस्तगतं वा तिष्ठेत्स पृथिवीप्रदेशो चैत्यभूतो सदेवकस्य लोकस्य। यस्य च धर्मभाणकस्यान्तिकादिमं धर्मपर्यायं श्रृणुयाद्वा उद्गृह्णीयाद्वा लिखेद्वा पर्याप्नुयाद्वा। तस्य धर्मभाणकस्या-

---

[232] Text enclosed in brackets (not in Tib.) – also cf. section 158 – preferably to be deleted.

[233] °स्कन्धप्रसुतो MS.

[234] After Tib. *luṅ 'bog na*; see Negi 1993ff. s.v. *luṅ 'bog pa*.

न्तिके एवंरूपं गौरवमुत्पादयितव्यं तद्यथापि नाम काश्यप तथागतस्य। *यश्च कुलपुत्रो वा कुलदुहिता वा धर्म*(81b)*भाणकं* सत्करिष्यति गुरुकरिष्यति *मानयिष्यति* पूजयिष्यति *तस्य व्याकरोम्यनुत्तरां सम्यक्संबोधिम्*। मरणकाले चास्य तथागतदर्शनं भविष्यति।

१६१

तथागतदर्शनेन च दश च कायकर्मपारिशुद्धि *प्रतिलप्स्यते*। कतमे दश। यदुत वेदनाया अपर्यादत्तचित्त कालं करिष्यति। चक्षुविभ्रमश्चास्य न भविष्यति न हस्तविक्षेपं च करिष्यति न पादविक्षेपं च करिष्यति। नोच्चारं करिष्यति। न प्रस्रावं करिष्यति। *न हृदयात् स्वेदः प्रघरिष्यति*। न मुष्टिं करिष्यति न चाकाशं परामृशति। यथा *निषण्णस्तथायुःसंस्कारान् संत्याजयिष्यति*। *इमा दश कायकर्मपारिशुद्धीः प्रतिलप्स्यते*[235]।

१६२

दश वाक्कर्मपारिशुद्धीः प्रतिलप्स्यते। कतमा दश। यदुत मञ्जुलवचनो मधुरवचनो मृदुवचनः प्रियवचनस्स्निग्धवचनो ऽप्रतिवहनवचन आदेयवचनो वन्द्यवचनो देवमनुष्यसंगृहीतवचनो बुद्धसंगृहीतवचनश्च। इमा दश वाक्कर्मपारिशुद्धीः प्रतिलप्स्यते।

१६३

दश मनःकर्मपारिशुद्धीः प्रतिलप्स्यते। कतमा दश। यदुत अक्रोधो ऽनुपनाहो ऽम्रक्षो ऽप्रदास आदीनवज्वरो वैरप्रणयज्वरो[236] *ऽसंज्ञाविपर्यासः प्रहाणाप्रमत्तो ऽलीनचेतसा परिशुद्धबुद्धक्षेत्रग्राही मानातिमात्रमानविगतश्च सर्वबुद्धधर्माभिनिर्हारसमाधिप्रतिलाभी भविष्यति। इमा दश मनःकर्मपारिशुद्धीः प्रतिलप्स्यते।*

---

[235] After Tib.; likewise the final sections 162–166; Tib. of section 164 is in verse, the retranslation in prose.

[236] For SH Tib. ... *khon bcugs la mi dga' ba* read ... *gcugs la* ... (Lhasa ed.).

१६४

तत्रेदमुच्यते॥

कालं न करिष्यति वेदनार्दितः। तस्य चक्षुविभ्रमो न भविष्यति। न हस्तपादविक्षेपं भविष्यति। नोच्चारं न प्रस्रावं करिष्यति। न प्रघरिष्यति तस्य हृदयस्वेदः। मुष्टिं न करिष्यति। नाकाशपरामर्शस्तस्य। यथा निषण्णस्सुखं कालं करिष्यति। इमा दश कायकर्मपारिशुद्धीर्लप्स्यते। मञ्जुलसम्पूर्णमृदुमधुरवाणी। स्निग्धमनापप्रिय [वाणी] भविष्यति। अपरप्रतिवहनादेयवाणी। जनवन्द्यवाणी भविष्यति। तस्य वाणी देवनागकिन्नरैः। अथवा सुगतेन प्रशस्ता। तद्वचनार्थस्यापि धारणा [भविष्यति]। स इमा वाक्कर्मविशुद्धीर्लप्स्यते। अक्रोधो ऽनुपनाहश्च। स्थिरो ऽम्रक्षो ऽप्रदासश्च। आदीनवज्वरश्च वैरप्रणयज्वरः। असंज्ञाविपर्यासस्सः। शिक्षासमादाने ऽलीनचेताः। प्रहाणप्रमत्तो न भविष्यति। अलीनचेतसा क्षेत्रशोधनं करिष्यति। मानातिमानं परित्यज्य। सर्वसंपन्नसमाध्यभिनिर्हृतं च। मनो ऽभिनिर्हृतधर्माँल्लँप्स्यते। एभिर्धर्मैः समन्वितस्य बुद्धभावो न भविष्यति दुर्लभः॥

१६५

यो हि काश्यप सर्वसुखोपधानेन मां सत्कर्तुकामस्सर्वपूजनपूजार्थिकश्च तेनायं महारत्नकूटो धर्मपर्यायः परिगृहीतव्यः पर्यवाप्तव्यो लेख्यः पठितव्यो धारयितव्यः[237]*। एवं हि काश्यप तथागतेष्वर्हत्सु सम्यक्संबुद्धेष्वनुत्तरपूजा क्रियते॥*

[237] For SH Tib. *bcad par bya'o* read *bcaṅ bar bya'o* (Lhasa ed.).

१६६

इदमवोचद्भगवान्। आत्तमना आयुष्मान् महाकाश्यपस्ते च विचित्रबुद्धक्षेत्रसमागता बोधिसत्त्वा महासत्त्वास्ते च भिक्षवः सदेवमानुषासुरगन्धर्वश्च लोको भगवतो भाषितमभ्यनन्दन्निति॥

आर्यमहारत्नकूटस्य शतसाहस्त्रिकपरिवर्तधर्मपर्यायात्त्रयश्चत्वारिंशत्तम आर्यकाश्यपपरिवर्तो नाम [परिवर्तः] समाप्तः॥

II. English Translation of the *Kāśyapaparivarta*

The Mahāyāna Discourse Called the Noble Kāśyapa Section

Homage to all the Buddhas and Bodhisattvas.

(**1b**) [May there be] success.[1]

Thus have I heard at one time [when][2] the Exalted One was staying on Mount Vulture Peak [near] Rājagṛha, together with a large order of monks [numbering] eight thousand, and with sixteen thousand *bodhisattvas* who had come to the assembly from various Buddha-realms, i.e. [those] who had to wait for [only] one [more] birth [before realizing] the highest and perfect enlightenment.

1

On that occasion the Exalted One said to the Elder Mahā-Kāśyapa: "These four personality traits, Kāśyapa, bring about a *bodhisattva*'s loss of wisdom. Which four? (1) He is disrespectful to the Teaching and to one who sets it forth. (2) He wants to keep [knowledge of] the Teaching to himself, (**2a**) unwilling to share what he knows ('the teacher's fist'). (3) He proves a hindrance to those persons who are longing for the *dharma*, he puts them off, frustrates them and does not teach but conceals [the *dharma* from them]. (4) Inflated with pride he shows off and disparages others. These four personality traits ... loss of wisdom." In this connection[3] these [verses were] uttered:

---

1 As for *siddham* as a word of auspiciousness at the beginning of a discourse, see Roth 1986: 241f.; cf. von Staël-Holstein 1933: xii, n. 6: "The word Siddham ... does evidently not belong to the preamble. It has no equivalent in any of the translations, and some scribe has probably prefixed it to the text for good luck (maṅgala)."

2 For a comprehensive survey of the scholarly discussion of the traditional openings of Buddhist *sūtras* see Klaus 2007: 309–322.

3 Lit.: 'then, in that case'.

He is disrespectful to the proclaimer of the *dharma,*
And in regard to teachings he is much given to
Niggardliness, maintaining the 'teacher's fist' as
Far as the *dharma* is concerned. He creates
Obstacles for those who seek the truth, frustrating
Them in many ways and putting them off. He does
Not teach the *dharma* proclaimed by the Conqueror;
He is always intent on showing off[4] **(2b)** and lazy,
[But] taking delight in disparaging others. These
Four personality traits, [as] has been declared by the
Conqueror, lead to loss of wisdom of the Conqueror's
Spiritual sons. Having given up these four, one should
Cultivate four other traits [as] shown by the Conqueror.

2

"These four traits, Kāśyapa, bring about a *bodhisattva*'s full-blown wisdom. Which four? (1) He is respectful to the Teaching and to one who sets it forth. (2) In detail he imparts to others the teachings according to what he has learnt and mastered. (3) With a mind free from desire he does not hanker after **(3a)** gain, honour and renown. (4) Having realized that from great learning wisdom is acquired, he strives for [*dharma*] knowledge [with a sense of urgency] comparable to a person in search [of water] whose head and clothes are on fire.[5] The teachings imparted to him he puts into practice; talking, words, statements are not his primary concern; what actually matters to him is practice. These four traits ... full-blown wisdom." These are the Exalted One's words. In this connection these [verses were] uttered:

He is respectful to one who sets forth the *dharma* and
Imparts to others the teachings as studied by him. [With
A mind] free from desire he does not hanker after, care
For gain, honour and renown. **(3b)** Having realized that
From learning wisdom is acquired, he always strives
For [*dharma*] knowledge [with a sense of urgency]

---

4 See BHSD, p. 120, s.v. *utkarṣaṇa.*

5 See BHSD, p. 94, s.v. *ādīptaśiraścailopama,* with references to Pāli and Sanskrit texts in which this comparison is made.

Comparable to a person in search of [water] whose
Head is on fire. As imparted to him, he puts the
Teachings into practice. Having done so, he is firm
In his practice. As one to whom practice actually
Matters, he is a [true] sage [whose] primary concern
Are neither talking nor words. Sages who cultivate
These four personality traits, acquire the
Wisdom that is praised by the Conqueror.

3

"A *bodhisattva*, Kāśyapa, who is given to four modes of behaviour, will fail in his [lofty] aspirations for enlightenment (*bodhicitta*). Which are the four? He will fail[6] (1) when he breaks his promise [and thus] deceives his preceptor, spiritual teachers and [other] venerable [persons]; (2) when he causes others, unaffected by mental disturbance, compunction; (3) when he **(4a)** belittles those who have wholeheartedly embarked on Mahāyāna [practice] by detracting from their good reputation and renown; (4) when he plays tricks on other[s] and treats them with dishonesty instead of [having a *bodhisattva*'s] lofty disposition. A *bodhisattva*, Kāśyapa, who is given to these four ... will fail ..." These are the Exalted One's words. In this connection these [verses were] uttered:

He does not heed the instructions of his spiritual
Teacher and [other] venerable [persons];[7] he
Causes[8] mental disturbance for others; he defames
And speaks ill of those who have embarked on a
Bodhi [*sattva*'s practice]. Contrary to a [*bodhisattva*'s]
Lofty disposition, dishonestly he makes use of
Other[s] by means of tricks and by fraud.[9] When

---

6 Lit.: 'that is to say'.

7 Lit.: 'what has been taught by his spiritual teacher ...'; as for °*dākṣiṇīye*, see Weller 1965: 64, n. 14; Karashima 2002: 52, § 9.16.2 (instr. pl. ... -*e*). As for *proktuṃ* for *proktaṃ*, cf. BHSG § 3.58.

8 As for confusion of person and number, notably 3 pl. forms for other persons and singular number (*upasaṃharanti* and further 3 pl. forms *passim*, in the KP often m.c.), see BHSG § 25.4, § 25.30.

9 I.e. *kaitava* for MS *ketava*.

These four modes of behaviour are adopted, they
Cause the aspiration[s] for supreme Buddhahood to
Fail; accordingly, [someone] who adopts these modes
Of behaviour **(4b)** remains far away from supreme and
Perfect enlightenment.[10] He, however, who follows
The opposite [modes of behaviour] will realize, [as]
Taught, supreme and perfect enlightenment.

4

"To a *bodhisattva*, Kāśyapa, who is given to four modes of behaviour, right from birth in all his existences his [lofty] aspiration[s] for enlightenment will present themselves, and in the meantime he will not fail [in them] until he takes his seat on the 'throne of enlightenment'. Which are the four? (1) Even for the sake of [saving] his life he will not deliberately lie, [not] even with a view to[11] [making] jokes. (2) Being free from trickery and dishonesty and with [a *bodhisattva's*] lofty disposition he is a close [friend] of all beings. (3) All those on their way to supreme enlightenment (*bodhisattva*) he acknowledges as [spiritual] teachers and speaks in praise of them in all directions. **(5a)** (4) All those beings whom he brings to [spiritual] maturity he inspires to [their realizing] unsurpassed and perfect enlightenment and without their being eager [to follow more] limited ways [to realize emancipation] (*prādeśikayāna*). To a *bodhisattva*, Kāśyapa, who is given to these four modes ... until he takes his seat on the 'throne of enlightenment'." In this connection these [verses were] uttered:

[Even] for the sake of [saving] his life he will not tell
Untruth[s], and what he says is always meaningful.
At all times being free from trickery and dishonesty,
He always looks on beings with [a *bodhisattva's*] lofty
Disposition. Those pure beings who have embarked on a
Bodhi [*sattva*'s practice] he regards as [spiritual] teachers
On their way to supreme enlightenment, **(5b)** speaking in
Praise of them in all directions after acknowledging[12]

---

10 Re °*bodhīya*, cf. BHSG § 10.104; °*bodhāya* VD (after Weller 1965: 64, n. 24).

11 Lit.: 'to be looked at'.

12 Lit.: 'having formed the notion' (*saṃjñām upasthapitvā* (= *upasthāpya*)).

Them for good[13] as [spiritual] teachers. Those beings whom
He brings to [spiritual] maturity he inspires to [their
Realizing] unsurpassed insight-knowledge. Those who
Ground themselves wholeheartedly[14] in these modes of
Behaviour, will never fail in [pursuing their goal:
Supreme] enlightenment.[15]

5

"O Kāśyapa, the karmically wholesome, repeatedly produced qualities of a *bodhisattva* who is given to four modes of behaviour, vanish on account of which he no [longer] grows in such qualities. Which are the four? [His good qualities vanish] because of his (1) enquiring into materialistic lore [owing to] his being self-conceited; (2) because of his looking out for high-ranking families [owing to] his coveting gain and honour; (3) because of his having an aversion to and slandering *bodhisattvas*; (4) because of his repudiating such discourses as were neither transmitted nor explained [to him]. **(6a)** O Kāśyapa, the karmically wholesome, repeatedly produced qualities of a *bodhisattva* who is given to these four modes of behaviour, vanish ..." In this connection these [verses were] uttered:

Full of self-conceit he enquires into materialistic
[Lore] and, coveting gain, he makes use of noble
Families. He is, moreover, hostile to *bodhisattvas*, the
Buddha's spiritual sons, speaking ill of them around.
He repudiates such discourses – [though] set forth by
The Conqueror – as were neither transmitted nor
Explained [to him]. For him who is given to these[16]
Modes of behaviour, there will be no growth in good
Qualities. So an intelligent *bodhisattva* should
Relinquish the[se] four modes of behaviour once

---

13 Re *sad* = *sadā*, see BHSG § 4.24.

14 Lit.: 'the mind of those who ...'

15 For the Romanized text of section 4, Tib. and an English translation see Skilling 2009: 77ff.

16 As for *tam-ehi*, see BHSD, p. 250 s.v. *tam-enaṃ;* cf. Karashima 2002: 57, § 16.9.

And for all.[17] A [*bodhisattva*] who is given to them is
Removed from enlightenment[18] just as the sky is
Very far away from the earth.[19]

6

(6b) "A *bodhisattva*, Kāśyapa, who is given to four modes of behaviour is not subject to suffering any loss, [but makes] for superior attainment.[20] To which four? (1) He searches for what is authentic, not what is unauthentic: [his quest is] the quest for the *bodhisattva* canon [enshrining] the 'six perfections'.[21] (2) Because of his humility towards all beings, moreover, he resembles an [endearing] dog. (3) Further, he is quite satisfied with what he has received rightfully; as one who has abandoned all wrong modes of gaining a living he is quite satisfied with the [four kinds of] 'noble usage';[22] he neither enquires as to whether others [have committed] an offence or not, nor searches out [one or] other [of their] faults or blunders. (4) [Whenever] there are profound [discourses] which are beyond his ken, then he admits, having invoked the Tathāgata to bear witness: 'The Tathāgata really knows, I do not know; the Buddha's enlightenment **(7a)** is infinite; the *dharma* is proclaimed in accordance with the needs of beings with their manifold inclinations.' A *bodhisattva*, Kāśyapa, who is given to these four ... [makes] for superior attainment." In this connection these [verses were] uttered:

He is always intent on the perfections, on skill in
Means and on the *bodhisattva* canon. Because of
His humility, in his nature, he resembles a dog,
Having overcome self-conceit vis-à-vis all beings.

---

17 Lit.: 'should leave far behind'.

18 As for *bodhaye*, see BHSG § 10.139.

19 For this analogy cf. *Aṅguttaranikāya* II (Kashyap 1960a): 53: Suvidūrasutta.

20 As for *viśeṣagāmitāyaiḥ* for °*tāyai*, see Karashima 2002: 44, n. 3, regarding the confusion between Visarga and *daṇḍa* in SH. Karashima states that at Pāsādika 1993: 216–217 '*viśeṣagāmitāyaiḥ* (*sic*)' is wrongly taken to be instr. pl. whilst, actually, in the given place (p. 216) the correct reading at ŚS 168, 5ff. is referred to: °*tāyai*; cf. BHSG § 9.60.

21 See BHSD, p. 341, s.v. *pāramitā*.

22 See BHSD, p. 105, s.v. *āryavaṃśa*; see also *Aṅguttaranikāya* II (Kashyap 1960a): 30f.: Ariyavaṃsasutta.

He is satisfied with what he has received
Rightfully and makes his living impeccably,
Conforming to 'noble usage'. He neither enquires
Into others' offences nor searches out their
Blunders. When he [can]not fathom out [profound
Discourses], he invokes the Tathāgata to bear
Witness: 'The Conqueror knows, I do not know. **(7b)**
The enlightenment, attested by the Blessed
One, is infinite. Having become acquainted with
These four modes of behaviour, he will never fall
Short of what is superior and uppermost. He who
Abides by these modes of behaviour will have no
Difficulty in realizing [such] enlightenment [as]
Commended by the Conqueror.

7

"A *bodhisattva*, Kāśyapa, who deviates from [his lofty] aspirations [in] these four [respects], should mend his ways.[23] In which four? (1) About all the Buddha's teachings he has his doubts, disagrees and brings them into question. (2) Towards all beings he is arrogant, conceited, hypocritical, angry and malicious. (3) When others thrive, he is envious and jealous. (4) [He deviates from his aspirations] because of his belittling *bodhisattvas* and his detracting from their good reputation and renown.[24] A *bodhisattva*, Kāśyapa, who deviates ... should mend his ways." In this connection these [verses were] uttered:

About the teaching he has his doubts and **(8a)**
Disagrees [with them]. Towards [his fellow] beings he
Behaves arrogantly, is conceited and irascible. When
Others thrive, he is envious and jealous. He never puts
His trust in the Conqueror and, in his foolishness, has
Been belittling[25] *bodhisattvas* all the time, detracting
From their good reputation and renown. A *bodhisattva*

---

[23] Lit.: 'dishonest aspirations should be abandoned'.

[24] Cf. above section 3 (3).

[25] Lit.: 'caused to spread ill repute' (... *cārayī*); see BHSG § 32.16.

Should stop deviating from [his lofty] aspirations
In four [respects as mentioned] and always be
A [helpful] friend of [his fellow] beings.

8

"There are, Kāśyapa, these four marks of honest[y] of an upright *bodhisattva.* Which are the four? (1) [Should] he have committed an offence, he does not conceal, [but] confesses, reveals it and [thus] becomes free from depravity.[26] (2) Even if through [any of] his words of truth serious damage [is caused] to the [country's] government or its finances [so that his] very life is in danger, he will tell the truth unreservedly[27] **(8b)** without falling back on prevarications. (3) [Even if] others are violent, abuse, revile, blame,[28] rebuke, beat, threaten, fetter or put [him] to death - [all these] offences he [considers] his own fault, accepting [them] as the result of [previous] actions [and thus] not being angry with others, nor bearing them any grudge. (4) He is firmly rooted in his faith, and with a pure mind he puts his trust in all the teachings of the Buddha, including [those - for persons inclining towards the Śrāvakayāna -] very difficult to believe.[29] These are, Kāśyapa, the four marks ..." In this connection these [verses were] uttered:

[Should] he have committed an offence, he does not
Conceal, [but] speaks about and reveals[30] it, [thus]
Ridding himself[31] of guilt. Neither in the interest of the
Government or [its] finances, nor for the sake of his
Life would he intentionally[32] tell untruths. **(9a)** [Even

[26] See BHSD, p. 335f., s.v. *paryutthāna.*

[27] Lit.: 'he does not hide'.

[28] See BHSD, p. 184, s.v. *kuṃsana.*

[29] See von Staël-Holstein 1933: 52: Sthiramati's comment on *aśraddheya* teachings of the Buddha: *theg pa chen po la lhag pa'i bsam pas mos par yoṅs su bstan pa yin no* | 'What is meant is [one's] devotion (*adhimukti*) to the Great Vehicle wholeheartedly (*adhyāśayena*).'

[30] As for *vivaraṃti*, see BHSG, p. 231 - √*vṛ*.

[31] Lit.: 'escapes from'.

[32] See Karashima 2002: 58, § 21.1: *vidadhīya* (gerund of *vi*-√*dhā*), lit.: 'having fixed awareness'.

If], abused, reviled, rebuked, fettered, imprisoned
Or put to death, he will not be angry with others,
[Considering all this suffering] his own fault; [knowing
That] he is responsible for [all his] actions, he bears
[Nobody] any grudge. He puts his trust in the
Enlightenment of the Blessed Ones and, with a pure
Mind, is [firmly] rooted in his faith. These are the
Marks of honest[y] mentioned by the Conqueror;
He who [aspires] to the most excellent goal
Should be endowed with[33] [them].

9

"Among the *bodhisattvas*, Kāśyapa, these four are [like] unruly [horses].[34] Which are the four? [The first formally] lives according to the *dharma*, [but] is [given to] agitation[35] because of what he has learnt [so that] he does not [actually] practise in accordance with the Teaching. [The second formally] lives according to the *dharma*, but [received and misunderstood] instructions agitate him[36] [so that] he does not want to listen [any more] to his spiritual teachers and preceptors. [The third, although] he has broken his vows, enjoys what has been offered with faith and [thus] causes such offering[s] to go waste. (**9b**) When [the fourth] sees *bodhisattvas* who, [perfectly] restrained, have become [well trained] thoroughbreds [, as it were], he does not show respect and holds his head high. These are the four among the *bodhisattvas*, Kāśyapa, who are [like] unruly [horses]." In this connection these [verses were] uttered:

The [first of the 'unruly ones'] is given to agitation
Because of what he has learnt, and in that state
Of mind he does not practise as he has been instructed.
The [second] adopts all the teachings, but being
[Given to] agitation, in no way whatever wants to

33 Lit.: 'should be employed'.

34 See von Staël-Holstein 1933: 54: *dper na rta ... de bźin du | byaṅ chub sems dpa' ...*

35 *Ibid.: thos pas g.yeṅ ba'i chos su gnas pa*; cf. Negi 1993ff. s.v. *g.yeṅ ba* (= *auddhatyam*).

36 See von Staël-Holstein 1933: 55: *rjes su bstan pa la g.yeṅ ba'i chos su gnas pa ... bstan na phyin ci log tu rtog pas ...*

Listen to the Noble Ones. The [third] has broken his
Vows, but is given to enjoying choice food offered
In [good] faith. When the [fourth] sees[37] 'thoroughbred'
bodhisattvas, he does not show respect; this 'unruly
One' has an inflated opinion of himself[38] instead
Of doing obeisance to the *bodhisattvas* free of pride.
These four the Blessed One has declared 'unruly ones';
The Conqueror's spiritual sons should avoid **(10a)** them.

10

"These four, Kāśyapa, are 'thoroughbred' *bodhisattvas*.[39] Which four? [The first of them] studies what has been correctly transmitted and then practises [in accordance with the *dharma* on whose] meaning he relies, not on the letter. [The second] takes a reverential attitude when [listening to] exhortations and instructions; he is gentle in speech, and [whatever] he does is a meritorious act; he really is at the service of his spiritual teachers. [The third] partakes of [offered] food as a 'thoroughbred', never being destitute of virtue and concentration. When [the fourth] sees [perfectly] restrained 'thoroughbred' *bodhisattvas*, he shows respect, reveres [them], is inclined, disposed to, tends to [follow] their [example] and wishes to [be endowed with] their virtue. These, Kāśyapa, are the four 'thoroughbred' *bodhisattvas*." In this connection these [verses were] uttered:[40]

What [the first] studies – the correctly transmitted
[*dharma*] – **(10b)** that he puts into practice; what
Really matters to him is the meaning of the *dharma* in
[Whose] practice he is firmly grounded. [The second]
Reverentially takes to the instruction[s he receives];
He is gentle in speech and, [out of] love of the *dharma*,
Is at the service of his spiritual teacher[s]. Always
Training himself[41] in virtue and concentration,

---

37 As for *paśyitva* (m.c. for *paśyitvā*), see BHSG, p. 220.
38 Lit.: 'increases his pride'.
39 Cf. *Aṅguttaranikāya* II (Kashyap 1960a): 264ff.: Ājānīyasutta.
40 In the following sections abbreviated to "The verses: ..."
41 Lit.: 'abiding in'.

Virtuous and restrained, [the third] partakes of the
Food [offered to him. The fourth] shows respect
And is full of admiration, being inclined, disposed to
[Follow the example] and wishing to [be endowed with]
The virtue of those of the Conqueror's spiritual sons
Who have become 'thoroughbreds'; at all times he
Beholds them with joy. These four 'thoroughbreds'
The Blessed One has mentioned as his [spiritual] sons.

11

"A *bodhisattva*, Kāśyapa, [may commit] these four errors. Which four? (1) He errs if he believes [alleged attainments of] beings who have not yet spiritually matured. (2) He errs if he reveals the sublime teachings of the Buddha to beings who have not become 'a [deserving] vessel' for [them]. **(11a)** (3) He errs if he reveals [teachings of] the Lesser Vehicle to beings who concentrate on the sublime [teachings of the Great Vehicle]. (4) He errs if he is disrespectful to beings who have arrived at the truth [of the *dharma*], are virtuous and have a good character and if [, on the other hand,] he is in favour of [persons] who are immoral and of bad character. These are, Kāśyapa, the four errors which a *bodhisattva* [may commit]." The verses:

Neither should one trust those who have not yet
Spiritually matured, nor should one communicate
The sublime *dharma* to anyone who is not 'a
[Deserving] vessel' for [it]. He [who aspires to be a
Conscientious] *bodhisattva* should never reveal
Hīnayāna [teachings][42] to those whose characteristic
Is [being intent on] sublime [Mahāyāna teachings].
He should neither be disrespectful to those who
Adhere to the truth [of the *dharma*], who are endowed
With virtue and excellence and have a good character,
Nor should he follow those who are immoral; he
Should shun [their] bad behaviour. Having recognized
These four errors [as such], **(11b)** a *bodhisattva* should

[42] See Karashima 2002: 52, § 9.15: *hīnayāne* – acc. pl. nt.

'Keep far away' from them. [Should] he behave[43]
In these four [ways], he will not realize
[Supreme] enlightenment. So a wise [person]
Will avoid these [ways of] behaviour.

12

"These are, Kāśyapa, the four 'ways' of [an unerring] *bodhisattva*. Which four? (1) Towards all beings he is upright and of an even disposition. (2) He inspires all beings to realize the insight of an Enlightened One.[44] (3) [It is] with the right attitude that he teaches [the *dharma*] to all beings.[45] (4) He is [endowed] with the right employment [of skill in means] for the sake of all beings. These are, Kāśyapa, the four 'ways' of [an unerring] *bodhisattva*." The verses:

May [a *bodhisattva*] always be upright and of an even
Disposition towards beings. May he inspire [them]
Now to realize a Buddha's insight,[46] and may he,
[Out of] his kindness, teach all beings the *dharma*
Set forth by the Conqueror. **(12a)** May he, firm in
His practice, be rightly employed in handling
[Salvatory means] for the sake of all beings alike.
These four 'ways' set forth by the Conqueror,
His spiritual sons will always cultivate.

---

[43] Re *niṣevaṃtu* m.c. for *niṣevantaḥ*, cf. BHSG § 18.8 (VD n. 72).

[44] According to Sthiramati (von Staël-Holstein 1933: 63), however, it would be a gross error to include here beings intent on the Hīnayāna: *theg pa chuṅ ṅu 'dod pa rnams ... ṅan par byas pa'i 'khrul pa sel bar rig par bya'o* ||

[45] According to Sthiramati (*ibid.*), it should be understood that he teaches Hīnayāna and Mahāyāna followers according to their respective requirements: *ci rigs par* = *yathā-yogam* (Negi 1993ff. s.v.).

[46] As for *samādapeyā(-d-iha)*, see BHSG § 29.28; regarding *buddhayāna* (m.c.) for *buddha-jñāna*, as in the prose part above, see Karashima 2002: 60, s.v. *jñāna/yāna*; in the verse part Tib. has *saṅs rgyas theg*, though.

13

"These four, Kāśyapa, are a *bodhisattva*'s bad friends, bad companions, whom he should avoid. Which four? [He should avoid] (1) a monk who, pursuing his own welfare, follows the Śrāvakayāna; (2) a follower of the Pratyekabuddhayāna who is modest, [but] inactive [as far as teaching the *dharma* to others is concerned]; (3) a materialist who is quickwitted, [drawing on] a variety of [materialistic] lore; (4) [someone] who, after making friends with some person, takes to the world's objects of enjoyment, not to the *dharma*. These four, Kāśyapa, are ... whom he should (**12b**) avoid." The verses:

> The Disciples, intent upon their own welfare,
> Those who have gone forth [into homelessness]
> And practise meditation; and also the
> Pratyekabuddhas who are modest, [but]
> Inactive, and who avoid contact [with others];
> Moreover, the fools, studying materialistic [lore],
> According to which[47] controversies are a must;[48]
> [Persons] who, while making friends with
> Someone, will take to objects of enjoyment and
> Not to the *dharma*[49]– having given up the[se] four
> [Types of persons], *bodhisattvas* will turn to four
> [Types of] spiritual friends. From those whom
> The Conqueror has declared bad friends,
> Bad companions, one should keep far away

14

"These four, Kāśyapa, are a *bodhisattva*'s truly spiritual friends. Which four? A *bodhisattva*'s truly spiritual friends are (1) a beggar (**13a**) to strengthen

---

47 Lit.: 'where'.

48 Lit.: 'taught, prescribed'; the whole *pāda*, viz. *vigrāhikā yatra kathopadiṣṭā*, after the emendation in Karashima 2002: 62, n. 147: "Also the foolish who study the *lokāyata*-philosophy, in which disputations are taught."

49 Lit.: 'and in whom (*yahiṃ* – see BHSG § 21.22) taking of the *dharma* is not likely to be'.

[him on his] way to [supreme] enlightenment; (2) a proclaimer of the *dharma* to strengthen [his] understanding of what [he] has been taught; (3) someone who inspires [him] to go forth [into homelessness] so as to strengthen all [his] 'roots of merit'; (4) the Buddha, the Exalted One, to strengthen the teachings of all Enlightened Ones. These are, Kāśyapa, a *bodhisattva*'s truly spiritual friends." The verses:

> A spiritual friend is he who receives [alms from]
> Donors for the sake of [their – the *bodhisattvas*' –
> Eventually] realizing [supreme] enlightenment. The
> Blessed One **(13b)** has called him a spiritual friend
> Who reveals the essence of the *dharma* [and thus]
> Promotes the understanding of what has been
> Taught. Further, those are called [spiritual] friends
> Who inspire [*bodhisattvas*] to go forth [into
> Homelessness, being] the 'root of merit'.[50] The Buddhas
> Are the friend[s] of the Blessed One's spiritual
> Sons so as to strengthen [them on their] way to
> [Become] Fully Enlightened Ones [too]. These four
> The Conqueror has declared the spiritual friends of
> The Blessed One's spiritual sons. Following them and
> Always being diligent, they will realize [supreme]
> Enlightenment [as] stated by the Blessed One.

15

"These four, Kāśyapa, are fake *bodhisattvas*. Which four? (1) [He who] covets gain and honour, [but] does not interest himself in the *dharma*; (2) [he who] covets good reputation and renown, [but] does not interest himself in virtue; (3) [he who] covets his own happiness, [but] does not interest himself in alleviating[51] the suffering of [other] beings; (4) [he who] covets an assembled multitude instead of **(14a)** seclusion. These four, Kāśyapa, are fake *bodhisattvas*." The verses

50 See Karashima 2002: 46, § 4.1. k/g: confusion of consonants (*sugatasya* for *sukṛtasya*).

51 Lit.: 'taking away'.

[A fake *bodhisattva*] covets gain, [but] he is not
Desirous of the *dharma*; he covets fame, [but] does not
Interest himself in virtue;[52] [he is a fake
Bodhisattva] who always covets his own happiness
And does not interest himself in alleviating
The suffering of [other] beings. [A fake *bodhisattva*]
Covets an assembled multitude, [but] is not desirous
Of seclusion; he clings to happiness, [but] is not
Intent on virtue. These four are called fake
[*Bodhisattvas*]; a [real] *bodhisattva* should avoid them.

16

"These four, Kāśyapa, are a *bodhisattva*'s real virtues. Which four? [The first is] his concentrating on emptiness and his having confidence in [the truth that] actions have consequences; [the second is] his approving of 'not-self' and his great compassion for all beings; **(14b)** [the third is] his being intent on *nirvāṇa* and also his applying himself in the round of rebirths; [the fourth is his] generosity in order to bring beings to spiritual maturity, [but] without expecting any resulting [merit for himself]. These four [modes of] character, Kāśyapa, are a *bodhisattva*'s real virtues." The verses:

[A virtuous *bodhisattva*] always concentrates on
[The truth that] 'facts' (*dharmas*) are empty and
Has confidence in[53] [the truth that] actions have
Consequences. Because he approves of 'not-self', he
Is firmly established in equanimity and shows
Constantly compassion for beings. He is always
Intent on *nirvāṇa* and also applies himself in the round
Of rebirths; he is generous in giving [help] in order
To bring [beings] to spiritual maturity, [but] he does
Not expect any [merit] resulting from [his] actions.

---

52 Lit.: 'does not want in respect of virtues'; see VD n. 84 on *guṇaibhir*: hypersanskritism for *guṇebhir*; cf. BHSG § 8.110.

53 See BHSD, p. 317, s.v. *pattīyati*.

17

"A *bodhisattva*, Kāśyapa, obtains these four great 'treasures'. Which four? (**15a**) (1) [The 'treasure' of his] paying homage[54] to the Buddhas [whenever they make their] appearance [in the world]; (2) [the 'treasure' of his] learning of the six perfections; (3) of his meeting - with receptiveness[55] - a proclaimer of the Teaching; (4) [of his taking] delight in living diligently in solitude. These are, Kāśyapa, the four great 'treasures' which a *bodhisattva* obtains." The verses:

Four conditions (*dharma*) the Blessed One has declared
Great 'treasures' of [his], the Conqueror's, spiritual
Sons: paying homage to the Buddhas whenever they
Make their appearance [in the world]; learning of the
Six perfections; furthermore, [a *bodhisattva*'s] being
Kindly disposed towards a proclaimer of the Teaching
[On] seeing [whom] he always [shows] respect,
And his living [as] diligently as ever in the forest -
The very [place] in which he always takes delight.

18

"These four attitudes, Kāśyapa, [bring about] a *bodhisattva*'s completely overcoming the ways of Māra. (**15b**) Which four? (1) [His] not abandoning his [lofty] aspirations for [supreme] enlightenment; (2) [his] being accomodating[56] to all beings; (3) [his] recognizing all instances of [wrong] views and (4) [his] not looking down on anyone. These are, Kāśyapa, the four attitudes [bringing about] a *bodhisattva*'s completely overcoming ..." The verses:

[Unerring *bodhisattvas*] do not abandon their [lofty]
Aspirations for [supreme] enlightenment and, by all
Means, give up [all] aversion to beings. They do not

---

54 See Negi 1993ff. s.v. *mñes par byed pa* (= *ārāgaṇam, ārādhanam*).
55 Lit.: 'whose mind is unimpeded' (*apratihatacittasya*).
56 Cf. above n. 55 (*apratihatacitta*).

Subscribe to wrong views and are respectful[57]
Towards the multitude of beings in this world.[58]
These four attitudes, says the Blessed One, surely
[Bring about] Māra's defeat. After cultivating
Them [unerring *bodhisattvas*] become Conquerors,
Aṃgīrasas,[59] incomparable leaders [in the world].

19

"These four attitudes, Kāśyapa, are conducive to a *bodhisattva*'s gathering all that is karmically wholesome. **(16a)** Which four? (1) [His really] having a predilection for living in the forest without his being a hypocrite; (2) [his employing] the four instances of kind treatment[60] without expecting[61] any requital; (3) dedicating in his quest for the true *dharma* his body and life to all beings and (4) [his] being keen on acquiring all 'roots of what is karmically wholesome'. These four attitudes, Kāśyapa, are conducive to ... wholesome." The verses:

[Living] in the forest, [an unerring *bodhisattva*] is free
From hypocrisy and the [four instances of] kind
Treatment of beings, set forth by the Conqueror, [are
His concern]. In his quest for the true *dharma* he
Dedicates his body and life [to all beings]. He is always
Keen on acquiring quite a few **(16b)** 'roots of what is
Karmically wholesome'. The Blessed One has set forth
The four attitudes for the sake of [one's]
Gathering all that is karmically wholesome.

---

57 As for MS *na cādhimanyanti*, cf. the Middle Indic *adhimāna* (arrogance, conceit).

58 After VD (')*ha* (= *iha*).

59 *Aṃgīrasa* – epithet of the Buddha; cf. *Khuddakanikāya* II (Kashyap 1959b): 320 (*Theragāthā*, v. 536): *Buddhassa ... Aṅgīrasass' appaṭimassa ...*

60 See BHSD, p. 548, s.v. *saṃgraha-vastu* (*dāna, priya-vacana, artha-caryā/-kriyā, samānārthatā/samānasukhaduḥkatā*).

61 Lit.: 'being desirous of'.

20

"These four, Kāśyapa, are a *bodhisattva*'s inestimable meritorious acts.[62] Which four? (1) [He] makes a gift of the Teaching with a mind free from sensual desire; (2) he [shows] great compassion for depraved persons, (3) tells all beings about aspiring to enlightenment and (4) patiently cares for the spiritless. These four, Kāśyapa, are ... meritorious acts." The verses:

With a pure mind, free from sensual desire, [as]
Praised by the Conqueror, [he] makes a gift of the
Teaching, and his compassion for the depraved is
Intense. He induces others to aspire to enlightenment
And patiently cares for the spiritless. Those [acts]
(17a) Are mentioned for the sake of gathering
Merit;[63] having performed them, [*bodhisattvas*]
Will become Conquerors. [So] they should
Always be performed by them.[64]

Having given up eight quadruple evils[65]
Which create obstacles to [realizing] awakening,
Having cultivated twelve other [tetrads] and in
Touch with the deathless, the sages will realize
[Supreme] enlightenment. The foremost beings
Who uphold this way of the *dharma*, recite and
Propagate [the Teaching], says the Conqueror, [will
Gain] limitless merit; he declares their [merit]
Immeasurable.[66] [If] anyone[67] were to fill myriads of

---

62 Lit.: 'equipment'.

63 For *dharmeṣu* Tib. has *dge chos, kuśaladharmeṣu.*

64 As for *bodhisatve*, see Karashima 2002: 52, § 9.16: Instr. pl. *-ai, -er, -eḥ, -e.* The lines that follow are set apart from the 'verses' belonging to section 20 proper because – partly being reminiscent of the *uddānas* of the *Aṅguttaranikāya/Ekottarāgama* – they a) summarily refer to good and bad *dharmas* dealt with in sections 1, 3, 5, 7, 9, 11, 13, 15 and 2, 4, 6, 8, 10, 12, 14, 16–20 respectively and, b) moreover, highlight ways of making immeasurable merit, anticipating by way of a résumé, as it were, the KP sections 158–159.

65 I.e. *pāpakā* for *pāpakāni.*

66 For *apramāṇaṃ* Tib. has *tshad, pramāṇaṃ.*

67 Cf. Karashima 2002: 57, § 16.11: Nom. sg. masc. *ye*?

Worlds, as numerous as the [grains of] sand in the
Gaṅgā, with jewels and then offer [them] to the
Conquerors,[68] and should someone recite [just a single]
Stanza of four metrical units from this [discourse],
The latter's merit will be incalculably [greater].[69]

21

"These four qualities, Kāśyapa, are conducive to a *bodhisattva*'s overcoming mental defilements that are connected with nescience. **(17b)** Which four? (1) [His] restraining himself in conduct, (2) his devoting himself to the true *dharma*, (3) his making a gift of the lamp [of the Teaching] and (4) [his making such a gift] at least to close friends. These four qualities, Kāśyapa, are conducive to a *bodhisattva*'s overcoming ... nescience.[70]

22

"These four qualities, Kāśyapa, are conducive to a *bodhisattva*'s [gaining] unobstructed insight-knowledge.[71] Which four? [They are] as follows: (1) [He exercises] restraint of the senses,[72] (2) reveals the deep meaning [of the true *dharma*],[73] (3) does not despise [others] on account of his being well off

---

68 'Conqueror(s)' after Tib.

69 The comparative is implicit in Tib. *phul ba bas*. Cf. *Vajracchedikā* (Harrison, Watanabe 2006), pp. 118, 124, 131f.: § 8: *yaś ca ... imāṃ tṛsāhasrāmahāsāhasrāṃ lokadhātuṃ saptaratnapratipūrṇaṃ kṛtvā dānaṃ da<d>yāt | yaś ceto dharmaparyāyad aṃtaśaś catuṣpadikām api gāthām udgṛhya parebhyo deśayet ... ayam eva tatonidānaṃ bahutaraṃ puṇyaṃ prasunuyāt* | § 13e: *yaś ca ... gaṃgānadīvālukopamān ... yaś ceto dharmaparyāyāc catuṣpadikām api gāthām ... pra<sunuyād ...>* § 16b: *asya ... puṇyaska(n)dh(a)sy(āṃ)t(i)k(ā)d (e)ṣa pū(r)v(a)k(aḥ puṇyaskandhaḥ śatatamī)m api kalā<ṃ> nopaiti ... saṃkhyām api ... na kṣamate* |

70 Unlike MS, Tib. has verses that conclude section 21: 'The verses: Self-restraint in conduct is duly exercised [by him] (prose reconstruction of Tib.: *śīlasaṃvaraḥ samyagādhīyate ca*), he follows the true *dharma* and makes a gift of the lamp [of the Teaching] (*saddharmaṃ gṛhṇāti pradīpaṃ ca dadāti*) – such a gift he makes at least to close friends (*evam antamaśaḥ saṃstutebhyo dadāti*); [these qualities] rid a wise [person] of that which is connected with nescience ([*te dharmā*] *avidyābhāgīyāt paṇḍitaṃ vivecayanti*)'.

71 As for *°jñānatāye*, see BHSG § 9.38.

72 Tib. has instead 'gift of the true Teaching (*saddharmadāna*)'.

73 Tib.: 'devotion to the true *dharma* (*saddharmaparigraha*)'.

himself [74] (4) and he does not covet what others have got.[75] These four qualities, Kāśyapa, are conducive to ... insight-knowledge.[76]

23

"Further, **(18a)** Kāśyapa, one is certainly not called *bodhisattva*, a 'great Being', in name only; one is [rightly] called *bodhisattva*, a 'great Being', Kāśyapa, [provided] one devotes oneself [77] to righteous living, to impartial conduct, karmically wholesome behaviour and to taking one's firm stand on [*bodhisattva*] practice.[78] He is called *bodhisattva*, Kāśyapa, [who] possesses thirty-two qualities. Which[79] thirty-two? [They are] as follows: (1) [His] determination [to work] for the good and happiness of all beings; (2) his initiating [them] into the Omniscient One's insight-knowledge; (3) [by thinking:] 'Am I of any worth?' his not being contemptuous of the knowledge of others [and] his being free from arrogance; (4) his resolve, (5) unfeigned loving kindness, (6) impartiality towards friends and foes and (7) his unbroken friendship lasting until **(18b)** *nirvāṇa*[80] [is realized].

24

"(8) Friendly speech[81] and speaking politely with a smiling face; (9) his being courageous after shouldering a heavy burden; (10) his unlimited compassion for all beings; (11) his being in high spirits; (12) his constant thirst for learning and [penetrating] the meaning [of what has been learnt] once he has set out to search for the true *dharma*; (13) his disclosing his transgressions in case of any wrongdoing on his part and calmly disapproving of

---

74 Tib.: 'he is not jealous (*anīrṣu*)'.

75 Tib.: 'no disrespect for others (*pareṣv anavamānanā*)'.

76 According to Tib., the verses *catuṣkakā aṣṭa* (Tib. has *bcu po/daśa*) *jahitva ... imasya puṇyasya na eti saṃkhyā*, occurring under section 20 of MS, conclude section 22.

77 Lit.: 'is endowed with'.

78 As for *dharmāśritābhiḥ* (for °*āśritaiḥ*), see BHSG § 8. 113. See von Staël-Holstein 1933: 97: Sthiramati's comment on *dharmāśrita*: *chos la gnas pas ni byaṅ chub sems dpa'i spyod pa* ...

79 As for *katame*, cf. Karashima 2002: 56, § 16. 2: Instr. pl. masc. *te* (Skt. *taiḥ*).

80 After Tib. corresponding to *atyaṃtamitratā yāvan nirvāṇaparyaṃtatāye*.

81 According to Tib.: 'moderate speech'.

offences in case of wrongdoings on the part of others; (14) on the whole, in his behaviour being devoted to his aspirations for enlightenment; (15) his being generous without expecting any reward; (16) his moral conduct without motivation[82] for being [re]born in any of the [various] states of existence (17) [and] his continual forbearance towards all beings.

25

"(18) [His] effort to acquire all 'roots of merit'; (19) steering clear[83] of the state of formlessness **(19a)** [in his] meditation; (20) his wisdom being congruous with[84] [skill in] means [and] his salvatory means being endowed with the four instances of kind treatment;[85] (21) loving kindness making no distinction between[86] moral and immoral persons; (22) his listening to the *dharma* with devotion and zealously living in solitude; (23) total indifference to all sorts of worldly things without his holding wrong views; (24) his having no liking for the Lesser Vehicle and [his having] manifested the blessings of the Great Vehicle; (25) giving up bad company and relying on spiritual friends; (26) his cultivating the four 'brahmic states',[87] (27) easy mastery of the five [kinds of] higher knowledge[88] (28) [and] his reliance on insight-knowledge; (29) concern for [all] beings [irrespective of whether] they follow the [right or] wrong path; (30) unequivocal speech, commitment to the truth **(19b)** [and] (31) his being indefatigable in his acquisition of all 'roots of merit';[89] [finally] (32) the first priority being his aspirations for [supreme] enlightenment.

---

[82] Lit.: 'unattached, free', i.e. *aniśrita* for MS *aniḥśrita*.

[83] Lit.: 'dragged out, extracted'; in SH, Tib. *rnam par gsal ba* does not correspond to *parikarṣita*, whereas the reading of the Lhasa ed., e.g., does: *rnam par bsal ba* (Negi 1993ff. s.v.): *vighaṭita* ('broken, separated'), *parikarṣita* (cf. *parikarṣa*, °*karṣaṇa*, 'dragging out'). See also Weller 1965: 88, n. 11, quoting from Sthiramati's commentary: *bral ba* (*apanīta*), tallying with *rnam par bsal ba*.

[84] Lit.: 'received, welcomed by'.

[85] Cf. above n. 60 of section 19; for MS *upāya* em. *upāyāḥ*.

[86] Lit.: 'of identity'; after Tib. em. °*advayatāyā*.

[87] See BHSD, p. 404, s.v. *brahma-vihāra*.

[88] *Ibid.*, p. 50, s.v. *abhijñā*.

[89] This latter item does not occur in Tib.

26

"[He who] possesses these thirty-two qualities, Kāśyapa, is called *bodhisattva*, a 'great Being'." The verses:

[The qualities are his being,] with determination,
Intent on the good and happiness of all beings;
His initiating [them] into the Omniscient One's
Insight-knowledge; [by thinking:] 'Am I of any
Worth?' his not being contemptuous [while forming]
An opinion about [others'] knowledge[90] and being free
From arrogance; his resolve and unfeigned loving
Kindness; unbroken friendship with beings
As long as the final goal, *nirvāṇa*, is not [realized];
Impartiality towards friend and foe, friendly speech
With a smiling face; being courageous[91] after
Shouldering a heavy burden **(20a)** and, likewise,
His unlimited compassion for [all] beings.[92]

27

[His being,] in search for the true *dharma*, in high
Spirits; his being eager for[93] learning and in case
Of any wrongdoing his seeing [through] the
Transgressions on his part; other[s, in case of any
Wrongdoing on their part,] he should not criticize
Angrily;[94] his being diligent in his aspirations [for
Enlightenment] in [all] modes of physical behaviour
And generosity without expectation of reward;
Moral conduct without his aiming for any state

[90] Lit.: 'knowledge-opinioned, ... -opining'; Tib.: 'opinion about oneself' (*bdag la dpog* (*ātmamāna*)).

[91] After Tib. *sgyid lug źum pa med*, *aviṣāda*; Tib. does not provide a clue to fill the lacuna in the MS (++*dāryaṇatvaṃ*, suggestive of *audārya*, 'magnanimity').

[92] See BHSG § 5.1: "The use of ... singular for plural forms, and vice versa ..."

[93] As for *atṛpte*, cf. Karashima 2002: 50, § 9.2: Nom. sg. masc. -*e*.

[94] Lit.: 'by one who is offended'.

Of existence; unreserved forbearance towards beings;
His effort to acquire what is karmically wholesome
And meditation without the state of formlessness
As its aim;[95] his wisdom being congruous with [skill
In] means and his salvatory means being congruous
With the four [instances of] kind treatment;[96] loving
Kindness and making no distinction between
Moral and immoral persons;[97] listening to the
Dharma with devotion for some time and
Zealously leading a tranquil life in solitude;
Refraining from taking delight in so many worldly
Affairs and in 'lesser **(20b)** vehicles'; he should be
Keen on 'sublime vehicles', give up bad company,
Always rely on spiritual friends and
Cultivate the four 'brahmic states'.[98]

28

Moreover, he should always have the five
[Kinds of] higher knowledge at his fingertips[99]
And constantly have recourse to insight-knowledge;
He should never forsake those who follow the [right]
Path nor the other fellow [beings following the wrong
Path]; he should always speak unequivocally and
[Thus] the truth is always esteemed by him.[100] After
Having given first priority to his aspirations for
Enlightenment he cultivates the qualities praised
By the Conqueror. These thirty-two qualities
Announced by the Blessed One should be developed
By his spiritual sons; those who possess these
Qualities the Blessed One declares *bodhisattvas*.

---

95 Lit.: 'removed from'.

96 See VD n. 140: °*saṃgraheḥ* – inst. pl.

97 Lit.: 'morality and ill-behaved (persons)'.

98 As for *brahmāś ca vihāra*, see BHSG § 8.93, § 8.94.

99 Lit.: 'he should always play with'.

100 As for *se* = *tasya*, see VD n. 144; cf. BHSG § 21.18.

29

"I will give you descriptions, Kāśyapa, by making comparisons (**21a**) by means of which one may make known a *bodhisattva*'s, a 'great Being's', virtues. Just as this great earth, Kāśyapa, is unchanging and sustains all beings without [expecting] any reward, so a *bodhisattva*, Kāśyapa, right from the time he has begun to aspire to Buddhahood until he takes his seat on the 'throne of enlightenment', is unchanging and sustains all beings without [expecting] any reward." The verses:

> Just as the earth sustains all beings, is unchanging
> And does not expect any reward, so a *bodhisattva*,
> Engrossed in unparalleled thought[101] until he has
> Become an Enlightened One, a Conqueror, the chief and
> Best, sustains all beings, is unchanging and does not
> Expect any reward (**21b**). He does not discriminate,[102]
> [Irrespective of anyone being either his] son or an
> Enemy,[103] and always seeks to [gain] enlightenment,
> Foremost and supreme.

30

"Just as the water element, Kāśyapa, makes all [vegetation] grow - grass, bushes, herbs and forest trees -, so a *bodhisattva*, Kāśyapa, strictly honest and having suffused all beings with loving kindness, spends his time, making all spotless qualities grow in all beings." The verses:

> Just as the water element [nourishes] grass, bushes,
> Herbs, trees and [all] kinds of plants and corn,
> So a strictly honest *bodhisattva* suffuses countless[104]
> Beings with loving kindness; having diffused manifold

[101] Alternatively, 'in initial thought'.
[102] Lit.: 'equal-notioned'.
[103] Cf. Weller 1965: 87, n. 2: ... *śatruṃhi* = *śatruṣmin* = *śatrau*.
[104] Lit.: 'endless'.

Teachings in regular order, [countless beings] grow[105]
In spotless qualities. In due course[106] **(22a)** he realizes
The Conquerors' enlightenment after defeating
Māra and his forces.

31

"Just as the heat element, Kāśyapa, causes all grains to ripen, so a *bodhisattva*'s wisdom, Kāśyapa, causes all spotless qualities in all beings to ripen." The verses:

Just as heat causes all grains, grass and herbs to ripen,
So the wisdom of the Blessed One's spiritual sons[107]
Brings spotless qualities in beings to maturity.

32

"Just as the air element, Kāśyapa, makes up[108] all Buddha-realms, so a *bodhisattva*'s skill in means, Kāśyapa, makes up all teachings of the Buddha." The verses:

Just as the air [element] **(22b)** makes up the various
Realms [issuing] from the Buddha's mind, so the
Means of the spiritual sons of the Conqueror make up
The excellent teachings set forth by the Blessed One.

33

"Just as all the gods, Kāśyapa, are certainly unable to defeat and overcome [for good] Māra's, the Evil One's, fourfould army,[109] so a strictly honest *bo-*

105 Cf. above n. 92 of section 26; Karashima 2002: 51, § 9.10: Nom. pl. *-aḥ*? – and BHSG § 8.83.

106 Lit.: 'in regular order'.

107 As for °*ātmajānān* = °*ātmajānām*, see BHSG § 2.65 (VD).

108 See BHSD, p. 486, s.v. *viṭhapayati* (cf. *vi-√sthā*).

109 I.e. elephants, chariots, cavalry and infantry.

dhisattva, Kāśyapa, cannot be defeated and overcome [for good] by Māra and his [forces]."

34

"Just as the moon's disc, Kāśyapa, waxes indeed and increases in the light half of a month, so a strictly honest *bodhisattva*, Kāśyapa, increases in all spotless qualities." The verses:

> Just as the moon's disc (**23a**) waxes, increases and does
> Not wane, so a strictly honest *bodhisattva* always
> Increases in spotless qualities.[110]

35

"Just as the sun's disc, Kāśyapa, gives indeed light to beings [even] by just a few sunrays which it emits, so a *bodhisattva*,[111] Kāśyapa, gives beings the light of insight-knowledge [even] by just a few rays of his wisdom which he emits." The verses:

> Just as the sun gives light to beings [even] by just a few
> Rays which he emits, so the Conquerors' spiritual son
> Gives beings the light of wisdom by the rays of insight-
> Knowledge.

36

"Just as the lion, Kāśyapa, king of beasts - whencesoever he proceeds -, certainly moves around everywhere fearless[ly] and not at all frightened,

---

[110] A number of comparisons in the KP might have been inspired by precursors in the *Nikāya/Āgama* literature of the Śrāvakayāna; as for this section's comparison, cf., for example, *Aṅguttaranikāya* IV (Kashyap 1960a): 115: Cetokhīlasutta: *seyyathāpi ... juṇha-pakkhe candassa yā ratti vā divaso vā āgacchati, vaḍḍhateva vaṇṇena vaḍḍhati maṇḍalena ... evam eva ... yassa kassaci ... ime ... cetokhīlā pahīnā ... tassa ... āgacchati vuddhi yeva ... kusalesu dhammesu no parihānīti.*

[111] As for *bodhisatvam*, see BHSG § 8.26 (nom. sg. *-aṃ/-am*).

(23b) so a *bodhisattva*, Kāśyapa, who has a firm footing in virtue, in learning, in special qualities and in *dharma* [practice],[112] – whencesoever he proceeds – certainly moves around everywhere fearless[ly] and not at all frightened." The verses:

> Just as the lion with his mane, king of beasts, moves
> Around fearless[ly] wherever he likes, so a *bodhisattva*
> Who has a firm footing in virtue, in learning and
> Insight-knowledge, goes wherever he likes [without fear].[113]

37

"Just as an elephant, Kāśyapa, a mighty, well-trained tusker, does not weary of carrying any kind of burden, so a *bodhisattva*, Kāśyapa, who has his mind perfectly under control, does not weary of carrying[114] for all beings any kind of burden." The verses:

> **(24a)** Just as a strong, well-tamed elephant carrying a
> Burden does not feel exhausted, so a *bodhisattva* who
> Has his mind perfectly under control, does not
> Become tired of [carrying] the burden of beings.

38

"Just as the lotus, Kāśyapa, [though] growing[115] in water, is certainly not soiled by it, so a *bodhisattva*, Kāśyapa, [though] born in [this] world, is not soiled by worldliness." The verses:

> Just as the red lotus grows in water, [but] is
> Neither soiled by water nor by mud, so a

---

112 Tib. differs: *thos pa daṅ | tshul khrims daṅ | bslab pa daṅ | sbyaṅs pa'i yon tan daṅ | yo byad bsñuṅs pa daṅ | tiṅ ṅe 'dzin daṅ | ye śes la gnas pa yaṅ* (*śrutaśīlaśikṣādhū(u)taguṇasaṃlekhasamādhijñānapratiṣṭhito*).

113 Cf. *Khuddakanikāya* I (Kashyap 1959b): 299: Munisutta, v. 214f.: *paññābalaṃ sīlavatūpapannaṃ, samāhitaṃ jhānarataṃ satīmaṃ | ... sīhaṃ va saddesu* ***asantasantaṃ****, ... taṃ vā pi dhīrā muniṃ vedayanti ||*

114 As for *sarvabhāravahanatā* (for °*vahanatayā*), see BHSG § 9.65.

115 Lit.: 'grown'.

Bodhisattva, [though] born in [this] world,
Is never soiled by worldliness.[116]

39

"Just as a tree, Kāśyapa, with its branches lopped off will certainly grow again [new] shoots [so long as] its root[s] are undamaged, so a *bodhisattva*, Kāśyapa, with his mental defilements 'lopped off' **(24b)** thanks to his skill in means will surely 'shoot up' again in the three states of existence[117] [so long as] the connection to[118] all his roots of merit is undamaged." The verses:

Just as a tree with its branch[es] lopped off will grow
[Again] shoots [so long as] its root[s][119] are unharmed
And healthy, so he whose [mental defilements] are
'Lopped off' thanks to [his skill in] means will 'shoot up'
[Again so long as] his connection to the root[s]
Is not abandoned.[120]

---

[116] As for the lotus *upamā*, cf., for instance, *Khuddakanikāya* I (Kashyap 1959b): 55 (*Dhammapada*, v. 401 (or the corresponding v. in its various parallel versions)); cf. *ibid.*: 395: *Suttanipāta*, v. 47 (= v. 812): *udabindu yathā pi pokkhare, padume vāri yathā na limpati (lippati) | evaṃ muni nopalimpati (°lippati), yad idaṃ diṭṭhasutaṃ mutesu vā ||*

[117] See BHSD, p. 259, s.v. *traidhātuka*.

[118] Perhaps a pun is intended here: *saṃyojana* = 'connection' and 'fetter binding to/ causing rebecoming'. Tib. additionally has *sñiṅ rje chen pos*, 'because of his great compassion'.

[119] As for *mūla* = *mūle*, *saṃyojana* = *saṃyojane*, see VD n. 159: 'Stem in *-a* as oblique case form'; cf. BHSG § 8.3; § 8.11.

[120] This *upamā* illustrates a *bodhisattva*'s postponing his final emancipation for the sake of his *bodhisattvacaryā*. Cf. Sthiramati (von Staël-Holstein 1933: 109): *dpe bcu pas ni kun nas ñon moṅs pa med kyaṅ ji ltar yoṅs su mya ṅan las mi 'da' ba ston to |* 'The tenth *upamā* illustrates [a *bodhisattva*'s] not entering complete *nirvāṇa* in spite of his being rid of mental defilements.' Sthiramati's referring to the 'tenth (instead of 'eleventh') *upamā*' is due to his not commenting on the above section 33 in which the verses are lacking.

40

"Just as the entire body of water, Kāśyapa, [stemming] from the great rivers from the various directions, [the cardinal and] intermediate points,[121] certainly takes on just a single taste, namely the taste of salt [once] it has flowed into the great ocean, so a *bodhisattva*'s 'roots of merit', Kāśyapa, gathered up by various means and dedicated to [the realization of supreme] enlightenment,[122] take on just a single taste, namely the taste of [ultimate] release." The verses:

> Just as the water of various rivers [once] it has flowed
> Into the great **(25a)** ocean, will take on a single taste, [so
> A *bodhisattva*'s] merits, accumulated by various means
> And dedicated to [the realization of ultimate release],
> Have a single taste, [the taste] of enlightenment.[123]

41

"Just as the gods, Kāśyapa, belonging to the group of the four World-Guardians and the Trāyastriṃśa gods are established on [Mount] Sumeru, so a *bodhisattva*'s [future] omniscience is established on [account of] his 'roots of merit' pertaining to his aspiring to Buddhahood." The verses:

> Just as the community of the gods belonging to the group
> Of the four World-Guardians and of the Trāyastriṃśa
> Gods reside on [Mount] Sumeru, so *bodhisattvas* are
> 'Established' in [their 'roots of] merit'; [once]
> They have gained omniscience, they set forth
> [The Blessed One's] teachings.

---

121 As for °*digvidikṣu*, see BHSG § 7.82: loc. for ablative.

122 As for *bodhāya*, see BHSG § 10.97.

123 This comparison occurs in several texts of the Pāli canon and in the Āgama literature, for instance at *Aṅguttaranikāya* III (Kashyap 1960a): 310: Pahārādasutta: *seyyathāpi, Pahārāda, yā kāci mahānadiyo ... tā mahāsamuddaṃ patvā ... seyyathāpi ... mahāsamuddo ekaraso loṇaraso; evam eva kho ... ayaṃ dhammavinayo ekaraso vimuttiraso* |

42

"Just as kings, Kāśyapa, run all state affairs by fully relying on their ministers, so a *bodhisattva*'s wisdom, Kāśyapa, **(25b)** brings about all actions of an Enlightened One by fully relying on salvatory means." The verses:

> Just as kings always run all [state] affairs by fully relying
> On their ministers, so a *bodhisattva*'s wisdom –
> Fully relying on salvatory means – always brings
> About [all] that is an Enlightened One's concern.

43

"Just as no rain can be awaited,[124] Kāśyapa, [so long as] the sky is clear and with no clouds, so no 'rain', Kāśyapa, of the true *dharma* can be awaited on the part[125] of a *bodhisattva* who has only limited knowledge." The verses:

> Just as it never happens that it rains when the sky is clear
> And without clouds, [so] it never happens that on
> The part of a *bodhisattva* who has only limited
> Knowledge the *dharma* is set forth.

44

"Just as a downpour, Kāśyapa, **(26a)** emerging from a compact mass of thunderclouds showers on the crops, so a *bodhisattva*'s 'rain' of the true *dharma*, Kāśyapa, emerging from the *dharma*-clouds of great compassion[126] showers on beings." The verses:

> Just as a thundercloud with flashes of lightning saturate
> The crops with rain, so a *bodhisattva* 'saturates'
> Beings with the downpour emerging from
> The clouds of the true *dharma*.

---

[124] Lit.: 'no source of acquiring rain'.

[125] Lit.: 'from the proximity'; as for °*antikā*, see BHSG § 8.46 (abl. sg.).

[126] Tib. additionally has °*bāhuśrutya*° (*daṅ/maṅ du thos pa'i*).

45

"It is like this, Kāśyapa: Wherever a universal monarch appears, there appear [his] 'seven jewels'.[127] Likewise, Kāśyapa, the thirty-seven *dharmas* pertaining to enlightenment[128] 'arise', wherever a *bodhisattva* arises." The verses:

Wherever a universal monarch appears, **(26b)**
There one will find his seven jewels,
And wherever a *bodhisattva* appears,
There one will find his seven enlightenment factors.[129]

46

"It is like this, Kāśyapa: Wherever jewels can be awaited,[130] there hundreds and thousands of *kārṣāpaṇa*-coins can be awaited. Likewise, Kāśyapa, wherever a *bodhisattva* can be awaited, there hundreds and thousands of Disciples and Pratyekabuddhas can be awaited." The verses:

Where there is a [priceless] jewel, for example, many
Kārṣāpaṇa-coins are obtained, and where there is
The approach of aspiring to supreme enlightenment,
Also many Disciples will approach[131] [a *bodhisattva*].

47

"Just as the pleasures, Kāśyapa, the enjoyments of the Trāyastriṃśa gods **(27a)** being established in the Miśrakā Grove,[132] remain the same all the time, so a strictly honest *bodhisattva*'s altruistic (*samyañc*) practice, Kāśya-

[127] They are described in the Pāli canon and Āgama literature, for example at *Dīgha-nikāya* II (Kashyap 1958a): 132–135: Mahāsudassanasutta.

[128] See BHSD, p. 402, s.v. *bodhipakṣya.*

[129] BHSD, p. 403, s.v. *bodhyaṅga.*

[130] Cf. above n. 124 of section 43.

[131] Lit.: 'an abundant approach of Disciples'; as for *bahū*, see BHSG § 12.14 (nom. sg. masc. -ū).

[132] Cf. BHSD, p. 433, s.v. *Miśrakāvana, Miśrāvana.*

pa, for the sake of[133] all beings remains [the same all the time]."[134] The verses:

The practices of the gods who stay in the Miśrakā Grove,
For example, remain[135] the same all the time;
Likewise a strictly honest *bodhisattva* practises
Altruism towards beings [all the time].

48

"Just as poison, Kāśyapa, does not cause [one's] death [if] one recites a *mantra* as an antidote,[136] so the poison of mental defilements pertaining to a *bodhisattva* who is 'taken up'[137] with insight-knowledge and skill in means, cannot cause [his spiritual] death." The verses:

Just as poison (**27b**) – because of [one's] being 'taken
Up' with a *mantra* – cannot harm anybody, so in this world
A *bodhisattva*, endowed with insight-knowledge, cannot
Be harmed[138] by mental defilements.

49

"Just as in cities, Kāśyapa, heap[s] of [dung] sweepings are useful for sugar cane fields, rice paddies and vineyards, so a mental defilement pertaining to a *bodhisattva*, Kāśyapa, is useful for his [maturing] omniscience." The verses:

Just as in towns foul [heaps of dung] sweepings[139] will
Make useful [manure] for sugar cane fields, so a

---

133 Lit.: 'in the presence of'.
134 After Tib. *mtshuṅs par 'gyur ro |*
135 As for *saṃsthihate*, cf. BHSG § 28.43.
136 Lit.: 'poison taken with a medicine-like *mantra*'; Tib.: '... taken with a *mantra* and medicine'.
137 Re °*parigṛhīto* for °*parigṛhītasya*, cf. BHSG § 8.10.
138 Lit.: 'killed'; as for *vinipātanāya*, see BHSG § 36.15 (BHS infinitives).
139 As for *saṃkāru*, see BHSG § 8.20 (nom. sg. -*u*).

Bodhisattva's mental defilement will prove
Useful in regard to the Conquerors' Teaching.[140]

50

"Just as someone, Kāśyapa, handles a bow **(28a)** who is untrained in archery,[141] so [one] should consider, Kāśyapa, a rather uninformed *bodhisattva*'s 'skilfully' [handling] 'discriminating comprehension' of the *dharma*, investigation and knowledge of how to grasp the [deep] meaning [of teachings].

51

"Just as a potter, Kāśyapa, makes a good fire for [baking] unbaked pottery, so [one] should consider, Kāśyapa, a *bodhisattva*'s inspiring exposition of the *dharma* for those whose wisdom is not fully developed.

52

"Then, Kāśyapa, a *bodhisattva* who wishes now to acquire [insight-] knowledge in respect of this Dharma-disquisition of the Great Collection of Jewels, should wisely apply himself to the *dharma*. How[142] then, Kāśyapa, does one wisely apply oneself to the *dharma*? One should[143] see all things as they really are. And how, Kāśyapa, does one see all things as they really are? If one does not conceive of a self **(28b)** of a being, a soul, personality, person, man or human being [as entities], Kāśyapa, it [can] be said that [one follows] the Middle Way [by] seeing things as they really are.

---

[140] Cf. Sthiramati (Staël-Holstein 1933: 113f.): *de'i ñon moṅs pa ñes par mi 'gyur ba daṅ | yon tan chen po byed pa'i phyir ro | ... byaṅ chub sems dpa' ... sems can thams cad kyi dge ba'i rtsa ba mṅon par sgrub pa'i gnas su gyur pas phan 'dogs pa ...* "His mental defilement does no harm (*doṣa*) because it creates great virtue (*guṇa*). Since a *bodhisattva* is the protector (*āśrayabhūta*) of the roots of merit of all beings, he is 'the benefactor' (*upakāraka*)."

[141] Lit.: 'bow'.

[142] Lit.: 'which is ...'

[143] Lit.: 'that is to say'.

53

"Moreover, Kāśyapa, the Middle Way - seeing things as they really are - [amounts to the following] contemplation: Neither permanence nor impermanence pertain to form; neither permanence nor impermanence pertain to feeling, perception, formations and to consciousness. This is called the Middle Way, Kāśyapa, [one's] seeing things as they really are.

54

"Contemplating that neither permanence nor impermanence pertain to the earth element, that neither permanence nor impermanence pertain to the elements or water, of heat and air, **(29a)** that neither permanence nor impermanence pertain to the elements of space and consciousness - this is called the Middle Way, Kāśyapa, [one's] seeing things as they really are.

55

"Furthermore, Kāśyapa, the Middle Way - seeing things as they really are - [amounts to the following] contemplation: Neither permanence nor impermanence pertain to the eyes - this is called the Middle Way ... as they really are. The same contemplation [applies to the other] sense organs: Neither permanence nor impermanence pertain to the ears, the nose, tongue, body and mind base - this is called the Middle Way ... as they really are.

56

"This is one extreme, Kāśyapa, [viz. positing] permanence; the second extreme is [positing] **(29b)** impermanence. The middle, [free] of these two [extremes, viz.] of permanence and impermanence, - that is the formless, the unseen, non-appearance, without designation, unsupported and abodeless.[144] This is called the Middle Way, Kāśyapa, [one's] seeing things as they really are.

---

[144] At *Dīghanikāya* I (Kashyap 1958a): 190, 9 (Kevaṭṭasutta), the noteworthy Pāli equivalent of *anidarśanam*, *anidassanaṃ*, occurs as an epithet of the consciousness of someone

57

"This is one extreme, Kāśyapa, [viz. positing] a self; the second extreme is [positing] not-self. The middle, [free] of [these] two [extremes, viz.] of a self and not-self, – that is the formless, the unseen, non-appearance, without designation, unsupported and abodeless. This is called the Middle Way, Kāśyapa, [one's] seeing things as they really are.

58

"This is one extreme, Kāśyapa, [viz. positing] the real[ity of] mind; the second extreme, Kāśyapa, is [positing] the unreal[ity of] mind. This is called the Middle Way, **(30a)** [one's] seeing things as they really are when no mind, no acts of will, no thought, no consciousness [are posited as entities].

59

"Thus [to maintain] the impurity of all 'facts' – [of the *dharmas* that are] karmically wholesome or unwholesome, mundane or supramundane, objectionable or unobjectionable, subject to the malign influences or free from them, conditioned or unconditioned, – that, Kāśyapa, is one extreme. The second extreme, Kāśyapa, is [to insist on] the purification [regarding all 'facts']. This is called the Middle Way ... as they really are, [viz. one's] neither positing nor stating nor expatiating on [any] of these two extremes.

---

who has realized final emancipation. See also Sthiramati's paraphrase of the epithets of *madhya* (von Staël-Holstein 1933: 119f.): *de ni rnam par mi rtog pa'i ye śes te | de rnam par brtag tu med pas dpyad du med pa'o* || ('It is insight-knowledge free of false discrimination (*avikalpajñāna*), being free of figurative illustration (*arūpaṇa* – for *arūpin*, the formless) because there is no false discrimination.'); *brjod du med ciṅ bśad du med pas bstan du med pa'o* || ('Being inexpressible (*anabhilāpya*) and indescribable (*anirdeśya*), it is without indicating/without appearance/the unseen (*anidarśana*).'); ... *'khor ba daṅ mya ṅan las 'das pa la mi gnas pas gnas med par rig par bya'o* || ('As it has no abode (*anavasthita*) either in *saṃsāra* or in *nirvāṇa* it should be understood to be abodeless.'). As for Tib.-Sanskrit equivalents/quasi-equivalents, see Negi 1993ff.

60

"This is one extreme, Kāśyapa, [viz. one's insisting on] 'it is'; the second extreme is [one's insisting on] 'it is not'. The middle, [free] of these two extremes, – that, Kāśyapa, is called the Middle Way, [one's] seeing things as they really are.[145]

61

"Although, Kāśyapa, I have made known to you [dependent origination and its cessation], namely (**30b**): 'Karma-formations are conditioned by ignorance; consciousness is conditioned by karma-formations; mental and physical phenomena are conditioned by consciousness, the six bases by mental and physical phenomena, contact by the six bases, feeling by contact, craving by feeling, clinging by craving, becoming by clinging, birth by becoming; conditioned by birth old age, death, sorrow, lamentation, pain, grief and despair manifest themselves; thus appears this whole great mass of suffering.

62

" 'With the cessation of ignorance karma-formations cease, with the cessation of karma-formations consciousness ceases, with the cessation of consciousness mental and physical phenomena cease, with the cessation of mental and physical phenomena the six bases (**31a, b**) cease, with the cessation of the six bases contact ceases, with the cessation of contact feeling ceases, with the cessation of feeling craving ceases ... with the cessation of birth old age, death ... and despair cease; thus this whole great mass of suffering ceases' – in this respect, [however,] Kāśyapa, both [true] knowledge

[145] Cf. *Saṃyuttanikāya* II (Kashyap 1959a): 17: Kaccānagottasutta: *sabbam atthīti kho, Kaccāna, ayam eko anto | sabbe natthīti ayaṃ dutiyo anto | ete te, Kaccāna, ubho ante anupagamma majjhena tathāgato dhammaṃ deseti* ... In the *Madhyamakaśāstra* (Vaidya 1960a: 117, 15, v. 7) Nāgārjuna refers to an *āgama* version of this *sūtra*: *Kātyāyanāvavāde cāstīti nāstīti cobhayam | pratiṣiddhaṃ bhagavatā bhāvābhāvavibhāvinā ||* See also P, *ibid.*, p. 118, 12–14, where KP section 60, including the epithets of *madhya* occurring in sections 56, 57, is quoted.

and ignorance [are not two and] that non-duality is not divided up into two. The insight-knowledge in this respect – that, Kāśyapa, is called the Middle Way, [one's] seeing things as they really are. Thus both karma-formations and the unconditioned, both consciousness and cessation of consciousness ... birth and cessation of birth, both old age and death and cessation of old age and death [are not two and] that non-duality is not divided up into two. The insight-knowledge in this respect **(32a)** – that, Kāśyapa, is called the Middle Way ... as they really are.

63

"Furthermore, Kāśyapa, seeing things as they really are does not [imply] that one renders things empty by dint of emptiness – things themselves are empty; it does not [imply] that one renders things signless by dint of the signless – things themselves are signless ... that one renders things undesired by dint of the undesired ... that one renders things unformed by dint of non-performance – things themselves are unformed; ... that one renders things unoriginated ... unborn ... unperceivable ... without malign influences ... without individual essence by dint of non-origination ... of the unborn[146]... of what is unperceivable ... of what is without malign influences ... without individual essence – things themselves are unoriginated ... unborn ... unperceivable ... **(32b)** without malign influences ... without individual essence. Contemplating thus – *that in this way not by dint of what is without individual essence there is the state of being without individual essence of things, that individual essence of things [simply] does not occur*[147] – that is called the Middle Way, seeing things as they really are.

64

"Again, Kāśyapa, emptiness [should] certainly not [be misunderstood as having been set forth] in order to destroy [the wrong notion of] the existence of a 'person' [as an entity]. A 'person' is just emptiness, emptiness is

---

146 As for *ajātā*, see BHSG § 7.46: abl. for inst.; cf. Weller 1965: 100, n. 14.

147 As for *upalabhate* as a passive form, see BHSG § 37.16. Italicized text is not found in Tib. The meaning seems to be that conceiving of instrumentality with regard to essencelessness is redundant.

just emptiness – absolute emptiness. [Likewise] emptiness [pertains to] the past, the future and the present. Go by[148] emptiness, Kāśyapa, not by a 'person'. So on account of [this] announcement I declare those, Kāśyapa, lost once and for all who nevertheless[149] go by emptiness by imagining **(33a)** that it [is tantamount to destruction]. Indeed, Kāśyapa, one had better subscribe to the notion – as high as [Mount] Sumeru – of a 'person' than to a [nihilistic][150] notion of emptiness insisted upon by someone who is insufferably conceited. For what reason? The means of getting rid of wrong notions [such as the notion of] a 'person', Kāśyapa, is emptiness; but by what [means], Kāśyapa, will someone be cured[151] who has a [nihilistic] notion of emptiness?

65

"Let us suppose, Kāśyapa, there is a sick person; a physician administers medicine to him which, gone [down] into the stomach and having rid [the patient] of all his ailments, remains [in the stomach and upsets it]. What do you think, Kāśyapa? Would the sick person be cured of his illness [after having taken] that medicine **(33b)** [which], gone [down] into the stomach and having rid [the patient] of all his gastric ailments, remains [in the stomach and upsets it]?" – "No, Exalted One," [Kāśyapa] replied, "that person's illness would be aggravated [after his having taken] the medicine ... remains [in the stomach]." – "Similarly, Kāśyapa," the Exalted One continued, "emptiness is the means of getting rid of all wrong notions. He, however, Kāśyapa, who has a [nihilistic] notion of emptiness – I declare him indeed irremediable." The verses:

> Just as a physician may give someone a purgative to
> Cure an illness [which], having rid [the patient] of his
> Ailments, remains [in the stomach and upsets it, and]
> Consequently no [pain] relief [is given], so for
> Those who resort to a thicket of notions, emptiness

---

148 As for *pratisaratha*, see BHSG § 26.13.

149 Lit.: 'indeed again'.

150 Cf. the KP quotation at P 108, 28: *abhāvābhiniveśikasya.*

151 Lit.: 'who will rid himself of?' or: '... by what [means] will a [nihilistic] notion of emptiness be got rid of?' – cf. BHSG § 31.2.

Definitely is the supreme antidote; but him who has
A wrong notion of emptiness, the Conqueror has
Declared indeed irremediable.

66

"Let us imagine, Kāśyapa, that somebody is frightened of empty space. Beating his chest and shedding tears, he cries: 'Take away that empty space.' – What do you think, Kāśyapa? Would it be possible to remove empty space?" – "Impossible," [Kāśyapa] replied. "Similarly, Kāśyapa," the Exalted One continued, "those ascetics and brahmins I declare greatly confused [who] are afraid of emptiness. For what reason? They just ramble about emptiness and so they are afraid of it." The verses:

Just as a person is frightened of empty space and
Cries [in] confusion: 'Take away that empty space,'
Although it is impossible to remove it [and only]
Foolish people speak like that, so as bewildered
Worldlings those ascetics and brahmins who
Are afraid of emptiness, just ramble about it
[As being annihilation] whilst it is absolutely
Impossible to reject it.

67

"Let us imagine, Kāśyapa, that a painter himself draws the frightening features of an ogre and then, paralysed with fear, falls headlong and thereafter is thrown into total confusion. Similarly, Kāśyapa, all unenlightened worldlings wander through the round of rebirths because of forms, sounds, smells, tastes and [objects of] touch created by themselves, not knowing what these things really are."[152] The verses:

---

[152] As for the *upamā* of the confused painter, cf. a) the *Mahāyānaviṃśaka* v. 8 (Bhattacharya 1931b): 11ff.; b) the *Karatalaratna* (Aiyaswami Sastri 1949): 34, 15. See also Martini 2008, providing further references to the painter *upamā* found both in Pāli and Mahāyāna sources.

Just as a painter, frightened of the terrible features of
An ogre drawn [by himself], falls headlong and then is
Thrown into total confusion, so all unenlightened
Worldlings, bewildered by their own creations – forms,
Sounds, etc. –, wander through the six states of existence.[153]

68

"Just as a magician, Kāśyapa, conjures up something magicked which then devours its very creator, so a monk, Kāśyapa, who engages in spiritual discipline,[154] sees, whatever he turns into an object of his contemplation, as being indeed void; everything appears to him as being just unreal, empty and insubstantial." The verses:

Just as a magician is devoured by something
Magicked which he [himself] has conjured up, so
What[ever] a meditator contemplates, appears to
Him as being utterly void and unreal.

69

"Just as fire is produced, Kāśyapa, depending on two pieces of wood,[155] and as the same [on being] produced does consume the two pieces of wood,[156] so the faculty of wisdom [pertaining to a] Noble [One] is produced, Kāśyapa, depending on [one's] seeing things as they really are, and [once] it

---

[153] As for *ṣaḍgatika*, see BHSD, p. 208, s.v. *gati/gatika.*

[154] Re *yogācāra* (also occurring in KP section 108), see Silk 2000.

[155] Sthiramati (von Staël-Holstein 1933: 130) gives a clue as to how the production of fire can be understood: It is produced by *gtsubs pa, mathana,* 'act of rubbing, friction', also meaning 'a kind of wood used to produce fire by attrition'; √*math* = 'to produce fire by rapidly rotating a dry stick'.

[156] The text's "fire ... [on being] produced does consume the two pieces" does not seem a particularly apt description: It would not make sense to let the stick as an indispensable implement for making fire be consumed by the same. However, √*dah* also means 'to scorch' so that it is not necessary to assume the said implement is being consumed by the fire that has just been produced.

is produced, it does 'consume' [one's] seeing things as they really are."[157] The verses:

> Just as fire, produced because of rubbing together two
> Pieces of wood and by blowing, consumes [the two
> Pieces], so the faculty of wisdom, once it is produced,
> Does 'consume' [one's] seeing things as they really are.

70

"Just as an oil-lamp, Kāśyapa, will not say: 'It's me that dispels darkness,' - but rather when an oil-lamp[158] is lit complete darkness vanishes because of [the lamp's] light, and as far as the oil-lamp, Kāśyapa, and complete darkness [as separate entities] are [concerned] - both are what [amounts to] emptiness which cannot be taken hold of, is 'immobile' and [just] empty - similarly, Kāśyapa, when insight-knowledge arises ignorance vanishes, and insight-knowledge, Kāśyapa, will certainly not say: 'It's me that dispels ignorance,' - but rather [when insight-knowledge arises] ignorance vanishes because of insight-knowledge, and as far as insight-knowledge and ignorance [as separate entities] are [concerned] - both are what [amounts to] emptiness which cannot be taken hold of, is 'immobile' and [just] empty." The verses:

> Just as because of a lamp all complete darkness
> Vanishes [which], however, neither comes from nor
> Goes [anywhere], so with the arising of insight-
> Knowledge ignorance vanishes which, too, neither
> Comes from nor goes anywhere. The lamp will not
> Say: 'I dispel darkness,' but with the appearance of
> Light darkness vanishes. [Both the lamp and
> Darkness] are empty, cannot be taken hold of and
> Are like 'flowers in the sky'. The same [applies

---

[157] Sthiramati (*ibid.*) gives a further clue to an understanding of *bhūtapratyavekṣā* being 'consumed' by *āryaprajñendriya* by stating that through the latter supramundane insight-knowledge (*'jig rten las 'das pa'i ye śes, lokottarajñāna*) arises which once and for all transcends even *bhūtapratyavekṣā* which is till *lokya.*

[158] Lit.: 'light' (*pradyota*).

To] insight-knowledge and ignorance –
Both are [what amounts to] emptiness.

71

"Let us suppose, Kāśyapa, that within a thousand years there had not been anyone to light an oil-lamp either in a house, in a cell or in an underground room. But then somebody would light an oil-lamp in that place. What do you think, **(37b)** Kāśyapa, would it in whatever way occur to complete darkness: 'I have been prevailing herein for a thousand years and will not move out'?" – "No, Exalted One," [Kāśyapa] replied, "it would be impossible for complete darkness not to move out once an oil-lamp is lit; it will have to disappear by all means." – "Likewise, Kāśyapa," the Exalted One said, "[one's] actions and mental defilement[s], in spite of [their] prevalence for an 'incredibly long time',[159] will 'disappear' once [the lamp of] the unique contemplation with wisdom [pertaining to] wise attention [is lit].[160] The oil-lamp, Kāśyapa, stands for the faculty of wisdom [pertaining to a] Noble [One], and complete darkness for [one's worldly][161] actions and mental defilement[s]." The verses:

Just as after a long [time] someone has lit a lamp
In a cell [or] house and as it will not occur to darkness
Therein: 'I have been prevailing herein for long and
Will not move out,' – it would be impossible for
Complete darkness not to move out once a lamp is
Lit; it is due to the lamp that darkness disappears,
And both [darkness and the lamp] are empty and
Without there being any illusory imagining [on their
Part]. Thus due to the insight-knowledge being free
From malign influences and [pertaining to a] Noble
[One], ignorance, increased by mental defilements,
Disappears. Between insight-knowledge and mental
Defilement[s] there never is any connection. It does
Not occur to insight-knowledge: 'Let there be no

---

[159] Lit.: 'one hundred thousand *nayutas* of crores of aeons'.
[160] Lit.: 'because of the unique ...'
[161] After Tib. *'phags pa ma yin pa* (*anārya*, 'vulgar, inferior').

Ignorance.' It is by depending on insight-knowledge
That spiritual darkness disappears; both knowledge
And ignorance are empty, cannot be taken hold of,
And both are like 'flowers in the sky'.

72

"Just as seeds, Kāśyapa, do not sprout in the sky, so it is absolutely impossible,[162] Kāśyapa, for the qualities of a Buddha [which] a *bodhisattva* [aspires after] to 'sprout' from the Unconditioned."[163] The verses:

Just as seeds do not sprout in the sky – neither did
They in the past nor will they in future –, so the
Qualities of a Buddha cannot definitely 'sprout'[164]
Anywhere from the Unconditioned.

73

"Just as all [kinds of] seed, Kāśyapa, do sprout in soil fertilized by manure,[165] so the qualities of a Buddha, Kāśyapa, [which] a *bodhisattva* [aspires after] do 'sprout' in attachment to the world 'fertilized' by the 'manure' of mental defilements." The verses:

Just as seeds sprout in [soil] that is fertilized and
Irrigated [well], but not in deserts, so the Conqueror's

---

[162] Lit.: 'non-existence, impossibility'.

[163] With reference to the *āryapudgalas* who – through their vision of the *āryasatyas* and experience of *asaṃskṛta* – are incapable of a *bodhisattva*'s aspiration for Buddhahood, whilst the latter's experience of *saṃskṛta* as the 'habitat' of mental defilements enables him to aspire after the qualities of a Buddha, see § 3, chapter VII of the *Vimalakīrtinirdeśa* (Takahashi *et al.* 2006: 78) which in all likelihood was inspired by this and the following KP sections 73–75: *na śakyaṃ kulaputra asaṃskṛtadarśinā niyāmāvakrāntisthitenānuttarāyāṃ samyaksaṃbodhau cittam utpādayitum | kleśāgārasaṃskṛtasthitenādṛṣṭsatyena śakyam anuttarāyāṃ samyaksaṃbodhau cittam utpādayitum | ... nāsaṃskṛtaniyāmaprāpteṣu satveṣu buddhadharmā virohanti |*

[164] Lit.: 'the coming forth is unreal and impossible'.

[165] Lit.: 'completely furnished with sweepings'; cf. section 49 above.

Qualities [after which] his spiritual sons [aspire] 'sprout
Up' in this world with [all] its defilements and falsity.

74

"Just as the lotus, Kāśyapa, does not grow in the wilderness and in deserts, so it is absolutely impossible, Kāśyapa, for the qualities of a Buddha [which] a *bodhisattva* [aspires after] to 'sprout' from the Unconditioned." The verses:

Just as the lotus grows in lakes and ponds, but
Never in deserts, so the qualities of a Buddha cannot
Definitely 'sprout' anywhere from the Unconditioned.

75

"Just as the lotus, Kāśyapa, grows in mud which is [like] manure, so the qualities of a Buddha, Kāśyapa, [which] a *bodhisattva* [aspires after] grow in the 'mud' of mental defilements which are [like] manure with sentient beings who are given to what is wrong." The verses:

Just as the lotus grows in muddy water which is [like]
Manure[166] and never on dry land, so the Conqueror's
Qualities [after which] his spiritual sons [aspire] 'grow'
In this world with [all] its defilements and falsity.

76

"Just as if the four great oceans, Kāśyapa, overflowed with ghee, so one should regard a *bodhisattva*'s achievement of his 'roots of merit'." The verses:

Just as if the four great oceans overflowed with ghee,
Pure and greatly appreciated by everybody, so a
Bodhisattva, the Blessed One's spiritual son, should

166 Lit.: 'containing sweepings'.

Be seen as constantly 'overflowing' with a stream
Of stream of goodness.

77

"Just as someone, Kāśyapa, would take out of the four great oceans a drop of water on the tip of a strand of a hundredth part of a hair,[167] so, Kāśyapa, one should regard a Disciple's achievement of his 'roots of merit' [as being comparatively minimal]." The verses:

Just as a person would take out of [that] body of
Water[168] a drop on the tip of [a strand of] a hundredth
Part **(40a)** of a hair,[169] so you should regard[170] the goodness
That a Disciple has accomplished and is endowed with.

78

"The insight-knowledge achieved by a Disciple, Kāśyapa, should be likened to the space within a mustard-seed bored by a worm." The verses:

The space within[171] a mustard-seed bored by a worm
Is indeed small; the insight-knowledge achieved by a
Disciple, you should know, is equally small and minute.

79

"The insight-knowledge achieved by a *bodhisattva*, Kāśyapa, should be likened to space [extending] in the ten directions."[172] The verses:

Just as space extends in the ten directions, in the
Whole **(40b)** world and without obstruction, so you

---

167 Lit.: 'on the tip of a strand of a hair split into a hundred pieces'.

168 As for °*rāśito*, see BHSG § 10.133 (abl. sg.).

169 Tentatively after BHSG § 7.22: miscellaneous accusatives – *vālam* here genitive.

170 As for *paśyatha*, see BHSG § 26.13.

171 As for *abhyaṃtarita*, see BHSD, p. 60.

172 I.e. including the four intermediate points and the two locations 'above and below'.

Should regard the insight-knowledge, foremost in
The whole world, achieved by a *bodhisattva.*[173]

80

"Let us suppose, Kāśyapa, the chief queen consort, [married to a duly] anointed king endowed with sovereignty, has an adulterous relationship with a pauper to whom afterwards a son is born. What do you think, Kāśyapa? Should that [child be called] a prince?" – "By no means, Exalted One," [Kāśyapa replied]. – "Similarly, Kāśyapa," the Exalted One continued, "my Disciples[174] should not be declared worthy of being consecrated the Tathāgata's spiritual sons although they have come forth from the realm of the *dharma.*" The verses:

Just as if a beautiful queen consort would cohabit
With a pauper and the son she consequently gives
Birth to **(41a)** would [neither] be [recognized] as a
Prince nor as the [would-be] king, so the Disciples,
[Though] free from desire, are not at all worthy of being
Consecrated my spiritual sons. This is due to the fact that[175]
They strive for their own welfare; the Buddha's spiritual
Sons work for both their own and others' sake.

81

"Let us [again] suppose, Kāśyapa, a [duly] anointed king endowed with sovereignty has an affair with a very low female servant and that afterwards a son is born to him. Although a very low female servant would have given birth to his [son],[176] one should nevertheless call him a prince. Similarly, Kāśyapa, at any rate a *bodhisattva* should be declared the Tathāgata's **(41b)** spiritual son, even though he [may] have just started aspiring after

[173] Lit. '*bodhisattvas*'; see above n. 64.

[174] Re *śrāvakār dharma°*, see BHSG § 4.42 (VD n. 201).

[175] Lit.: 'that is to say'.

[176] Lit.: 'he is born from the presence of ...'

[supreme enlightenment], not [yet] being able, while wandering through the round of rebirths, to lead beings." The verses:

Just as a universal monarch, while cohabiting with
A female servant, may father a son whom [later on]
The world addresses as 'prince', though he is born of
A female servant, so a *bodhisattva* is called the
Conqueror's spiritual son, 'a pure being', [though] he
May have just started aspiring after [Buddhahood],
Wandering through the 'triple states of existence'[177]
And wanting in ability to lead[178] beings through
His skill in means [such as] liberality.

82

"A universal monarch, for instance, Kāśyapa, might have a thousand sons; should, however, none among them[179] bear the characteristic marks of a universal monarch, then [none of them] would be recognized as the universal monarch's son. Similarly, Kāśyapa, even though the Tathāgata is surrounded by countless[180] Disciples, yet none [of them] **(42a)** is a *bodhisattva*, then none is recognized as the Tathāgata's spiritual son." The verses:

Just as a king might have a thousand sons but not
Even one [of them] would bear the marks [of a
Universal monarch], all [of them] thus being unable
To carry[181] the burden [of universal rule, and as] then
[None] among them [would] be recognized as [son]
Of the chief of men, so the Buddha is surrounded by
Many crores [of Disciples]. Should, however, none
Among them be a *bodhisattva*, none of them is

---

177 See BHSD, p. 258, s.v. *tribhava*.

178 As for *vinayaṃn*, tentatively taken as infinitive after BHSG §§ 35.4, 36.20. Tib. has *sems can mi 'dul yaṅ*, 'although he does not discipline beings' – cf. the reading of SH.

179 Lit.: 'there, in this respect'.

180 Lit.: 'hundreds of thousands of crores'.

181 As for *voḍhū*, see BHSG §§ 3.3, 36.5.

Recognized as the Blessed One's spiritual son –
On the grounds that a *bodhisattva* is not there.

83

"The chief queen consort, Kāśyapa, of a universal monarch may be, for example, pregnant with a son [who], seven days [after conception already], bears the characteristic marks of a universal monarch; although he is [being carried] in the womb, his sense faculties are [still] undeveloped and he is in an embryonic stage of development in respect of his 'great primary elements', on that occasion the divinities are all the more[182] delighted;[183] **(42b)** [their delight], however, does not [refer] to the [other] princes who are strong, swift, smart and have stamina. For what reason? Because he, [still developing in the womb,] will live to [ensure] the continuation of the *cakravartin* lineage. Similarly, Kāśyapa, a *bodhisattva* who has just started aspiring after [supreme enlightenment and] whose spiritual faculties[184] are undeveloped, still is in an 'embryonic stage of development in respect of his great primary elements' [(under the influence) of the mental defilements].[185] In that case, however, the divinities who had met the previous Buddhas, are all the more delighted. [Their delight,] though, does not [refer] to the *arhat*s who, in their meditation, abide in the eight [kinds of] liberation.[186] For what reason? Because he, [still under the influence of the mental defilements, though], will live to [ensure] the continuation of the Buddha lineage." The verses:

Just as a universal monarch's chief queen consort
Is pregnant with a being [endowed] with the 'marks'
And merit [on which account] the divinities are all
The more delighted, not [because] of the [other]
Princes [in spite of their] strength, [so] because of a

---

[182] As for *balavantatarā*, in the verse section *balavaṃtaraṃ* (em. *balavattaraṃ* (VD n. 209)), Tib. has *śin tu stobs daṅ ldan pas, stobs daṅ ldan pas – balavattaraṃ, balīyas*; see Negi 1993ff. s.v.

[183] Re *spṛham*, VD n. 207: acc. sg. fem.; cf. BHSG § 9.16.

[184] See BHSD, p. 115, s.v. *indriya*.

[185] Enclosed words in brackets after Tib.

[186] See BHSD, p. 497, s.v. *vimokṣa*.

Bodhisattva, practising single-mindedly (**43a**) while
Wandering through the round of rebirths in his
Quest of [187] Buddhahood, the divinities and *nāgas* are
Delighted, not because of the Disciples who, in their
Meditation, abide in the three [kinds of] liberation.[188]

84

"The chick of the Indian cuckoo, Kāśyapa, for example, [though] it is [still] contained in the egg and has not yet opened its eyes, surpasses all other birds which is [due to] its sonorous and melodious distinct note. Similarly, Kāśyapa, a *bodhisattva* who has just started aspiring after [supreme enlightenment], surpasses all Disciples and Pratyekabuddhas,[189] [although] he is still contained in the 'egg of ignorance', his eyes [still] being covered with 'the film of karmic darkness and of the dimness of the mental defilements'. [He surpasses others] because of his 'note of accomplishment' in dedicating his 'roots of merit'[190] [to all beings].[191]... (**43b**)

85

"Just as a single [semi-] precious stone, [viz.] a lapis lazuli, Kāśyapa, surpasses [in value] a heap[192] – even of the size of Mount Sumeru – of crystal,[193] so a *bodhisattva*, Kāśyapa, who has just set out on his way [to Buddhahood], surpasses all Disciples and Pratyekabuddhas." The verses:

---

[187] Re *ghaṭamāna*, see BHSG § 8.11: loc. sg. (VD n. 210).

[188] See BHSD, *ibid.*, s.v. *vimokṣa.*

[189] Re °*buddhām* for °*buddhān*, see BHSG § 8.90 (VD).

[190] Lit.: 'note and sound of accomplishment in the practice of diverting to [all beings' use] his roots of merit'.

[191] Since the remaining portion of this section is virtually identical with the prose part of KP section 86, its translation is given below in that section. As for another comparison of the *bodhisattva* with the *karaviṅka*, cf. Vaidya 1961: 7, 11ff., with a quotation from the *Ratnakaraṇḍakasūtra*; on this comparison, with further references, see also de Jong 1977: 255.

[192] Re *rāśi* for *rāśiṃ*, see BHSG § 10.48.

[193] Re °*maṇikān* for *maṇikānām*, see BHSG § 8.118 (VD n. 215).

Just as a brightly shining lapis lazuli surpasses
[In value] any amount of crystal, so a *bodhisattva*
[Who has] just begun to aspire [after Buddhahood],
Surpasses a multitude of different Disciples.[194]

86

(44a) "[Here is another] comparison, Kāśyapa: As soon as the chief queen consort of a [universal] monarch has given birth to a son [bearing the marks of a *cakravartin*], everybody will do obeisance to him - guild-leaders, townsfolk, country people and vassal princes. Similarly, Kāśyapa, no sooner has a *bodhisattva* started aspiring after [supreme enlightenment] than the world, including its divinities, does obeisance [to him]." The verses:

Just as to the [supreme] ruler, to the Lord of the
World, a son is born whose body is adorned with
The 'marks', to whom vassal princes and townsmen
Will do obeisance as soon as they have seen the newly
Born prince, so, with a trusting heart and great respect,
The world with its divinities pays homage to the
Bodhisattva as soon as he has appeared, the royal
Scion of the Conqueror, endowed with the 'marks'.[195]

87

"All medicinal [herbs], for example, Kāśyapa, growing [in] the Himālaya, the king of mountains, are **(44b)** without desire, without avarice[196] and false discrimination. Whenever they are given for a disease they cure it. Similarly, Kāśyapa, all the medicine of insight-knowledge that a *bodhisattva* provides who has just set out on his way [to Buddhahood], that he pro-

---

194 Lit.: 'multitudes having different Disciples'.

195 The *upamā* of the vassal princes following the *cakravartin* is already employed at *Saṃyuttanikāya* II (Kashyap 1959a): 371, or at *Aṅguttaranikāya* III, IV (Kashyap 1960a): 78, 116 respectively: Appamādasutta. As for the 'marks', cf. sections 23–28 above.

196 Tib.: 'unprejudiced'.

vides, being free from false discrimination; he gives medical care to all beings [with] a mind [regarding all] as equal." The verses:

> The medicinal [herbs] growing in the Himālaya,
> The king of mountains,[197] are not selfish and do not
> Falsely discriminate. Whenever administered, they
> Cure the disease; some also rejuvenate. Likewise
> The Conqueror's spiritual sons provide, free
> From false discrimination, the medicine of insight-
> Knowledge. They provide everything [that is]
> For the good of beings and give [them] medical
> Care with a mind [regarding all] as equal.

88

"Just as **(45a)** the new moon indeed is worshipped and certainly not the full moon, Kāśyapa, so by those who put trust in me, Kāśyapa a *bodhisattva* should be revered all the more,[198] [but] not the Tathāgata. For what reason? [Because] it is from the *bodhisattvas* that the Tathāgatas originate." The verses:

> Everybody worships the new moon, but not the full
> [Moon]; similarly, he who puts trust in [me], let him
> Pay homage to a *bodhisattva*, the Conqueror's spiritual
> Son,[199] but not to the Conqueror[200] [himself].

89

"Just as [the taking note of] tabulated summarie[s], Kāśyapa, precedes an understanding of and knowledge about all treatises, so a *bodhisattva*'s beginning to aspire after [supreme enlightenment], Kāśyapa, precedes all incomparable miracles and powers of an Enlightened One."

---

[197] As for ... *parvatarāja*, cf. BHSG § 8.11; Karashima 2002: 49, § 9.1: Stems in *-a* as locative.

[198] Lit.: 'stronger'.

[199] As for *jinātmajo*, see BHSG § 8.36: acc. sg.

[200] Re *jinā*, see BHSG § 8.38: acc. sg.

90

"Just as **(45b)** nobody, Kāśyapa, would ever dismiss the moon's disk and worship[201] first a [faintly luminous] heavenly body, a star, so the wise would never dismiss[202] a *bodhisattva* who has practised according to my instructions[203] and pay homage [first] to a Disciple." The verses:

> Nobody would ever worship heavenly bodies, having
> Ignored[204] the moon. Similarly, one would never pay
> Homage to a Disciple, having disregarded a spiritual son
> Of mine who has practised according to [my] instruc-
> tions.[205]

91

"Let us suppose, Kāśyapa, the [whole] world, including its gods, would polish a crystal; that crystal [, however,] would never become a lapis lazuli, a [semi-] precious stone. Similarly, Kāśyapa, a Disciple will never **(46a)** take his seat on the 'throne of enlightenment' and attain the highest, full and complete enlightenment, even though he is possessed of all [the accomplishment of] virtue, learning, of the qualities of someone who is purified [through ascetic practices] and of concentration." The verses:

> Just as the world with its gods would polish a
> Crystal so as to make it become[206] a lapis lazuli –
> The crystal would never become one [because of]
> Its being just of a different kind –, so a Disciple,
> Although he is possessed of virtue, learning, [the
> Accomplishment of] meditation and of all qualities

---

[201] Re *namaskṛta* for *namaskṛtaṃ*, cf. BHSG § 6.1ff.

[202] Lit.: 'leave behind'.

[203] Re *śikṣāpratipanna*, see BHSG § 8.32: acc. sg. masc.

[204] Lit.: 'avoided'.

[205] Cf. the *upamā* of the 'light of the stars not worth a sixteenth part of the light of the moon' at *Saṃyuttanikāya* II (Kashyap 1959a): 371: Aniccasaññāsutta; *Aṅguttaranikāya* II (Kashyap 1960a): 300: Sumanasutta; *ibid.* III: 78: Appamādasutta (a); *ibid.* IV: 116: Appamādasutta (b); *Khuddakanikāya* III, 1 (Kashyap 1959b): 379: Sambhavajātaka.

[206] Lit.: 'for purification'.

[Resulting from ascetic practices], will not sit on the
'Throne of enlightenment' and become a Blessed One
After defeating Māra and realizing enlightenment.

92

"When, for example, an impressive [specimen of] the [semi-] precious stone lapis lazuli is polished,[207] Kāśyapa, this[208] will be a means to make hundreds and thousands of *karṣāpaṇa* coins. Similarly, Kāśyapa, when the 'polishing' of a *bodhisattva*[209] is accomplished, **(46b)** this will be a means [to cause] hundreds and thousands of Disciples and Pratyekabuddhas to appear." The verses:

[When] a precious lapis lazuli is polished, it will
Bring many *karṣāpaṇas*. Similarly, the 'polishing'[210]
Of the Buddha's spiritual sons will 'bring
Forth' indeed numerous Disciples.

93

Again the Exalted One addressed the Elder Mahā-Kāśyapa: "The country, Kāśyapa, in which is found the [worm called] 'camel-smoke', black-headed and lying on its back, that country is in distress, is afflicted and in despair. If, however, Kāśyapa, there is a *bodhisattva* in the country, it will not be in distress, [it will be] without affliction and free from despair. Therefore, **(47a)** Kāśyapa, a *bodhisattva* should work for the sake of beings. He should duly collect all 'roots of merit' and [then] offer them all to all beings. He who is in quest of the medicine[211] of [supreme] knowledge should go in all directions and give 'real' medical care to all beings; it is the 'real' medical care that [all] beings should be given.

---

207 Re *parikarma*, cf. BHSG § 17.1 (*n*-stems adapted to the *a*-declension) and § 8.11 (loc. of *a*-stems).

208 Lit.: 'on that occasion'.

209 Tib.: 'the polishing of a *bodhisattva*'s merit'.

210 Re *parikarmanaṃ*, abl. sg. nt. (Karashima 2002: 55: § 14.2).

211 I.e. *bhaiṣajya* for MS *bheṣajya*.

94

"Then, Kāśyapa, what is 'real' medical care? The treatment for lust – that is [the contemplation of] foulness, the treatment for hatred is loving kindness, for delusion [one's] wisely contemplating dependent origination; the treatment for all wrong views is [the liberating insight into] emptiness, for all fancying, false discrimination, imaginary assumption, conceiving ideas and fixing [them] in one's mind it is [the liberating insight into] signlessness,[212] **(47b)** for one's giving up all [attachment to] the world of sensual desire, fine-materiality and immateriality it is one's [liberating realization of] desirelessness; the treatment for all perverted [views] are the four [kinds of] factual [knowledge]: (1) the treatment for the false notion of permanence in respect of what is [actually] impermanent is [the insight that] all conditioned states are impermanent; (2) for the false notion of pleasure in respect of what is [actually] suffering it is [the insight that] all conditioned states are suffering; (3) for the false notion of [something] possessed of a self in respect of what is [actually] not possessed of a self it is [the insight that] all things are without self and (4) for the false notion of beauty in respect of what is [actually] foulness it is [the insight that real beauty is] the peace [of] *nirvāṇa*.

95

"The medical care given to those dependent on the body, feelings, on mind and mind-objects [in terms of 'I' and 'mine'] is the four[fold] application of mindfulness: Engaged in contemplating one's body with regard to the body[213] and one's feelings **(48a)** with regard to feelings, one does not, in doing so, fall [prey] to the wrong view that a self [exists]; engaged in contemplating one's mind with regard to mind and mind-objects with regard to mind-objects, one does not, in doing so, fall [prey] to the wrong view that a soul or personality [ultimately exist]. The treatment for getting rid of all that is karmically unwholesome are the four [kinds of] right exer-

---

[212] Cf. the lexicographical definition of 'sign' as 'an event, an action or a fact that shows that something really exists or is happening'.

[213] I.e. contemplating bodily aspects with one-pointedness of mind by directing one's mindfulness to them again and again.

tion[214] conducive to the accomplishment of all that is karmically wholesome. The medical care conducive to getting rid of attachment to body and mind – as a whole [supposed to constitute a self] –,[215] are the four bases for success.[216] The treatment for faithlessness, indolence, forgetfulness, inattention, carelessness and obtuseness are the five spiritual faculties [or] powers,[217] and bewilderment[218] **(48b)** and spiritual ignorance in respect of the *dharma* are cured by the seven enlightenment factors. The noble eightfold path is the treatment for the weak-minded, for all false teachers and those gone astray. This, Kāśyapa, is what is to be understood[219] by 'real' medical care which a *bodhisattva* should zealously provide.

96

"Of all[220] doctors or their assistants in Jambudvīpa, Kāśyapa, Jīvaka, 'the king of doctors', is reckoned[221] foremost. [If], Kāśyapa, all the beings in the world system [consisting] of a 'triple thousand great thousand' [worlds] were like Jīvaka, 'the king of doctors', and [if] they were asked,[222] 'Which is the medicine [to cure] him who is rooted in – his downfall – [wrong] views and mental disturbance?' – they would be unable[223] to reply and describe [the medicine because of their] **(49a)** not knowing [it]. A *bodhisattva* then, Kāśyapa, should deliberate thus: 'I must not be satisfied with worldly medicine; I must search for[224] the supramundane medicine of insight-knowledge and do my best to collect all 'roots of merit'.' Thus he should deliberate. When he has acquired the medicine of [supreme] knowledge, he should go

---

214 See BHSD, pp. 380, 389 s.v. *pradhāna, prahāṇa.*

215 Cf. Sthiramati (Staël-Holstein 1933: 170): *phan tshun du ṅa rgyal gyis mṅon par zin pa de'i gñen por rdzu 'phrul gyi rkaṅ pa rnams so* | 'The four bases for success are the remedy (*pratikāra*) for one in the grip of self-consciousness (*ahaṃkāra*) concerning (*prati*) [body and mind]'.

216 See BHSD, p. 151f. s.v. *ṛddhipāda.*

217 See above section 83, n. 184.

218 I.e. °*sammūḍha*° for MS °*samūha*°.

219 Lit.: 'is called'.

220 Lit.: 'as many as'.

221 Lit.: 'is called'.

222 Re *paripṛcchyeran* for *paripṛccheran*, cf. BHSG § 37.32 (VD n. 236).

223 Re *śaknonti* for *śaknoti*, cf. BHSG § 28.62 (VD n. 237).

224 I.e. *paryeṣṭavyaṃ/°eṣitavyaṃ* (Karashima 2009: 392) for MS °*eṣṭitavyaṃ.*

in all directions and give 'real' medical care to all beings; it is the 'real' medical care that [all] beings should be given.[225]

97

"Then which is the supramundane medicine of insight-knowledge? It is the insight-knowledge[226] of causes and conditions, of concentration on 'facts' [as being] not-self, without a being, without a soul, without individuality or personality; it is fearlessness with regard to 'facts' being baseless because of their being empty, and it is **(49b)** the exertion of contemplating[227] [one's] mind. One contemplates one's mind, [pondering] thus: Which mind is passionate, malicious or confused? Is it one's past, one's future or present mind? In case of its being past, it no longer exists; one's future mind has not yet occurred, and one's present mind is evanescent.

98

"The mind, to be sure, Kāśyapa, does not occur within, or outside, or in between both. The mind, to be sure, Kāśyapa, is formless, unseen, unobstructive, without appearance, without designation, unsupported and abodeless.[228] The mind, Kāśyapa, has never been seen by any of the Buddhas; they are neither seeing it, nor will they see it.[229] What none of the Buddhas **(50a)** have [ever] seen, what they are not seeing and what they will not see, how should one consider its 'occurrence' unless [in the sense] that 'facts' occur on account of mistaken perception.[230] The mind, to be sure, Kāśyapa, is like an illusion; having falsely imagined what [actually] is unreal, it grabs manifold states of existence. The mind ... is like the wind,

---

225 Cf. the last sentence of section 93 in the Devanāgarī text; as for *satvāni*, see BHSG § 8.86: nom. pl. masc. *-āni*.

226 Re °*jñānaṃ* for *jñānaḥ*, see BHSG § 6.12.

227 Lit.: 'looking intently for'; re *parigaveṣatāye*, see BHSD, p. 321, s.v. *parigaveṣatā*. As for the foll., cf. Conze 1954: 162. In n. 1 on p. 162, Conze points out that 'this meditation is a development of the mindfulness as to mind' described in the *Satipaṭṭhānasutta*.

228 Cf. above section 56, n. 144.

229 ŚS omits *paśyiṣyanti*.

230 Transl. after Tib., tallying with the reading of ŚS.

blowing here and there,[231] elusive and without manifesting itself. The mind ... is like the current of a river, fleeting, broken up as soon as formed and dissolving. The mind ... is like the flame of a lamp, occurring/shining through causes and conditions.

99

"The mind, to be sure, Kāśyapa, is like lightning, transient, coming to an end in an instant. The mind ... is like space, being defiled by adventitious defilements.[232] **(50b)** The mind ..., desiring sense objects, is like a monkey because of its being involved in[233] multifarious action. The mind ... is like a painter because of its shaping multifarious action. The mind ... is fleeting because of the occurrence of divers mental defilements [in conjunction with it]. The mind ... occurs singly[234] because no second mind [instant] coincides with it. The mind ... is like a king because it rules over[235] all 'facts'. The mind ... is like an enemy because it causes all suffering.

100

"The mind, to be sure, Kāśyapa, is like a sandcastle[236] due to its false notion of permanence with regard to what is impermanent.[237] The mind ... is like a bluebottle due to its false notion of purity with regard to what is impure.[238]

---

231 Lit.: 'far-going'; as for *dūraṃgamam ...*, cf. *Khuddakanikāya* I (Kashyap 1959b): 20 (Dhammapada, v. 37 (or the corresponding v. in its various parallel versions)).

232 Cf. *Aṅguttaranikāya* I (Kashyap 1960a): 10: *pabhassaram idaṃ, bhikkhave, cittaṃ | taṃ ca kho āgantukehi upakkilesehi upakkiliṭṭhaṃ* ... According to Sthiramati (Staël-Holstein 1933: 175), since the mental defilements are not conducive to purification (*rnam par dag par mi ruṅ ste* (*na yujyante*)) so that liberation (*mokṣa*) cannot be realized (*thar par mi 'thad do*) and in order to get rid of one's faults (*ñes pa spaṅ ba'i phyir* (*doṣaprahāṇāya*)), the mind has been likened to space (*nam mkha' daṅ mtshuṅs par ston to*) (symbolizing purity).

233 Lit.: 'standing together-ness'.

234 Cf. above section 98, n. 231 (Dhammapada v. 37).

235 As for *adhipateyā* (cf. Pāli *adhipatiya*), see BHSD, p. 13, s.v. *adhipatya*; re °*pateyā*, see BHSG § 8.46: abl. sg. -*ā*.

236 Lit.: '°house'.

237 Tib.: ' ... due to its destroying all 'roots of merit''.

238 Tib. in this place: 'The mind ... is like dew due to its false notion of permanence ...'

The mind ... (**52a**) is like a fish-hook due to its false notion of pleasure with regard to what is suffering. The mind ... is like a dream due to its false notion of what is possessed of a self with regard to what is without self. The mind ... is like an adversary because it causes divers agony. The mind ... is like a blood[239]-sucking ghost because it always searches for [an opportunity of] alighting on something.[240] The mind ... is like a fiend because it always searches for [an opportunity of] taking delight in[241] shortcomings.

101

"The mind, to be sure, Kāśyapa, always has its ups and downs and is [always] afflicted with [the dilemma of] being 'for or against'. The mind ... is like a thief because it steals all 'roots of merit'. The mind ... enjoys colourful forms like a butterfly's eye, ... sounds like (**52b**) a battle-drum, ... it always enjoys smells like a pig on a muck [heap],[242]... tastes like a female servant savouring the remains of dainties,[243]... touch[ables] like a fly in a pot of sesamum oil.

102

"The mind, to be sure, Kāśyapa, when it is contemplated, is not found, and what is not found does not occur. What does not occur, that is not past, future or present. What is not past, future or present, that is entirely beyond the three [dimensions of] time. What is entirely beyond them, that neither is nor is not. What neither is nor is not, that is unborn. What is unborn, has no individual essence; what has no individual essence, does not come into existence; what does not (**53a**) come into existence, is not annihilated; what is not annihilated, does not cease; [where there is] no cessation, there is no coming and going, neither death nor rebirth. Where there is no coming and going, neither death nor rebirth, there are no con-

239 Lit.: 'bodily strength'.

240 ŚS reading: ' ... searches for weak spots'.

241 Tib. has no equivalent of *ārāma*.

242 After the ŚS reading; for MS *mīḍakuṇape* read *mīḍha°* ('on a corpse in faeces').

243 After the ŚS reading; MS: 'like a female servant with regard to dainties to be enjoyed'.

ditioned states whatever – that is the unconditioned, that is the 'lineage of the Noble Ones'.

103

"As for the 'lineage of the Noble Ones', there is no moral conduct, no basis [of it] and no non-basis. Where there is no moral conduct, no basis [of it] and no non-basis, there is no disregard of moral conduct. Where there is no disregard of it, there is neither restraint nor non-restraint. Where there is neither restraint nor non-restraint, there is no practising, no non-practising and no application. Where these are not, there is no mind and there are no mental concomitants [as] 'facts'. **(53b)** Where these are not, there is no mind [element] and there is no consciousness [as individual essence]. Where these are not, there is no action and there is no result [of action]. In their absence there are neither pleasure nor suffering. Where these are not – that [refers to] the 'lineage of the Noble Ones'. As for this lineage, there is no action and no performance of action, and in this lineage no bodily, vocal or mental action is performed. Moreover, in this lineage there is no differentiation between deficiency, superiority and what is middling. Because of its being like space, this lineage is 'oneness'; it is absolute 'oneness' because all 'facts' have one and the same flavour, [namely that of being without individual essence].

104

"This lineage is free because of its 'holy indifference' to body and mind. Unsullied by any mental defilements, this lineage is taintless and 'conforms to' *nirvāṇa*. This lineage is desireless **(54a)** and rid of egotism and selfish attachment. It originates with the identity of what actually exists and what does not exist and is [thus] in [perfect] harmony. Because of the ultimate truth this lineage is [at one with] the Truth; it is absolutely unborn and [thus] imperishable; it lasts forever because of the everlasting true nature of things. Because *nirvāṇa* is the highest, this lineage is [supreme] happiness;[244] it is [ultimately real] 'beauty' without any blemish whatsoever; it is not [related to] a self because a self is not ascertain[able even if] one

244 After Tib. and Sthiramati (Staël-Holstein 1933: 204, 15).

searches for it intently. This lineage is pure because of its being absolutely holy.

105

"[I advise my disciples,] Kāśyapa, [thus]: Look within, do not rush around the outside [world]. For what reason? In the future, Kāśyapa, there will be monks resembling dogs chasing after lumps of earth [thrown at them]. How [is it], Kāśyapa, [that] monks will bear (**54b**) such a resemblance? A dog, for example, Kāśyapa, scared away by a clod, will pursue that very clod, not him who has thrown it. Similarly, Kāśyapa, there will be some ascetics and brahmins who, afraid of the [potential] dangers of forms, sounds, smells, tastes and touch[ables], will abide in forests. [Although] they will lead their solitary lives there as hermits in strict seclusion, [sooner or later] they will encounter seductive and at once stimulating[245] forms, ... and touch[ables]. Then paying attention [to them][246] and diverting themselves, they will become addicted to worldly pleasures.[247]

106

"They will not understand, it will be beyond their grasp as to how to be immune[248] to [the lures of] forms, ... (**55a**) and touch[ables]. Ignorant, unaware of the disadvantage [inherent in] their enjoying the sense objects and [not knowing how to] be immune to the [enticements] and having made their way to villages, towns, market-places, districts or to the capital, they will come to harm again because of [the lures of] the sense objects. When [those] forest dwellers will have died, they will be reborn in a heaven [because of their] having been restraint-based [ascetics] with worldly [interests]. Even there they will come to harm because of [the lures of] the

[245] Re *tajja(k)kriyā* (not in Tib.) tentatively rendered as a *bahuvrīhi* compound, lit.: 'of instantaneous action'; cf. Karashima 2002: 62, n. 150 (obscure words).
[246] Tib.: *btaṅ sñoms su 'jog ciṅ* (*audāsīnyaṃ kalayantaḥ* – after Negi 1993ff. s.v.), 'being negligent'.
[247] Tib. additionally: *naṅ du so sor rtog pa la mṅon par mi brtson te* (*adhyātmaṃ pratyavekṣānabhiyuktāḥ*), 'without applying themselves to thoroughly looking within'.
[248] Lit.: 'escape'.

five heavenly strands of sensual desire.[249] After their death as divinities,[250] as before, they will not have escaped the four evil states, [viz. that of] the hells, the existence as animals, in Yama's realm [as ghosts] or as *asuras*. Thus, Kāśyapa, monks will resemble dogs **(55b)** chasing after lumps of earth.

107

"How, Kāśyapa, will a monk not resemble a dog chasing after a lump of earth? The monk, Kāśyapa, who will not, having been abused, beaten, reviled, derided or exasperated, in return abuse, beat, revile, deride or exasperate.[251] He will look within, wisely contemplating [his states of] mind [and meditating on the question]: Who has been abused, beaten, reviled, derided or exasperated? Thus, Kāśyapa, a monk will not resemble a dog chasing after a lump of earth." The verses:

As a dog, being scared away by a clod, chases after
The clod, not after [him] who has thrown it, just so
There will be some ascetics or brahmins who, afraid
Of sense objects, will take to forest-dwelling. **(56a)**
When they, dwelling in the jungle, will have come
Across[252] enticing sense objects, they will be
Negligent, not knowing their inner selves. Not
Knowing as to how to avoid[253] the misery[254] [inherent
In the unrestrained enjoyment of sense objects],
They will take again to inhabited places, and [thus]

---

249 I.e. 'the objects of the five senses'; see BHSD, p. 177 s.v. *kāmaguṇa*.

250 Lit.: 'fallen from that place'.

251 Cf. *Bhikṣuṇī-Vinaya* (Roth 1970): 51, § 69: *catvāraḥ śramaṇīka(kā)rakā dharmā ākhyātā* | *ākruṣṭāya na pratyākrośitavyaṃ roṣitāya na pratiroṣitavyaṃ* | *bhaṇḍitāya na pratibhaṇḍitavyaṃ tāḍitāya na pratitāḍitavyaṃ* ||

At § 69, n. 1, Roth also refers to a *Karmavācanā* parallel: "the four qualifications which determine a *śramaṇa* (*śramaṇa-kāraka-dharmā*)." Cf. also *Khuddakanikāya* IV, 1 (Kashyap 1960b): 341, 8f.: *akkosantaṃ na paccakkoseyya, rosantaṃ nappaṭiroseyya, bhaṇḍanaṃ nappaṭibhaṇḍeyya*.

252 As for *eta* (*ā*+√*i*), 'come near, reached', see Weller 1965: 126, n. 3.

253 Lit.: 'which means to get rid of'.

254 Re *ādīnavān*, see BHSG § 8.124: gen. pl. (VD n. 253).

They will come to harm again because of [alluring]
Forms ... So after enjoying heavenly pleasures and
After their death – some [having left] celestial [worlds,
Others that of] human beings[255] –, some will be reborn in
Evil state[s].[256] The Blessed One has compared them to
Dogs [chasing after] clods who in their bewilderment,
Existence after existence,[257] will have to suffer, thus
Being in the grip of so much pain. The Conqueror has
Not likened him to a dog [chasing after a clod], who
Will not, [himself] abused and beaten, abuse [and beat]
In return; who will not, himself reviled, revile anybody,
Not deriding others in return, derided [though]
Himself, not exasperating [but remaining] calm,
Himself [though] exasperated [by others], following
Virtuous conduct of such a kind [while] seeking to
Pacify his mind by being mindful and introspectively
[Counteracting each defilement] by its opposite.[258] **(56b)**

108

"Let us suppose, Kāśyapa, [there is] a charioteer who is an expert at breaking in horses. In any place on earth where there is a horse that stumbles, rears or acts viciously,[259] there he tames it. He tames it in such a way that it will no longer be unruly. Similarly, Kāśyapa, a monk who applies himself to spiritual discipline exercises self-control [by being particularly mindful] whenever he becomes aware that his mind is wandering. He 'tames' his mind in such a way that it will no longer be 'unruly.' " The verses:

There may be, for instance, a charioteer,
Expert at [breaking in] horses, and [whenever]

---

[255] Re *cyutāś ca ... manujaiś ca* ('fallen from ...'), see BHSG § 7.35: instr. for abl.

[256] As for °*bhūmiḥ*, see BHSG § 10.60: nom. sg. for acc.

[257] Lit.: 'again and again fallen from'.

[258] Cf. above KP section 94.

[259] After BHSD, p. 121 s.v. *utkumbhati*; see also Karashima 2002: 59, n. 121–123; re *khaḍuṃka*, Pāli *khaḷuṅka*, cf. *Aṅguttaranikāya* III (Kashyap 1960a): 301f.: Assakhaḷuṅkasutta.

A horse is stumbling, **(57a)** he takes hold of[260] it.
Similarly, a meditator, on becoming aware
That his mind is wandering, exercises
Self-control so that it will calm down.[261]

109

"Just as compression of the throat, Kāśyapa, affects all faculties of the senses and endangers one's life, so of all wrong views, Kāśyapa, attachment to the self [-view] endangers the 'life' of the Teaching." The verses:

Just as compression of the throat certainly
Endangers one's life and causes but one's suffering,
So among the wrong views the self-view is likely
To destroy the very 'life' of the Teaching.

110

"Just as a person, Kāśyapa, should indeed be freed from whatever he is bound to, so [one's] mind, Kāśyapa, should indeed be freed from whatever **(57b)** it clings to." The verses:

Just as a person who is tightly bound should be freed
From all [fetters], so a meditator should free his
Bewildered mind from whatever it is attached to.

111

"[There are,] Kāśyapa, these two [kinds of] attachment [as useless as attachment to] vacuity[262] pertaining to someone who has gone forth into

---

260 Re °*graheti*, see BHSG, p. 211 s.v.

261 As for the *assadamaka* and the 'thoroughbred colt' *upamā*, see *Majjhimanikāya* II (Kashyap 1958b): 129f.: Bhaddālisutta. On the Āgama parallels see also Anālayo 2011: 358ff.

262 As for *paligodha* and [*pali*]*bodha* of the verse part below, in Tib. they have the same meaning. As Weller (1965: 127f, n. 19) points out, both terms are used interchangeably

homelessness. Which two? [Attachment in the way of] (a) his enquiring into materialistic lore and (b) his hoarding alms-bowls and robes. These are the two." The verses:

> Applying oneself constantly to putting
> Materialistic [lore] into practice and then
> One's hoarding alms-bowls and robes –
> These are established as the two [kinds of]
> Attachment [as useless as attachment to]
> Vacuity.[263] A *bodhisattva* should avoid them.

112

"These two strong fetters,[264] Kāśyapa, pertain to someone who has gone forth into homelessness. Which two? (a) There is the fetter of the self-view **(58a)** and (b) the fetter [in the way of] gain, honour and renown. These are the two ...[265] " The verses:

> The two strong fetters pertaining to an
> Ordained person are, [so] the Noble Ones have
> Said, the fetter of the [self-]view and the fetter
> [In the way of] gain, honour and fame. An
> Ordained person should always shun them.

113

"These two attitudes, Kāśyapa, prove an obstacle to someone who has gone forth ... Which are the two? (a) His predilection for the class of householders and (b) his aversion to the group of the Noble Ones. These are, Kāśyapa, the two attitudes ... " The verses:

---

in the 5th rock edict of Aśoka. Re *ākāśa*, the gloss in brackets after Sthiramati (Staël-Holstein 1933: 217), quoted at Weller, *ibid.*

263 See Karashima 2002: 51, § 9.7: Nom. du. masc. -*e*? 57b4: *ākāśabodhe* (read: °*godhe*?) *imi dve* (')*pratiṣṭhite*; *ibid.*, n. 37 (alternatively): "These two kinds of sky-like attachment ... are groundless."

264 Re *gāḍhabandhano*, see Karashima 2002: 51: § 9.8 Nom.-acc. du. nt. -*o*.

265 *Ibid.* § 9.9 Nom.-acc. du. nt. -*aṃ*?

One's predilection for the class of
Householders and one's finding fault with
The group of spiritual guides[266] – these two
Obstacles causing [serious] obstruction,
A **(58b)** *bodhisattva* should avoid.

114

"These two taints, Kāśyapa, pertain to someone who has gone forth ... Which two? (a) There is the [taint of] putting up with one's [own] mental defilements and (b) of one's taking to attachment to families of friends and to those that give alms food. These are, Kāśyapa, the two taints ..." The verses:

An ordained person's putting up with his
Mental defilements[267] and his predilection for
Friend[s] and families that give almsfood –
These two the Chief Conqueror has declared
Taints. A *bodhisattva* should avoid them.

115

"These two [attitudes], Kāśyapa, are [like] flashes of lightning striking down someone who has gone forth ... Which two? (a) His repudiation of the true *dharma* and (b) his enjoying what has been offered with faith [although he has] broken the rules of moral conduct.[268] These are, Kāśyapa, the two attitudes being [like] flashes of lightning striking down someone ..." The verses:

One's repudiating the true *dharma* **(59a)** and
Enjoying [almsfood although one has] broken the
Rules of moral conduct – these two [attitudes

266 Acc. to Tib. 'Noble Ones'.

267 Lit.: 'who, gone forth into homelessness, is likely to put up with *kleśa*s'.

268 Cf. above KP section 9.

Resembling] lethal flashes of lightning, the
[Spiritual] sons of the Protector of Men should avoid.

116

"There are, Kāśyapa, these two 'sores' of someone who has gone forth ... Which two? (a) His focusing on the faults of others and (b) hiding his own. These are, Kāśyapa, the two 'sores'..." The verses:

One's covering up one's own faults and
Observing those of others – these two 'sores,'
Like burning poison, the scrupulous should shun.

117

"There are, Kāśyapa, these two afflictions pertaining to someone who has gone forth ... Which two? (a) His wearing the yellow robes, though he is [full of] impure thoughts and (b) [in this state of mind] his accepting the service and homage done by persons of virtue and merit. These are, Kāśyapa, the two afflictions ..." **(59b)** The verses:

Wearing the yellow robes, though being [full of]
Impure thoughts, and [one's accepting] being
Honoured, worshipped, served and revered by the
Virtuous[269] – these two attitudes should be given up.[270]

118

"There are, Kāśyapa, these two [kinds of] lasting weakness pertaining to someone who has gone forth ... Which two? (a) His [theoretically] contemplating [states of] mind and [being] self-conceited, and (b) his dissuading those who have embarked upon the Great Vehicle from [following it]. These are, Kāśyapa, the two [kinds of] lasting weakness ..." The verses:

---

[269] Lit.: 'from the virtuous honouring, homage ...'

[270] Re *parivarjanīyā*, see Karashima 2002: 51: § 9.6 Nom.-acc. du. masc. -*ā*.

[Theoretical] contemplation of [states of] mind
[On the part] of the self-conceited and dissuasion
From the Buddha Vehicle[271] – these two the
Unequalled Conqueror has declared the two [kinds
Of] weakness pertaining to an ordained person.

119

"There are, Kāśyapa, these two debilities beyond remedy pertaining to someone who has gone forth ... Which two? **(60a)** (a) The state of repeatedly committing offences and (b) of not being rehabilitated.[272] These, Kāśyapa, are the two debilities beyond remedy ... [273]

120

"There are, Kāśyapa, these two [kinds of] mental torment pertaining to someone who has gone forth ... Which two? (a) His [having] broken rules of moral training and (b) dying without his having realized what is the heart [of the *dharma*]. These, Kāśyapa, are the two [kinds of] mental torment ..." The verses:

[One's] having broken rules of moral training
And one's death without having realized what is
The heart [of the *dharma*] – these are the two
[Kinds of] mental torment pertaining to an
Ordained person as the Omniscient One, the
Teacher of gods and men, has declared.

---

[271] Re *buddhayānaṃ*, see BHSD, p. 484 s.v. *vi(c)chandnā* : read °*yānād(t)*, abl.? Cf. above section 12, n. 46. See also Karashima 2002: 50: § 9.4.

[272] As for *avyutthānatā*, cf. *Saṅgītisūtra* (Stache-Rosen 1968: II.8): *āpatti-vyutthāna-kauśalya* ('expertise in regard to rehabilitation after an offence'); cf. also *Dīghanikāya* III (Kashyap 1958a): 169, 14: Saṅgītisutta.

[273] KP section 119 is missing in Tib.

121

"One always speaks of ascetics, Kāśyapa. How many [kinds of] ascetics then, Kāśyapa, [can] be mentioned? There are, Kāśyapa, these four [kinds of] ascetics. Which four? (1) There is the ascetic who [only] looks like a *śramaṇa* because of the colour [of his robes] and [other outer] marks of appearance; (2) the ascetic [of the second type] is a hypocrite, guarding [outwardly] proper conduct; (3) the ascetic [of the third type is interested just in] a name, in fame and praise, and (4) the ascetic [of the fourth type] actually practises in accordance with [the *dharma*]. **(60b)**

122

"Who then, Kāśyapa, [only] looks like an ascetic because of the colour [of his robes] and [other outer] marks of appearance? Here there is, Kāśyapa, some *śramaṇa* who, because of ... bears the [following outer] marks of appearance: He wears the outer patch-work robe, is shaven-headed and carries in his hands a shiny alms-bowl. Nonetheless, his behaviour, his bodily, vocal and mental actions are impure. He is unprincipled, caught up [in worldliness], uncurbed, restless, unguarded, misbehaving, greedy, lazy, a reprobate of wicked conduct. This is, Kāśyapa, the [so-]called [*śramaṇa*] who only looks like an ascetic because of ...

123

"Who then, Kāśyapa, is the ascetic who is a hypocrite, guarding [outwardly] proper conduct? **(61a)** Here there is, Kāśyapa, some *śramaṇa* who is on his best behaviour and meticulous in his conduct; he is perfectly mindful of his four postures and deportment (sitting, standing, lying, walking); he partakes of poor food and drink and is satisfied with the four [kinds of] 'noble usage;'[274] he neither has contacts with householders nor with those gone forth into homelessness; he is taciturn and monosyllabic. His deportment, [however,] is artificial because of his hypocrisy and [implicit] boasting and is not [conducive] to [real] self-restraint, calmness, purity and pea-

[274] See above KP section 6, n. 22; see also Karashima 2002: 52: § 9.16.2. Instr. pl. *-er*, *-e*.

ce of mind. He holds the wrong view that [things] are perceived as ['facts'].[275] When he hears that with respect to 'facts' [these] do not exist [ultimately] because of their being empty, he recoils, and [when] monks discourse on emptiness, he takes offence. This is, Kāśyapa, the [so-]called *śramaṇa* who is a hypocrite guarding proper conduct **(61b)** [outwardly].

124

"Who then Kāśyapa, is the ascetic [interested just in] a name, in fame and praise? Here there is, Kāśyapa, some *śramaṇa* who observes the rules of moral conduct after considering, 'How might others know me to be virtuous?' He masters the Teaching after considering, 'How might others know me to be erudite?' He stays in the jungle after considering, 'How might others know me to be a forest dweller?' Calculatingly he lives in solitude, is contented and easily satisfied – [but] just with a view to showing off and not for the sake of disgust for worldliness, freedom from passion, cessation [of suffering], ultimate peace and supreme enlightenment; not for the sake of [true] asceticism, of a life of purity, not for the sake of [realizing] *nirvāṇa*. This is, **(62a)** Kāśyapa, the [so-]called *śramaṇa* who is [interested just in] a name, in fame and praise.

125

"Who then, Kāśyapa, is the ascetic actually practising in accordance with [the *dharma*]? It is the monk, Kāśyapa, who does not set store by his body and life, let alone by gain, honour and renown.[276] When he hears that [all] things are empty, signless and undesired, he is pleased. He has realized [ultimate] truth and leads a life of purity, not even wishing [to realize] *nirvāṇa*, let alone [his] wishing for [any of] the three realms (of desire, fine-materiality or immateriality). He does certainly not set store by view[s] on emptiness, let alone on a self, on a being, on a soul, on individuality or personality. What he relies on is the [essence of] the *dharma*. Instead of seeking irrelevancies, he seeks inwardly to be ultimately free from the mental

[275] Tib. additionally has *ṅar 'dzin pa daṅ | ṅa yir 'dzin pa la gnas śiṅ* (*ahaṃkāra-mamakāra-samāśrita*), 'following [the way of] being arrogant and selfish'.

[276] Re °*śloke*, VD n. 282: I.e. instr. pl.

defilements. [By] realizing that all things are absolutely pure **(62b)** and by their very nature undefiled he relies on himself, not on others. He does not consider the Tathāgata even from the [angle of the essence of] the *dharma*, let alone [from that of] his bodily appearance. He does not adhere to the *dharma* even from the [angle of] passionlessness, let alone [from that of] declarations by the range of articulate speech. He does not form a mental image even of the Order of the Noble Ones [in relation to] the Unconditioned, let alone of an assembly of a group [of *saṅgha* members]. He is not intent on giving up anything [karmically unwholesome]; he neither strives to develop anything [karmically wholesome] nor to realize[277] anything. He neither 'thrives' in the round of rebirths nor 'enjoys' *nirvāṇa*; he neither seeks liberation nor bondage. Having understood that by their very nature all things are 'ultimately released', he neither moves about in the round of rebirths nor realizes final **(63a)** emancipation. This is, Kāśyapa, the description of the ascetic who actually practises in accordance with [the *dharma*]. One should exert oneself in conformity with[278] [the kind of] asceticism of actually practising in accordance with [the *dharma*]; one should not be [an ascetic] in name [only].[279] These are, Kāśyapa, the four [kinds of] ascetics." The verses:

126

He who is impure in his bodily, vocal and mental
[Actions], uncurbed, unguarded, misbehaving and
Greedy, shaven-headed, [wearing] the robes, an
Alms-bowl in his hands, is called an ascetic[280] [only]
Because of his outer marks of appearance. Though
Meticulous in his conduct and eating coarse food,
Though being fully endowd with the four [kinds of]
'Noble usage' and keeping far away from contacts, the
Second ascetic guarding proper conduct, **(63b)** [but]

---

[277] I.e. *sākṣātkriyāyai* for MS *sākṣīkkriyāya* (cf. BHSG §§ 9.55, 56).

[278] Re *śrāmaṇyā*, cf. BHSG § 8.42: instr. sg. -*ā*.

[279] Lit.: 'on account of the name'; Tib. *miṅ gis gnod par ni mi bya ste* (*nāmnā cāhitaṃ na kartavyam*), '... and because of the name no damage should be done'.

[280] Lit.: 'with regard to ascetics'.

Being a hypocrite, does by no means act[281] for the sake
Of [real] self-restraint, peace of mind and also disgust
For worldliness; when [all things are declared] empty
And signless, he recoils. The third ascetic is [interested
In] fame and praise; [through] his morality, learning,
Meditation and virtues [resulting from special] ascetic
Practices[282] he surprises others greatly;[283] his aim,
[However,] is neither peace of mind nor disgust for
Worldliness. He who does not set store by his body
Or life and turns his back on[284] gain and honour, does
Not wish for any of the realms of existence after
Hearing about the approaches to [ultimate] release.[285]
Having realized that [all] things are absolutely empty,
He neither sees extinction nor non-extinction.
Being free from desire, he always experiences the
[Essence of] the *dharma*. Having beheld it as the
Unconditioned, he is ultimately released.

127

"Let us suppose, for example, Kāśyapa, that a pauper is called a 'millionaire'. What do you think, Kāśyapa? Would this be an apt **(64a)** designation for a pauper?" – "By no means, revered Exalted One," [Kāśyapa replied.] – "Similarly, Kāśyapa," the Exalted One continued, "those who are ascetics and *brāhmaṇas* in name [only, but] wanting in a *śramaṇa*'s or *brāhmaṇa*'s virtue, I call 'paupers'." The verses:

Just as if a pauper were called a millionaire –
That would be a misnomer[286] – [so] a *śramaṇa*
Wanting in [real] asceticism is an embarrassment –
Just as if a pauper were referred to as a rich man.

---

281 Lit.: 'all of them ... are not conducive to'.

282 See BHSD, p. 286 s.v. *dhūta-guṇa*.

283 See BHSD, p. 504 s.v. *visvāpana*: read *vismāpana*, 'causing astonishment'.

284 I.e. *parāṅmukhaś* for MS *parāmukhaś*.

285 See BHSD, p. 497 s.v. *vimokṣa*.

286 Lit.: 'it looks bad'.

128

"Someone, Kāśyapa, for example, may be swept away by a huge ocean wave and die of thirst.[287] Similarly, Kāśyapa, some ascetics and *brāhmaṇas* [who] have mastered many teachings [but] do not overcome thirst **(64b)** [in the form of] greed and are unable to overcome thirst [in the form of] hatred and delusion, are swept away by the huge 'ocean wave' of teachings and, after dying of thirst [in the form of] mental defilements, will meet with evil destinies." The verses:

> As a man being swept away by an ocean wave
> May die of thirst, so experts,[288] though 'swimming'[289]
> In an ocean of teachings, will meet with evil
> States because of their thirst [in the form of]
> So many theories [without practice].

129

"A physician, Kāśyapa, for example, may shoulder his medicine-bag and set off. When, however, he is afflicted with disease, he might be unable to cure it. Similarly, Kāśyapa, one should regard the disease of mental defilements pertaining to an erudite person who – by dint of his learning – is unable to cure himself of that disease. Such learning will be of no use to him." **(65a)** The verses:

> Just as a physician carrying[290] his medicine-bag,
> May wander all over the world; afflicted with
> Disease, however, he might not cure it and his
> [Medicine] might prove useless, – so a monk, though
> Virtuous and learned [but] superficial, may not

---

[287] The translation of the following, i.e. the prose parts of the KP sections 128–135, is based mainly on de Jong's ed. and reconstruction of the fragments in the Hoernle and Mannerheim Collections; see also the ed. of the same fragments in Karashima 2004: 106–109, and in Karashima 2009: 354–356.

[288] Lit.: 'reciters, readers'.

[289] Lit.: 'being'.

[290] Lit.: 'being with'; re. °*saṃsthe* for °*saṃsthaḥ*, see BHSG § 8.25 (VD n. 301).

Cure his disease originating from mental defilements,
His exertion and learning being in vain.

130

"A sick person, Kāśyapa, for example, may take a medication, suitable and good enough for a king, and [yet] he may die because of [his taking it] indiscriminately.[291] Similarly, Kāśyapa, one should regard the disease of mental defilements pertaining to an erudite person who dies [a 'spiritual death'] because of his not guarding against [mental defilements]. [292]By not doing so, [though] in possession[293] of a 'medication suitable and good enough for a king', he will meet with evil states." The verses:

Having swallowed (**65b**) a medication suitable
And good enough for a king, a [sick] person may
Meet his death because of his indiscriminate use
[Of the medication. Similarly,] there is the disease
Of mental defilements pertaining to a learned
Person who dies now [a 'spiritual death']
Because of his not being self-controlled.

131

"An invaluable and big jewel, Kāśyapa, for example, that has fallen into faeces is not fit for use.[294] Similarly, Kāśyapa, one should regard an erudite man's 'fall into the faeces' of gain and honour; [thus fallen,] gods and men [will take him to be] indigent." The verses:

Just as a jewel fallen into faeces is disgusting[295] –
Thus it will not [certainly look] like before –, so,
I say, is a monk's fall into the 'excrement of
Honour', however erudite he may be.

---

291 Lit.: 'without restraint'.

292 The foll. sentence is neither is found in de Jong 1977: 250, nor in Tib.

293 Lit.: 'having mastered'; see BHSD, p. 335 s.v. *paryāpuṇati, °nati.*

294 See BHSD, p. 133 s.v. *-upaka/-upaga.*

295 I.e. *jugupsitaṃ* for MS *juguspitaṃ.*

[296]"That same invaluable and big jewel, for example, Kāśyapa, [when] taken out of foul ordure, washed, cleansed and polished with care, will not have lost **(66a)** its quality[297] as a jewel. Similarly, Kāśyapa, an erudite man rids himself of all mental defilements with a little bit of effort and thus does not lose the quality of his jewel-like great wisdom.

132

"The yellow robes, Kāśyapa, worn by [a monk] who has broken his vows, are comparable to a golden crown on a corpse's head." The verses:

> Just as a golden crown or a garland of flowers put
> On a corpse's head, so [one should look at] the
> Yellow robes [worn by] an ill-behaved [monk];
> Having done so, one should guard against depravity.[298]

133

"The yellow robes, Kāśyapa, worn by **(66b)** a virtuous[299] and erudite [monk], are comparable to a wreath of *campaka* flowers placed on the head of a guild-leader's son or [on that] of a prince, who is well purified by bathing, well anointed, with his hair and nails cut carefully, being clad in white clothes and anointed with the most excellent sandalwood unguent." The verses:

> Just as a wreath of *campaka* flowers, delightful
> And of a pleasant smell, is an ornament on the
> Head of a guild-leader's son who is well purified
> By bathing and well anointed, so one should
> Regard the yellow robe[s worn by] a man of

---

[296] The following neither is found in de Jong 1977: 250, nor in Tib.

[297] Lit.: 'does not lose its individual essence'.

[298] Lit.: 'one should not commit any offence due to one's mind', Tib.: *yid ni daṅ* (v.l. *dad*) *mi 'gyur*, ' ... one's mind does not become pleased (... *na prasīdati*)'.

[299] Deciding on *śīlavato* instead of MS *duḥśīlavato* is confirmed by *śīlasaṃpanna* in the verse part below and also by Tib. and Sthiramati (von Staël-Holstein 1933: 232: *tshul khrims daṅ ldan źiṅ*).

Virtue and merit, by the Conqueror's spiritual
Son, erudite and well restrained.

134

"These four [persons], Kāśyapa, are badly disposed and their moral conduct is just apparent. Which four? (1) Here there is a monk, Kāśyapa, living restrained with the restraint according to the code of monastic training, practising right behaviour and seeing danger in the slightest imperfections. Having undertaken [monastic training] and applying himself to the rules of that training,[300] his bodily, vocal and mental actions are pure, and pure is his livelihood. However, he **(67a)** subscribes to the self-theory. Thus, Kāśyapa, one should regard the first [person], badly disposed and with a moral conduct being just apparent. (2) Moreover, Kāśyapa, there is a monk who is an expert in the code of monastic discipline; he devotes himself to that code and firmly guards monastic discipline. [However,] he cleaves to the personality view. This, Kāśyapa, is the second [person], badly disposed and with a moral conduct being just apparent. (3) Moreover, Kāśyapa, there is a monk who abides in loving kindness which he cultivates towards [all] beings. However, when he hears that all things are unborn, he is frightened, terrified and panic-stricken. This, Kāśyapa, is the third [person] ... (4) Moreover, Kāśyapa, there is a monk who is endowed with the virtues [resulting from] the twelve [kinds of special] ascetic practice. **(67b)** However, he holds the [wrong] view that [things] exist [as facts] and arrogantly adheres to [it].[301] Thus, Kāśyapa, one should regard the fourth [person] ... These four [persons], Kāśyapa, one should regard as being badly disposed whose moral conduct is just apparent.

---

300 Cf. *Aṅguttaranikāya* II (Kashyap 1960a): 25f. (Dutiya-Uruvelasutta): *cattārome, bhikkhave, therakaraṇā dhammā | katame cattāro? idha, bhikkave, bhikkhu sīlavā hoti, pātimokkhasaṃvarasaṃvuto viharati ācāragocarasampanno aṇumattesu vajjesu bhayadassāvī, samādāya sikkhati sikkhāpadesu ... yo uddhatena cittena ... asaddhammarato ... pāpadiṭṭhi ...*

301 Lit.: 'is devoted to selfishness/arrogance'.

135

"One always speaks of moral conduct, Kāśyapa. [What is the Noble Ones' moral conduct?] Where there is no [false notion of] a self, of [anything] possessed of a self; where there is neither action nor inaction, neither doing nor non-doing, neither progression nor retrogression, neither manifestation nor non-manifestation; where there is neither mentation nor corporeality, neither a sign nor signlessness, neither quietude nor cessation,[302] neither grasping nor abandoning; where there is neither anything to be accepted nor anything to be refused, neither substance nor a statement about substance, neither speech nor a statement about speech, neither the mind nor a statement about it; where there is neither the world nor not the world, neither a basis nor a non-(**68a**)basis, neither commending one's own virtue nor depreciating the virtue of others, neither conceit nor one's fancying on account of one's virtue, one's being free from false discrimination and imaginary assumption – that, Kāśyapa, is called 'the Noble Ones' moral conduct', free from malign influences, uninvolved, beyond the three realms of existence[303] and absolutely independent."

136

On that occasion then the Exalted One spoke the following verse[s]:

"Pure is the man of moral conduct, calls nothing his
Own, free from presumption and independent; being
Without fetters, there is nothing obscure to him.
Passionless and without blemish, the man of virtue is
At peace, absolutely tranquil in his mind. [He who] is
Free from evil, from fancying and false discrimination,
Free from all agitation and conceit – that, Kāśyapa,
[According to] the Buddha's Teaching, is the man of
Moral conduct. (**68b**) He [who] sets no store by his
Body or life and does not desire to be born in any of
The realms of existence, who has taken the right

[302] Tib.: 'non-quietude'.
[303] Cf. above section 125.

[Path], is indeed firmly established in [moral] conduct –
That, Kāśyapa, [according to] the Buddha's teaching,
Is the man of virtue. [He who lives in this] world
Unsullied and uninvolved, unselfish and owning
Nothing, but having a brilliant [mind], who has no
[Discriminatory] notions in respect of himself and
Others; whose conduct is pure thanks to his
Insight-knowledge of thought;[304] for whom there
Is no 'here', no 'beyond' and no 'middle', who is not
At all attached to either a 'here' or a 'beyond',
Fetter-free, without clinging, unpretentious and
Without malign influences – that, Kāśyapa,
[According to] the Buddha's teaching, is
The man of moral conduct.

137

"He whose mind, collected and well restrained, is
Neither attached to mentation nor to corporeality,
Who now has no [false notion of] a self, of [anything]
Possessing a self, is on that account[305] declared
'Established in moral conduct'. **(69a)** Because of his
Learning regarding the code of monastic training
He is not conceited and also now does not take that
[Code] as an end in itself,[306] but looks for something
Superior – for the paths of the Noble Ones. These are
The characteristics of a [person] whose conduct is
Pure. For him virtue is not the highest, and
Meditation he does not take as an end in itself;
In his contemplation he strives further to develop
Wisdom. The lineage of the Noble Ones which is
Inconceivable – that is [ultimately] pure conduct
Extolled by the Blessed One. In his mind the

---

304 After Tib. *'du śes yoṅs su śes pas*; re *saṃjñāparijñāya*, see BHSG § 9.59: instr. *-āya*; alternatively Karashima 2002: 60: ***parijñāya***: "having comprehended and given up" (?) ...
305 Lit.: 'to that extent', tallying with Pāli *ettāvatā*.
306 Lit.: 'is not absorbed in it'.

[Ultimately virtuous one] is free from personality
View[s] and does not conceive of 'I' and 'mine'.
He is intent upon emptiness, the sphere of the
Buddhas, [and] his moral conduct is without equal.
Having [ultimately] established himself in virtue,
His meditation is pure. Collected through meditation,
He develops wisdom, [and] through wisdom pure
Insight-knowledge is gained; he whose insight-
Knowledge is pure, has accomplished moral conduct."

138

When these verses were being **(69b)** uttered, the minds of eight hundred monks, without their clinging [any more], were freed from the malign influences. Moreover, to thirty-two thousand beings [arose], with regard to existential conditions,[307] the pure, immaculate and untarnished vision of the Unconditioned.[308] Five hundred monks [, however,] who had realized [tranquillity-]meditation [but] did not penetrate this profound exposition of the Teaching which proved too deep for them and who were [therefore] displeased, rose from their seats and went away.

139

Then the Elder Mahā-Kāśyapa said to the Exalted One the following: "These five hundred monks, Exalted One, versed in [tranquillity-]meditation, have risen from their seats and gone away. They have not penetrated this profound exposition of the Teaching which has proved too deep for them and [therefore] they are displeased." – "These monks, Kāśyapa," said the Exalted One, **(70a)** "are conceited; they are displeased [because] on hearing me utter those profound verses dealing with the purity of moral conduct,

---

[307] Cf., e.g., *Catuṣpariṣatsūtra* (Waldschmidt 1957: 152, 13.1): *asmin khalu dharmaparyāye bhāṣyamāṇa āyuṣmataḥ kauṇḍinyasya virajo vigatamalaṃ dharmeṣu dharmacakṣur utpannam* ... ; in the Pāli parallel, instead of *dharmeṣu*, at *Mahāvagga* (Kashyap 1956: 15): ... *Koṇḍaññassa virajaṃ vītamalaṃ dhammacakkhuṃ udapādi – yaṃ kiñ ci samudayadhammaṃ sabbaṃ taṃ nirodhadhammaṃ ti.*

[308] Lit.: 'eye of the [*asaṃskṛta*-]*dharma*'.

free from the malign influences,[309] they have not penetrated [them because they] proved too deep for them, [and so] they are displeased. For what reason? Profound, Kāśyapa, are those verses that have been uttered, profound is the enlightenment of the Buddhas, of the Exalted Ones, which those beings who have not 'planted any roots of merit', who are completely under the influence of bad company and are quick to take offence, are unable to appreciate, penetrate or master.

140

"Moreover, Kāśyapa, when the Tathāgata Kāśyapa, the Worthy One, the Fully and Completely Enlightened One, was expounding [the Teaching], these five hundred monks were disciples of the head of another ascetic school. In the presence of the Tathāgata Kāśyapa (**70b**) they were listening to his exposition of the Teaching with a view to finding fault with [it]. After listening, however, faith arose in them. 'Marvellous,' they exclaimed, 'how melodious, how pleasant the Tathāgata Kāśyapa['s], the Worthy One['s] ... setting forth [of the Teaching]!' After they had died – their minds being undistracted and full of faith when breathing their last –, they were born in the celestial realms of the 'Thirty-three'. [When their (time) there had come to an end, they were born (again) here (on earth).][310] It is just for this reason[311] that they have gone forth here, [following] my Teaching. [However, since] these five hundred monks had [previously] fallen into wrong views, they have not penetrated[312] that profound exposition [of mine which] has proved too deep for them, [which] they fail to appreciate and have no faith in. Nevertheless, through the exposition of the Teaching their [minds] have been prepared. They will not further on (**71a**) be destined for [states of great suffering]; they will definitely realize final *nirvāṇa* in their present existence."[313]

---

309 According to Tib. and P 144, 4 – MS *anāsravaṃ* inaptly goes with °*nirdeśaṃ*.

310 After Tib.: *de nas śi 'phos nas 'dir skyes te.*

311 I.e. because they had previously faith in the *dharma*.

312 Lit.: 'do not penetrate'.

313 Lit.: 'with these very aggregates'. This story of the five hundred monks who did not appreciate what the Buddha had said, reminds one of the end of the Mūlapariyāyasutta, *Majjhimanikāya* I (Kashyap 1958b): 10: *idam avoca bhagavā | na te bhikkhū bhagavato bhāsitaṃ abhinanduṃ ti |* According to the commentary, the *Papañcasūdanī*, five hundred

141

Then the Exalted One said to the Elder Subhūti: "Go, Subhūti, and make those monks understand." – "When those monks," Subhūti replied, "are opposed to the words even of the Exalted One, what, again, would be [the use] of my speaking [to them]?" – On that occasion then the Exalted One magicked two monks on the way which those monks had taken. Those five hundred monks followed the way until they reached the two monks created by magic whom they asked: "Where are you going, venerable sirs?" – Both of them answered: "We are going to our forest haunts **(71b)** where we shall stay happily and comfortably [, practising tranquillity-meditation]. For what reason? We do not penetrate the Teaching set forth by the Exalted One; it proves too deep for us, [and therefore] we fail to appreciate it. We are afraid, we are terrified and panic-stricken. [Therefore we have set out and] will happily stay in our forest haunts."

142

Those five hundred monks said the following: "We also, venerable sirs, do not penetrate the Teaching set forth by the Exalted One; it proves too deep for us ... we are ... panic-stricken. Therefore we shall stay in our forest haunts and experience the happiness of [tranquillity-]meditation." – The magically created [monks] replied: "Venerable sirs, let us be united; we should not quarrel, **(72a)** because harmony is foremost in an ascetic's conduct. Speaking of [this topic], namely of 'final *nirvāṇa*', venerable sirs, which 'fact' is it that will reach final *nirvāṇa*? Is there any self in this body that will reach final *nirvāṇa*, any being, soul, creature, individuality, personality, human being, man, any doer, maker, experiencer, knower, perceiver, animator or rouser?"[314]

---

brāhmaṇa monks, though excessively proud of their learning, failed to understand the Buddha's exposition and thus could not appreciate it. The commentary then narrates that after further instructions of the Buddha in the end those monks realized final emancipation.

[314] According to Tib., also the following, quoted at P 144, 24f., is part of section 142: *kasya vā kṣayāt parinirvāṇam*, "... or with the termination of what is final *nirvāṇa* [real-

143

The [five hundred monks] said: "Nowhere is there any self in this body that will reach final *nirvāṇa*, any being ... personality, animating principle ... any rouser." - The two magically created [monks] asked: **(72b)** "Does one reach final *nirvāṇa* through realization?" - The [former] answered: "Final *nirvāṇa*, venerable sirs, [will be reached] with the termination of desire, hatred and delusion." - The two illusory [monks] asked again: "Your desire, hatred and delusion which you are going to eradicate, venerable sirs, - do they [really] exist?" - "They do not occur within, or outside, or in between both," the [five hundred monks] replied, "and, moreover, they will not occur [provided that] they are not vainly imagined."[315] - "Therefore, venerable sirs," the illusory [monks] said, "do not vainly imagine and do not falsely discriminate; what you do not vainly imagine and falsely discriminate - that you will neither be attracted by nor become averse to. He who is neither attracted by nor averse to [any 'thing'], venerable sirs, **(73a)** is called 'passion-free'.

144

"Moral conduct, venerable sirs, neither is involved in the round of rebirths nor in final *nirvāṇa*. [Likewise,] venerable sirs, meditation, wisdom, deliverance and insight-knowledge-cum-vision pertaining to deliverance neither are involved in the round of rebirths nor in final *nirvāṇa*. By [means of] these *dharmas*[316] [doubly uninvolved,] venerable sirs, *nirvāṇa* is pointed out. These *dharmas*, moreover, are empty, detached and unseizable. As for the

---

ized]?" As for the enumeration of *ātman* synonyms (*ātmā vā ... samutthāpako vā*), cf. *Mahāvyutpatti* (Sakaki 1926): 4667ff.: *Tīrthakātma-paryāyaḥ* (Weller 1965: 147, n. 22).

[315] Cf. *Vimalakīrtinirdeśa*, chapter III, § 34f. (Takahashi *et al.* 2006:) 30: *cittaṃ ca bhadantopāle nādhyātmapratiṣṭhitaṃ na bahirdhā nobhayam antareṇopalabhyate | ... saṃkalpo bhadantopāle kleśaḥ, akalpāvikalpā ca prakṛtiḥ |*

[316] The five *dharmaskandhas* are mentioned in numerous places, e.g. at *Aṅguttaranikāya* I (Kashyap 1960a): 149: *asekkhena sīlakkhandhena ... samādhi- ... paññā- ... vimutti- ... vimuttiñāṇadassanakkhandhena samannāgato hoti.* Whilst in the *Aṅguttaranikāya* these five pertain to the 'adept' (*arhat*), in the *Vimalakīrtinirdeśa*, chapter II, § 12 (Takahashi *et al.* 2006: 18f.), e.g., they, inter alia, give birth to the *dharmakāya/tathāgatakāya*: *dharmakāyo ... śīlanirjātaḥ ... samādhinirjātaḥ ...* For further references see Lamotte 1962: 139, n. 30.

notion of final *nirvāṇa*, venerable sirs, give it up, and do not have any notion regarding a notion. Do not conceive any notion regarding a notion.[317] He who does, will become entangled in his notions. Venerable sirs, attain the 'cessation of perception and feeling';[318] we assure [you] that **(73b)** a monk who has attained the 'cessation ...' has no higher [stage] to attain."[319]

145

During this investigation into the *dharma* then the minds of those five hundred monks, without [their] clinging [any more], were freed from the malign influences. With their minds [thus] freed, they went[320] to the Exalted One. Having approached him, they bowed down at his feet and then sat down at one side. Then the Elder Subhūti asked those monks: "Venerable sirs, where on earth did you go and from where have you come?" – "Venerable Subhūti," they replied, "the Exalted One has set forth the *dharma* so as to [bring home to us that] there neither is proceeding to nor coming from anywhere." – Subhūti asked [again]: "Who then, venerable sirs, is your teacher?" – "He who neither is born nor will reach final **(74a)** *nirvāṇa*," they replied.

---

317 MS additionally has: 'regarding a non-notion'.

318 MS additionally has: 'Do not vainly imagine, do not falsely discriminate'.

319 With reference to the five hundred monks 'who have not planted any roots of merit ...' (cf. KP section 139), Sthiramati (von Staël-Holstein 1933: 293) states that the two illusory monks' *dharma* exposition is a means to bring about the extinction of the malign influences with the former: *zag pa zad par* (*āsravakṣaya*) *bya ba'i thabs*. The latters' recommendation for attaining the 'cessation ...' is, according to Sthiramati (*ibid.*), their advice on a means to dwell at ease: *bde bar gnas par* (*sukhavihāra*) *bya ba'i thabs*. Furthermore, the attainment of the 'cessation ...' is recommended to the five hundred monks because of their being 'covered with dust and lacking in equipment consisting of merit and insight-knowledge': *bsod nams daṅ | ye śes kyi tshogs* (*puṇya-, jñānasaṃbhāra*) *daṅ mi ldan pa'i phyir śin tu rdul daṅ ldan pa* (*rajasvala*) *rnams so* ...

320 Re MS *upasaṃkkramann* for *upasaṃkrāman*, cf. BHSG § 32.3 (VD n. 353).

146

Subhūti inquired [again]: "Whose disciples are you[321] and from whom have you received guidance?" – [The monks: "From him] who has not attained [anything] and who has not won supreme enlightenment." – Subhūti: "From whom have you learnt the *dharma*?" – [The monks: "From him] to whom the aggregates, elements and bases for contact do not pertain." – Subhūti: "Moreover, in what manner have you learnt the *dharma*?"[322] – [The monks:] "So as to be beyond bondage and release." – Subhūti: "How have you exerted yourselves?" – [The monks:] "So as not to apply and exert ourselves and not for the sake of abandoning [anything]." – Subhūti: "Who has been your guide?" – [The monks:] "He who is beyond bodily perfection and concentrated effort." – Subhūti: "How did you exert yourselves[323] and how have you been freed?" – [The monks:] **(74b)** "Neither with a view to overcoming nescience nor for the arising of true knowledge."

147

Subhūti: "In how long a time will you reach final *nirvāṇa*?" – [The monks:] "We shall reach final *nirvāṇa* as soon as the Tathāgata's illusory [monks] reach it." – Subhūti: "Have you attained your goal?" – [The monks: "We have not] because there is no goal which one attains." – Subhūti: "Have you effected what should be effected?" – [The monks: "We have not] because nobody is perceived who effects [anything]." – Subhūti: "Who are your companions in the holy life?" – [The monks: "Those] who are not engaged in the three realms of existence and who do not busy themselves [in them]."

---

321 Re *yuṣme* = *yūyaṃ*, see BHSG § 20.63.

322 Re *dharmaṃ*, see BHSG § 6.6: confusion of gender in BHS.

323 Lit.: 'How do you exert yourselves?' As for the BHS text, tentatively: *yuṣma* (BHSG § 20.63: pl. nom. *yuṣma* (?) for *yūyam*) *abhiprayujyamānā* (cf. BHSG § 37.22: 'seemingly passive forms with active meaning').

148

(75a) Subhūti: "Have your mental defilements been brought to an end?" – [The monks: "They have] because of the absolute termination of all 'facts'." – Subhūti: "Have you overcome the Evil One?" – [The monks: "We have not] because no Evil One [as quasi-personification of] the aggregates is perceived." – Subhūti: "Have you paid homage to the Tathāgata?" – [The monks: "We have] not, neither by deed, nor by word or thought." – Subhūti: "Are you[324] intent upon the stage of those worthy of gifts?" – [The monks: "We are not] because there is neither clinging to nor receiving [anything]."– Subhūti: "Have you terminated[325] the round of rebirths?" – [The monks: "We have not] because neither annihilation nor eternity [hold good]." – Subhūti. "Have you reached the stage of those worthy of gifts?"[326] – [The monks] again: "[We have reached] that which is beyond attachment and release." – Subhūti: **(75b)** "Where are you going, venerable sirs?" – [The monks: "We are going] where the Tathāgata's illusory [monks] are going."

149

Thus, while the Elder Subhūti was asking questions and while those monks were answering, the minds of eight hundred monks and five hundred nuns in that assembly, without [their] clinging [any more], were freed from the malign influences. Moreover, to thirty-two thousand beings in the world with its gods and men [arose], with regard to existential conditions, the pure, immaculate and untarnished vision of the Unconditioned.[327]

150

Now then the 'great Being', the *bodhisattva* Samantāloka asked the Exalted One: "How, Exalted One, should a *bodhisattva*, who wishes to acquire knowledge of this Dharma-disquisition of the Great Collection of Jewels,

---

324 Re *yuṣmākaṃ* as nom. pl. , see BHSG § 20.63.

325 Re *chinnā* 'with active meaning', cf. BHSG § 34.15 (VD n. 360).

326 After Tib. and Sthiramati (von Staël-Holstein 1933: 310) for MS *śramaṇabhūmau*.

327 See above section 138, n. 308.

apply himself; how should he study and practise?" – The Exalted One replied **(76a)**: "Once knowledge of this Dharma-disquisition is acquired, son of good family, [and once] knowledge [of] this Dharma-disquisition is communicated, it[328] will prove most helpful to worthy men whose main concern is their putting it into practice.

151

"Let us suppose, son of good family, someone would seat himself in a boat made of clay with the intention of crossing the River Gaṅgā. What do you think, son of good family? Of what kind would that man's effort be so as to make the boat cross [the river]?" – [Samantāloka] replied: "His effort, Exalted One, [would be] tremendous. For what reason? [He would think with great anxiety:] 'May not the boat sink just in the middle [of the river] while I have not reached the opposite bank. I am at the mercy of the waves and strong current. May not indeed this boat burst in the middle [of the river].' " – "Similarly, Samantāloka," said the Exalted One, "[but] with much more **(76b)** effort a *bodhisattva* should [practise in order to] realize [supreme] enlightenment, and with heroic effort he should master the Buddha's teachings.

152

"A *bodhisattva* [should exert himself], contemplating thus: 'Alas, this body, made up of the four primary elements and originating with mother and father and from the foetus, is impermanent, changeful, unreliable and subject to alteration; it is [continually in need of] being anointed, bathed and massaged, subject to breaking up, to destruction and disintegration; [though] built up with boiled rice and gruel, it is transient and does not subsist without food.[329] In its debility it resembles a ramshackle house; I am at the mercy of the waves and strong current [of *saṃsāra*]; may [I] not indeed die in the midst [of life] without having realized what ultimately mat-

---

[328] Re *iyaṃ* here as nom. sg. masc., cf. BHSG § 21.85.

[329] Cf. *Aṅguttaranikāya* IV (Kashyap 1960a): 32 (Gaṇḍasutta): *gaṇḍo ti ... imass-etaṃ cātumahābhūtikassa kāyassa adhivacanaṃ mātāpettikasambhavassa odanakummāsūpacayassa aniccucchādanaparimaddana-bhedanaviddhaṃsana-dhammassa* |

ters. I will rig the great Dharma-ship in order to save [all] beings afflicted with one hundred and four diseases[330] and adrift **(77a)** [in the floods of *saṃsāra*]. With that[331] Dharma-ship I will save all beings adrift and at the mercy of the ocean of the round of rebirths.

153

"What kind of Dharma-ship then, Samantāloka, should a *bodhisattva* rig? Now a *bodhisattva,* Samantāloka, should rig a Dharma-ship that is equipped[332] with a mind that [regards] all [beings] as equal, laden with endless merit and constructed out of the boards of moral conduct.[333] [His ship should be] embellished with the ornament-like crew of liberality.[334] [She should be] stabilized carefully by means of the strong and durable ropes of [firm] intention and secured with the pegs[335] of patience, gentleness and mindfulness; [the ship should be] equipped with the seven enlightenment factors[336] and rigged with the timbers of unswerving effort and good qualities of character. [She should be] made navigable[337] with the mind of the absorptions, **(77b)** well finished thanks to the distinguished and excellent workmanship of self-restraint and peace of mind; [she should be] held together by great compassion characterized by absolute steadfastness, carrying the four 'instances of kind treatment'[338] and heroic thoughts [of aspiring after Buddhahood], well protected against 'pirates' by wisdom and in-

---

330 Cf. *Vimalakīrtinirdeśa*, chapter II, §§ 8, 11 (Takahashi *et al.* 2006): 17f.: *evam anityo 'yaṃ ... kāyaḥ, evam adhruvaḥ, evam anāsvāsikaḥ, evaṃ durbalaḥ ... evaṃ jarjaraḥ ... evaṃ vipariṇāmadharmā ... ucchādanaparimardanavikiraṇavidhvansanadharmā | upadruto 'yaṃ kāyaś caturuttaraiś caturbhī rogaśataiḥ |* See Lamotte 1962: 135, n. 26, listing numerous places according to which the reading corresponding to 'four hundred and four diseases' seems preferable to that of the KP MS.

331 Lit.: 'with which'.

332 Re °*saṃbhārāḥ* for °*saṃbhārā*, see BHSG § 9.10; re *bhavaṃti*, see *ibid.* § 25.5.

333 As for *phala* = *phalaka*, see Silk 2010: 904f.

334 Tentatively *parivāra* = 'followers, crew'; for *alaṃkāra* Silk alternatively reads *laṃkāra* 'sail'; cf. PTS Pali-English Dictionary, s.v. *lakāra*: 'for *alankāra* – a sail'.

335 After Weller 1965: 154, n. 3; Silk 2010: 908.

336 See BHSD, p. 403, s.v. *bodhyaṅga.*

337 For °*kkramanīya*° read °*kramaṇīya*°; lit.: 'made being in the action regarding that which is to be gone to'.

338 See above section 19, n. 60.

sight-knowledge. [The ship should be] carefully put together by skill in means [and kept] spick and span by the four brahmic states.[339]

154

"[A *bodhisattva*'s Dharma-ship should be] steered[340] by a body that is well contemplated through the four[fold] establishment of mindfulness. [Having] put out [to sea][341] with right exertion,[342][she should be] running full speed thanks to the bases for success.[343] [For a seaworthy Dharma-ship the following is prerequisite:] After close inspection - without any bribery involved-[344] through the spiritual faculties (faith, wisdom etc.) and [having] been launched[345] with the impetus of the spiritual powers (concentration, energy etc.), on the sea [she should] be on course,[346] promoting the enlightenment factors. She gives up Māra's, the malignant enemy's course and keeps to that of the [Noble Eightfold] Path; she gives up the 'fording places'/instructions of bad sectarians. [The Dharma-ship should be] announced as profound tranquillity-meditation united with **(78a)** insight-[meditation].[347] [Her cargo should be] endowment with the 'teaching of reason' and detachment from the extreme [standpoints of eternity and annihilation; she should be] unlimited in extensive, wide-ranging and unflagging exertion [on the part of her crew. The Dharma-ship should] have [someone on board with] a stentorian voice [who] shouts out[348] in the ten

339 See BHSD p. 404, s.v. *brahma-vihāra*.

340 Lit.: 'brought to an end'.

341 For MS *prasaṭhā* read *prasṛtā*; see Karashima 2002: 61, nn. 142, 143.

342 See above section 95, n. 214.

343 See above section 95, n. 216.

344 Lit.: 'free from dishonest(y) regarding gifts'. Tentatively after MS and VD: *°sunirīkṣita(ā) dānavakravigata(ā)*; cf. Silk 2010: 915f., reading *°dāruvakra°* (after Tib.).

345 Lit.: 'come forth'.

346 Lit.: 'between not unsteady'.

347 Cf. *Majjhimanikāya* III (Kashyap 1958b): 391, 393: Mahāsaḷāyatanikasutta: *tassime dve dhammā* ***yuganaddhā*** *vattanti - samatho ca vipassanā ca* | On other Pāli and Āgama parallels see also Anālayo 2011: 842f.

348 Re *ādāyati*, cf. BHSG § 28.24: presents in *-āyati*, e.g. √*dhā, dhāyati*

directions: 'Come, come! Mount on[349] the great Dharma-ship. She is bound for the City of *nirvāṇa*, en route for the peace [of *nirvāṇa*], parting with the personality view of this shore and sailing for the Further Shore without a whole load of wrong views.

155

"For the sake of all beings, son of good family, a *bodhisattva* should rig such a Dharma-ship, [taking him,] without feeling weary in mind, vast, countless numbers of aeons [to do so]. With this ship of the true *dharma* all beings should be saved that are adrift in the four floods.[350] Such **(78b)** a ship, son of good family, a *bodhisattva* should rig. What then, Samantāloka, is the immediate [result] of a *bodhisattva*'s higher knowledge? It is his unfeigned employing [skill in means] for [the sake of] all beings. On account of his pure intentions, with great zeal, he wishes [all beings well]. His fervent efforts [are directed] to the acquisition of all 'roots of merit'. Through wise attention he earnestly wishes for the karmically wholesome. For the accomplishment[351] of wisdom he does not content himself with what he has been taught. He gives up [all] pride in order to grow[352] in wisdom [and] sets his mind to homelessness for the accomplishment of all virtues; [from time to time] he lives in the forest [so as to devote himself], body and mind, to solitude.[353]

156

"By avoiding malignant persons[354] [a *bodhisattva*] has no [undesirable] contact. By relying on the [exact] meaning of absolute [truth], his aim is the [essence of] the *dharma*, [and] due to the fact that he aims at absolute

---

349 Cf. BHSD, p. 55, s.v. *abhi-rohana*; for *abhiru[ha]ta* Weller (1965: 156, n. 6) and Silk (2010: 920) prefer to read *abhi[d]ruta[ṃ]* on the strength of Tib. *myur du (drutam)*; *abhi-druta*, however, normally means 'attacked'.

350 See BHSD, p. 111f., s.v. *āsrava*, p. 158, s.v. *ogha*.

351 Re SH °*paripūryaiḥ*, see Karashima 2002: 44, n. 3.

352 Lit.: 'for strengthening'.

353 Re °*vivekatayā*, see BHSG §§ 9.29, 9.43.

354 Re *durjanāna*, see BHSG § 8.117.

steadfastness,[355] his objective is insight-knowledge. By seeking for **(79a)** insight-knowledge he aims at the [essence of] the *dharma*. With the intention of [always] keeping his word his aim is truthfulness. Determined to [apply himself to] correct practice, his aim is [the full realization of] emptiness. Desiring perfect tranquillity of mind, he is intent on solitude. This, Samantāloka, is what is called the immediate [result of] a *bodhisattva*'s, a great Being's higher knowledge."

157

Then the Elder Mahā-Kāśyapa said to the Exalted One: "It is wonderful, Exalted One, it is marvellous, Blessed One, how this 'King of Discourses', the Great Collection of Jewels, benefits sons and daughters of good family who have embarked on the Great Vehicle. How much merit, Exalted One, will a son or daughter of good family make who explains from this Collection of Jewels, the 'King of Discourses', just a single verse?"

158

After these words the Exalted One **(79b)** said to the Elder Mahā-Kāśyapa: " [Suppose], Kāśyapa, a son or daughter of good family were to split[356] in as many world-systems as there are grains of sand in the River Gaṅgā [all] small particles of matter, infinitesimal in size. Having split [them], he [or she] were to scatter treasures,[357] same in amount as [the split atoms], and they were to fill, exactly same in number, all world-systems with seven [kinds of] jewels. Then they were to offer them to the Tathāgatas, the Worthy Ones, to the Fully and Completely Enlightened Ones. For each Tathāgata, moreover, of Buddhas, Exalted Ones, as numerous as there are grains of sand ..., they were to have equally countless monasteries built.

---

[355] According to Tib. °*akopana*° tallies with °*akopya*° of section 153.

[356] Re *bhindeya*, see BHSG § 29.28: *-eya*, 3rd sg. opt., and *ibid.*, p. 223: √*bhid, bhindati*. As for *bhidya* in the corresponding part of section 159, see BHSG § 29.42: athematic opt. in *-ya* (VD n. 384).

[357] See Karashima 2002: 61, n. 145.

159

"Furthermore, [suppose] for as many aeons as there are grains of sand ... he [or she] were to wait, with all (**80a**) that makes for well-being, on an infinite community of Disciples belonging to each of so many Tathāgatas ... as there are grains of sand ...; [suppose], by serving and attending to those Buddhas, Exalted Ones, throughout [his or her] life by pleasing 'bodily, vocal and mental actions', he [or she] were to esteem, pay homage, (**80b**) revere and respect so many Buddhas, Exalted Ones, as there are grains of sand ..., and after their having realized final *nirvāṇa*, he [or she] were to have in their [honour] *stūpas* built, made of seven [kinds of] jewels. [But if] a son or daughter of good family learns and bears in mind just one verse of this Great Collection of Jewels, of all Buddha-words 'the King of Discourses', the former amount of merit will not equal a hundredth, a thousandth – an infinitesimally small part of this amount of merit [gained thanks to the *Ratnakūṭa*] which defies [all] clever calculation, counting, exemplification or comparison. He [or she] who listens [to this discourse] and thereafter does not reject [its teachings] will, therefore, make all the more merit. If a woman pays attention during an exposition (**81a**) [of this discourse], understands it and has it copied, she will never again [experience] extreme suffering and will not be reborn as [a woman].[358]

160

"The spot on earth where this Dharma-disquisition of the Collection of Jewels is set forth, taught, written down or, after having been committed to writing, exists in book form,[359] has become for the world of gods [and men] a sanctuary. The same homage, Kāśyapa, [that one pays] to the Tathāgata one should also pay to a proclaimer of the *dharma* from whom[360] one hears and learns this Dharma-disquisition [and with whose help] one copies and masters it. A son or daughter of good family who will esteem, pay homage, revere and respect a proclaimer (**81b**) of the *dharma* will, [so] I

[358] After Tib.: *de ñid de'i bud med kyi lus kyi tha ma yin no* | See also Sthiramati (von Staël-Holstein 1933): 314.

[359] Re *pustagataṃ*, see BHSG § 8.26 (i.e. nom. sg. m.) (VD n. 386).

[360] Lit.: 'from whose proximity'.

predict, realize the Highest, Full and Complete Enlightenment and, when breathing their last, he [or she] will 'perceive' the Tathāgata.

161

"By 'perceiving' the Tathāgata one will gain ten [kinds of] 'purity of bodily action'. Which ten? (1) One will breathe one's last with a mind free from agony; (2) one will not hallucinate;[361] (3) one will neither have trembling hands (4) nor trembling legs; (5) there will be neither defecation (6) nor one's passing urine; (7) no 'vapour' will ooze from one's heart, (8) one will neither clench one's fist (9) nor clutch at the air; (10) as one is sitting one will forsake the conditionings of one's life. These are the ten [kinds of] 'purity of bodily action' [which] one will gain.

162

"One will gain ten [kinds of] 'purity of vocal action'. Which ten? (1) One will have a pleasing voice, (2) one's speech will be delightful, (3) soft, (4) agreeable, (5) friendly, (6) inoffensive, (7) pleasant, (8) laudable, (9) received kindly by gods and men and (10) welcomed by the Buddha. These are the ten ... [which] one will gain.

163

"One will gain ten [kinds of] 'purity of mental action'. Which ten? (1) One will be free from anger, (2) free from malice, (3) free from hypocrisy (4) and spite; (5) one will grieve about the misery [of beings] (6) and manifestations of hostility; (7) one will be free from false notions and perverted [views], (8) with unflagging exertion[362] and (9) intrepidly getting hold of 'pure Buddha-lands', (10) realizing, without any arrogance or vanity, the meditation in which [the aim] of all the Buddha's teachings is accomplished. These are the ten ... [which] one will gain."

---

361 Lit.: 'rolling one's eyes'.

362 See above section 95, n. 214 (and n. 342).

164

The verses:

One will gain these ten [kinds of] 'purity of bodily
Action': [When] breathing one's last, one will be free
From pain; one will not hallucinate; one will neither
Have trembling hands nor trembling legs; one will
Neither defecate nor pass urine; no 'vapour' will ooze
From one's heart; one will neither clench one's fist
Nor clutch at the air; as one is sitting one will die
Peacefully.[363] One will gain these [kinds of] 'purity of
Vocal action': One's voice will be pleasing, full, soft
And delightful; it will be friendly, charming and
Agreeable; others will not take offence at it; one's
Voice will be pleasant and will deserve people's
Praise; it will be commended by the gods, the *nāgas*,
Kinnaras or by the Blessed One, and also the meaning
Of one's words will be kept in good memory. [As for
The kinds of 'purity of mental action',] one will be
Free from anger, free from malice, steady, free from
Hypocrisy and spite; one will grieve about the misery
[Of beings] and manifestation of hostility; one will be
Free from false notions and perverted [views] and,
With unflagging exertion, in pursuit of [superior]
Training,[364] one will be undaunted; intrepidly, [as
Bodhisattva], one will purify the [Buddha-]lands;[365]
Having forsaken arrogance and vanity, one will
Gain all that is accomplished [by dint of] perfect
Meditation, the *dharmas* accomplished by [an empty]
Mind; being fully endowed with these *dharmas*, one
Will have no difficulties in realizing Buddhahood.

---

363 Lit.: 'easily, comfortably'.

364 Cf., e.g., *Aṅguttaranikāya* I (Kashyap 1960a): 214ff.: Paṭhamasikkhāsutta: *tisso imā ... adhisīlasikkhā, adhicittasikkhā, adhipaññāsikkhā ...*

365 Cf., e.g., *Vimalakīrtinirdeśa* chapter I, § 13 (Takahashi *et al.* 2006:) 10: *... śīlakṣetraṃ bodhisatvasya buddhakṣetraṃ, tasya bodhiprāptasya sarvābhiprāyasaṃpannā daśakuśalakarmapathasaṃrakṣakāḥ satvās tatra buddhakṣetre saṃbhavanti* |

165

"He who wishes to honour me, Kāśyapa, with all that makes for happiness and who intends to pay homage by all [conceivable means of] doing so,[366] should accept, master, copy and recite this Dharma-disquisition of the Great Collection of Jewels and put [its teachings] into practice. Thus, Kāśyapa, the highest [kind of] homage will be paid to the Tathāgatas, the Worthy Ones, the Fully and Completely Enlightened Ones."

166

Thus spoke the Exalted One. Delighted the Elder Mahā-Kāśyapa, the *bodhisattvas*, the great Beings, who had gathered from various Buddha-lands, the monks and the [whole] world with its gods, men, *asuras* and *gandharvas* praised the Exalted One's speech.

The *Noble Kāśyapa Section*, the forty-third [section] of the Dharma-disquisition consisting of one hundred thousand sections of the *Great Collection of Jewels*,[367] is completed.[368]

---

[366] Lit.: 'with all respect'.

[367] Lit.: '*Noble Great Collection* ...'.

[368] The colophon of Tib. runs: "The Indian Master (*upādhyāya*) Jinamitra, Śīlendrabodhi and Bhante Ye śes sde, reviser-in-chief and translator, have translated [the text], made revisions and decided on the final [version of the translation]."